MOR

A TOUCHSTONE BOOK
PUBLISHED BY SIMON & SCHUSTER
NEW YORK   LONDON   TORONTO   SYDNEY

A PORTRAIT OF

THIS CHARMING MAN

BY AN ALARMING FAN

SAINT RIISSEY

MARK SIMPSON

TOUCHSTONE
Rockefeller Center
1230 Avenue of the Americas
New York, NY 10020

Originally published in Great Britain in 2004 by SAF Publishing
Published by arrangement with SAF Publishing

First Touchstone Edition 2005

TOUCHSTONE and colophon are registered trademarks
of Simon & Schuster, Inc.

For information regarding special discounts for bulk purchases, please
contact Simon & Schuster Special Sales at 1-800-456-6798 or
business@simonandschuster.com.

Designed by William Ruoto

Manufactured in the United States of America

10 9 8 7 6 5 4 3 2 1

Library of Congress Cataloging-in-Publication Data

Simpson, Mark, 1965–
    Saint Morrissey : a portrait of this charming man by an alarming
    fan / Mark Simpson.—1st Touchstone ed.
        p. cm
    Originally published: London : SAF, 2004.
    Includes index.
    1. Morrissey. 2. Rock musicians—England—Biography. I. Title.
    ML420.M635S56 2005
    782.42166'092—dc22
    [B]   2005050699

ISBN-13: 978-0-7432-7690-0
ISBN-10:   0-7432-7690-6

FOR THE OTHER **STEVEN** IN MY LIFE.

ALSO A **RUFFIAN**
BUTTERFLY COLLECTOR.

CONTENT'S

Saints should always be judged guilty until they
are proved innocent.

—George Orwell, *SHOOTING AN ELEPHANT*

Every great man nowadays has his disciples, and it is always
Judas who writes the biography.

—Oscar Wilde, *INTENTIONS*

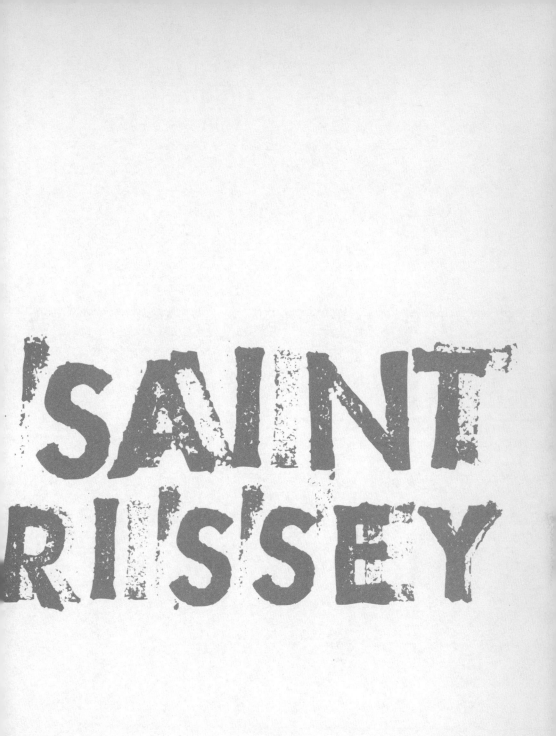

THE ANTI-POP IDOL

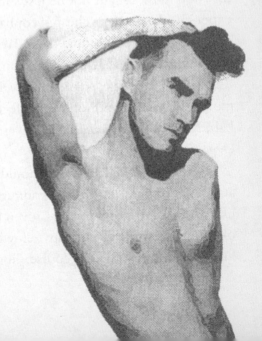

1.

*orrissey.*

The name, like the artist, like the unmistakable if somewhat dated hairdo, stands apart. Aloof in an age of ghastly accessibility. Aristocratic in an age of dumb democracy. Inimitable. Indigestible. *Irredeemable.*

Instead of being famous for being famous, Morrissey has the breathtaking petulance to be famous for being Morrissey.

And this from a pop performer! The former frontman of Manchester indie legends the Smiths and long-distance solo artist since their demise, in 1987, is the anti–Pop Idol: a reminder that pop music might not be just something you have to do, like expensive dentistry or cheap sycophancy, to become what everyone *really* wants to become these days—a TV presenter.

A reminder that pop could in fact be literally an end in itself: a (dangerously careening) vehicle for someone's prodigious, provocative, poisonous, perfectly beautiful scorn. Like his hair, Morrissey has succeeded in fashioning his shyness into an elegant weapon.

Truth be told, Morrissey should never have been a pop star at all—he should, by his own admission, have been a librarian, like his mum (though perhaps, given the gallows humor of many of his lyrics, he did end up following in the footsteps of his hospital-porter dad). Of course, librarians are very dangerous people and bear more grudges than High Court judges—so you can imagine what happens when one ends up on *Top of the Pops* with the words MARRY ME scrawled on his scrawny chest in Magic Marker.

Morrissey was the last, greatest, and most gravely worrying product of an era when pop music was all there was and all anyone could want. As anyone *young* enough to remember that time knows, sex, drugs, and materialism are piss-poor substitutes for pop music. Gloriously, terrifyingly, pop music was invested with far too much meaning by a whole generation of young people back then. And no one had overinvested pop music with more meaning than Steven Patrick Morrissey, spending the seventies in his box bedroom in his mother's Manchester council house, listening to the New York Dolls and Sandie Shaw, and wondering how he was going to become that strange, transfigured, transmitted thing, a pop star.

In that brief window of opportunity called the early eighties, the ultimate fan somehow spectacularly managed to become the ultimate star—one with a global following that to this day displays the kind of devotion unmatched by the fans of any other contemporary artist. The kind of devotion that only dead stars command. Or deserve.

Worse, this criminally shy, working-class Anglo-Irish boy from the mean Manchester suburb of Stretford managed to become a pop star on his own terms, in his own right, and in his own words: bizarre enough back then, but an unheard-of outrage in today's music business.

Bookish, reclusive-but-pugnacious—avowedly *celibate*—with an almost Puritan disdain for cheap glamour and armed with a deeply unhealthy interest in language, wit, and ideas, Morrissey succeeded in perverting pop music for a while and making it that most absurd of things, *literary*. Some were moved to talk of how much Morrissey owed that blowsy, Anglo-Irish nineteenth-century torch singer and stand-up comedian Oscar Wilde, the "first pop star." Arguably, poor Oscar was merely an early, failed, and somewhat overweight prototype for Morrissey.

NOW THAT THE twentieth century itself has already been counted down like a particularly tedious Sunday-evening singles chart and the world has woken up to a Hit-me-over-the-head Parade of Boy Blands and Girl Gropes, even to his enemies Morrissey is looking more and more like the man he told us again and again he was: the celibate climax to the once splendid and now well and truly spannered tradition of English pop.

The man from whom, in other words, pop music and England never really recovered.

You think I exaggerate? You think me partisan? Well, of course . . . but even the *NME,* Britain's most famous music newspaper and his sworn enemy since the early nineties, when it tried to assassinate him in one of the greatest *crimes passionels* in music history, in 2002 finally faced facts (and all those torrid Morrissey centerfolds they ran in the eighties), naming him the "most influential artist ever."

Morrissey may stand apart and aloof, but he still casts a long, disdainful shadow over the current British music scene, *almost* without trying, even from the distant, sybaritic comfort of Hollywood, where he has lived since the late nineties, partly to be closer to his largest fanbase, partly to be within idolatrous distance of the grave of his secret heroine, Bette Davis, the "difficult" diva who defied the studio system and almost won, but mostly because of a fabulously sulky desire to continue punishing the English for their ingratitude by the most painful means possible—depriving them of himself.

But then, one of the central paradoxes of the Morrissey phenomenon has been that while no one gives more of himself in his art and performance, no one is more selfish in the purest sense of the word. Morrissey is possibly the last privately owned company in a world where artists are floated on the stock exchange of public opinion.

As a result, he has somehow managed to hang on not only to his integrity, but also to his privacy in an age when transparency and confession are increasingly compulsory even for mere nobodies, let alone artists who have been globally famous for nearly two decades. Even in an hour-long TV documentary on Britain's Channel 4 in 2003 (his first major TV appearance in sixteen years), he managed to give nothing away except his relationship with hair dryers. Like his private life, his personality remains for most a puzzle to be unlocked. To the world, Morrissey remains a baffling enigma, an almost *occult* mystery.

Yet there is something rather pertinent here, something that everyone except his fans seems to have overlooked: *Morrissey is not a mystery at all.* There is no need to train a telephoto lens on his bathroom window or rummage through his dustbin in search of evidence of lesbianism. To get to the melancholic heart of Morrissey's condition, to get inside the wasteland of his head—or his bed—there is only one thing you need to do.

Listen to him.

Granted, this requires a certain amount of recklessness. Not only is Morrissey one of the greatest pop lyricists—and probably *the* greatest-ever lyricist of desire—that has ever moaned, but he is fully present in his songs as few other artists are, in a way that fans of most other performers, quite rightly, wouldn't tolerate for a moment. In an age when "truth" is whatever keeps the customer (vaguely) satisfied, Morrissey resolutely delivers only his own. Frequently unpalatable, it is often as hilarious as it is mortifying; after all, since desire is his subject—or, rather, his tormenter—frustration is frequently his material.

Morrissey's work is his life: There is no "clocking off," as he puts it. That is the key to his greatness—and to his tragedy. Morrissey is a record to be played, never a life to be lived. One day, perhaps, in spite of all the evidence to the contrary, a fascinating secret life of scandal and debauchery may be revealed (and I suspect that no one would be happier than Morrissey at such an exposé). But who would bet money on it?

In his singular oeuvre, which must include his interviews, in themselves frequently riotously entertaining performances, Morrissey offers himself up, dandy-Christlike, as a fascinating, foppish "fuckup" atoning for all our neuroses. As the novelist and Morrissey's "sister-in-law" Michael Bracewell has suggested, for his audience, Moz represents not only the ultimate pop star but the ultimate patient, one it wants to kiss better.

Hence, like its subject, *Saint Morrissey* is not a conventional biography. Instead, it is a "psychobio"—one that does not presume to put the performer on the couch, since he's already chained himself there, but does try to listen carefully and, informed more by literary than by clinical psychoanalysis, offers an interpretation and a kind of diagnosis of this famous patient's extraordinarily creative if rather disturbing symptoms. And the ways in which he has succeeded in turning them into a global epidemic.

Saint Morrissey is an inquiry conducted through words, images, and music into the beautiful but damaged soul of a man who has willed *himself* out of words, images, and music. It is a history of a man as a history of ideas, not all of them terribly wholesome.

It does not, however, promise any cure.

BUT BEFORE ANY of *that,* before we start rummaging around inside Mr. Morrissey's enormous head, please indulge me for a moment as I presume to lie on the couch myself and tell you something about Mr. Morrissey and me.

THI's CHARMING
MELANALGIA

I think writing about unhappiness is probably the source of my popularity, if I have any. After all, most people are unhappy, don't you think?

—Philip Larkin

All people are lonely in some ways. Some people are lonely in all ways.

—*Now, Voyager*

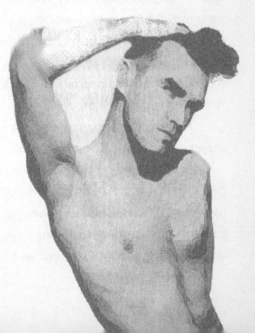

2.

remember it clearly. All too clearly. Seems like only yesterday and several lifetimes ago. It was teatime, November 1983. I had just turned eighteen and had hardly ever been kissed. It happened in my parents' sitting room in Upper Poppleton, a nice, sleepy, normal village in North Yorkshire, where such things aren't even supposed to be imagined.

I was minding my own business, slouching on the sofa, picking wax out of my ear, and watching a pop-music program called *The Tube* on Channel 4 while I waited for my tea. Then, without warning, this pale, emaciated James Dean double, clearly much more in need of my fish-fingers and chips than I was and wearing some woman's blouse, a plastic necklace, a pair of jeans two sizes too large, and a head three sizes too big, leaped out at me with his mouth open.

I stopped picking my ear. Of course, I should have jammed my fingers in both ears.

He was singing at me, right at me, in the most indecently direct and alarmingly fey way. He'd singled me out for his warped attentions, I could tell. And it wasn't just any old pop lyric you could hear at that time—the sort of thing that's a bit pretentious, like the Associates, or daft, like the Cure, or kinky and daft and pretentious, like Soft Cell, but basically harmless. Oh, no. It was, well . . . *bloody poetry.* How are you supposed to get over that?

Bloody poetry like I'd never heard before, but which spoke directly and assuredly to a happy-sad part of me that I barely knew existed. So how the hell did he know it was there? Such strange things to sing in a pop song. Such disturbing things. Such things that shouldn't really mean anything but that you couldn't help notice, even without those intense, overly expressive beetle-black eyebrows aimed at you, meant far too much. Such things that made it sound as if I'd never heard a pop song before.

And that voice, coasting, feet off the pedals, over the chiming, tearful, bright guitar chords that also sounded entirely new and familiar, young and ancient all at once; so naive and wise, wistful and lustful, carefree and very, very controlled, and—this is the really ill part—so clearly taking pleasure from the feeling of the words in his mouth: *"This charm-ming m-mann."* A pleasure in possession, for these were incontrovertibly his words and no one else's, with more lyricism in a single syllable than most popsters had in their entire back catalogs: *"It's gruesome / That someone so handsome should care."* This was an alliteration of the soul.

Oh, yes. I knew he was a wrong'un. But I couldn't help myself. There he was, blouse billowing, junk jewelry jiggling, economy-size Adam's apple bobbing, and his skinny arm windmilling a poor, abused bunch of gladiolus . . . round and . . . round and . . . round, like a floral mace, hitting me over the head again and again until I felt so dizzy that I didn't know what was the right or the wrong thing to do anymore. Petals were raining everywhere, like fairy dust, like free drugs, like jism, like poison. And all this well before the nine o'clock watershed.

I was alone with this man for less time than it takes to boil an egg. But he knew what he was doing, all right, and he made sure it was two and a half minutes I would never get over.

Accomplices? Well, I have a vague memory of three fresh-faced, slightly shifty lads looking on, smirking behind their instruments. I think he must have hit them over the head with his gladiolus, too, because whenever they stole glances at him, they had big, round, dazed eyes, as if they'd do anything he asked. I tried to get away, really I did. But I was rooted to the spot, like an especially pathetic victim in a Freddy Krueger film. This strange man's sense of abandon, his openness, his archness, his tenderness, his viciousness couldn't be resisted. I just couldn't look away. He was simply the funniest, saddest, smartest, loveliest, deadliest thing I'd ever seen.

I also knew the moment I saw him that he was the man my parents had warned me about: the man who steals children from their destiny and makes good sons bad. But when I tried to open my mouth to call out for help, I just found myself singing along.

I can still hear that unearthly noise he made—*YOW!*—a falsetto animal yelp of release and abandon not heard since Little Richard found God, Elvis joined the army, or Ziggy climbed back inside his spaceship. It was the cry of something unwholesome, unearthly, and unfed, unleashed upon a world too flabby and too soft to get away, to want to get away.

A yell of triumph, I think, at having caught me: I'd accepted the ride this charming-alarming man offered.

As if there were any other possible response.

LIKE MANY SUCH victims at the time, I was in deep denial about what had happened. I pretended it was just a bit of fun, a laugh. That it was just "pop music." I tried to forget about it. Put it down to experience. After all, I didn't have time for such foolishness. I was Going to University. I was Going to Experience Life—or at least leave home, make some new friends, get drunk, and maybe even get laid. I certainly wasn't going to let this blousy madman spoil it all.

The reality is that I'd taken a lift to a place from which I'd never quite be able to come back; I'd just met someone I would never quite manage to get rid of.

Within just a few months, I was to give up higher education as a bad mistake and find myself, in January 1984, on the dole and shivering in a rented room in Levenshulme, a depressed and dilapidated district of South Manchester without the romance of Whalley Range. I kidded myself that I was still in control, that I was hot on the trail of Real Life now—and somehow managed to overlook the fact that I'd ended up in Morrissey's hometown.

And then the Smiths' eponymous debut album was released.

I can't remember how I came to buy it. I didn't plan to; it just happened. In a haze. But listening to/mainlining that album, as I did constantly for weeks, I was happy to be shipwrecked in Manchester, and Morrissey was both siren and man Friday to me—the seductive architect of my doom and my sole, loyal companion in the wilderness. I lay on my mattress gasping and panting as I listened (above the sound of my teeth chattering): *"Under the iron bridge we kissed."*

Who needs heroin or analysis when you have lines like these? With their curiously hypnotic, self-sufficient, self-mocking nostalgia, they speak of a longing for something lost that was almost certainly never possessed in the first place and that could never be recaptured anyway, even if it had been. The mixture, the intimacy of longing and lack, is so acute, so intense, that it even produces "sore lips." It's a song of innocence and experience that is entirely adolescent but at the same time seems to do away with adolescence altogether.

The pathology at the root of "Still Ill" and *The Smiths* and Morrissey's art is the familiar modern malaise of self-reflexivity—an illness that the singer makes entirely his own but somehow universal at the same time. It's melancholia mixed with nostalgia and incubated in Morrissey's heart, head, and mouth to produce . . . *melanalgia. "Does the body rule the mind / Or does the mind rule the body? / I dunno."*

Sickness had never sounded or felt so good. For my part, sharing that box room and mattress with him, I was like thousands of others at that time, rapidly developing a full-blown case of melanalgia myself. I may have felt unloved and unlovable, but I also derived an exquisite, narcotic satisfaction from the knowledge of these things and the ability to laugh under my breath at the perversity of that knowledge. Instead of feeling eighteen and inept, I felt a thousand years old and wiser than the hills, and somehow, this allowed me to float above the pathetic reality of my life. To this day, Smiths songs reek of cheap hair gel, unwashed sheets, damp walls, badly ventilated gas fires, and impossible, intoxicating expectations. That's to say, a time when I had everything.

I had precisely one love affair to my credit at that point. Yet, according to Morrissey, in that one long, drawn-out, pathetic, spotty disappointment, I had experienced everything there is to experience in Love. He cooed in my ear that, yes, adolescence, like the Smiths and pop music, might be a moment that passes, that one day you might be laughing and dancing and finally living, but that feeling of aloneness and the bittersweet prospect of a life of disappointment stretching out before you—like a football supporter who chooses the wrong team to follow—is the purest, truest, noblest feeling you will ever have.

In other words, he told me terrible, venomous, mad things that innocent teenagers should never ever be told. Precisely because, of course, they're true.

In fact, *The Smiths* and the Smiths were experiences from which not only I but, I'd like to think, the whole of Western civilization has never recovered. *The Smiths* was not so much an album as it was a serious illness—the kind that you secretly relish because in the grip of its fevers and sweats, its aches and agues, it transforms your view of the world and leaves you so charmingly debilitated, so thoroughly exhausted, that afterward you almost find the idea of yourself quite likable. To this day, there are precious few Smiths songs that can't mist my vision; but pretty much every track on *The Smiths* can have me abashedly wiping my eyes, if I make the mistake of really listening to it.

Not because they are "sad" or "miserable," but because they are so unutterably, unfeasibly, unlawfully *handsome*. Which is the deadliest drug of all. If ever there was proof that Keats's assertion "Beauty is truth, truth beauty" is anything more than just a trite line or simply wishful thinking, then it is in *The Smiths*.

THE SMITHS IS the greatest of the Smiths' albums, making it, of course, the Greatest Album of All Time. The first Smiths album had to be the best. It's the most immediate, the freshest, the purest, and the most depraved. Its power and poignancy is in the final emergence into the light, blinking and gasping, of all the passions and preoccupations that consumed Morrissey for years, alone in his darkened bedroom.

Like the first single, "Hand in Glove," the first album has an evangelical brilliance, an urgency and malice that fills you with a lust to go out shoplifting expensive perfume with which to spray bus shelters, or to seditiously stay in bed all day picking your nose. With bafflingly beautiful tracks such as "Still Ill," "Reel Around the Fountain," "Suffer Little Children," and "I Don't Owe You Anything," *The Smiths* did nothing short of reinvent desire and turn it into something palpable, something communicable, something transmissible, something catchable—the inevitable effect of capturing the fickle, fleeting essence of it so definitively.

The much-mentioned poor production on the album, apparently a source of great disappointment to Morrissey and Marr, sounded and still sounds perfect to my ear. Its very lack of high-tech professionalism, the slightly muffled, distant quality, especially of some of the vocals, even the rough mixing that allows Mike Joyce's drums to dominate too often, lends it an innocence and energy that underscore the remarkable depth of its knowledge, as well as reminding you where this album is coming from: someone's bedroom, someone's past, someone's bottomless frustration. *The Smiths* represents a once-in-a-lifetime explosion of suffocated ambition, disappointed desire, and blocked aggression that could never be repeated, not even by Morrissey.

The official rock critic best album, *The Queen Is Dead* (decreed Best Rock Album Ever by *Melody Maker* in its All-Time Top 100 Albums of 2000), is a very fine album and, in fact, the second-best album in the world. But the problem, or, rather, a slight and minor flaw in *Queen* compared with *The Smiths,* is that it sounds just a little too accomplished, a little too professional, a little too grown-up.

Not content with just reinventing/perverting desire, Morrissey also reinvented/perverted the eighties, or at least the version of it that I and other losers like me inhabited. Thousands of young people fled to Morrissey's version of that decade, abandoning in self-righteous disgust the shiny High Street one that everyone else seemed to live in: the wake-me-up-before-you-go-go-Kajagoogoo-morning-in-America-do-they-know-it's-Christmas-the-price-is-right-for-I-am-your-laydee-and-yoo-are-my-maan-this-lady's-not-for-turning-this-time-you've-gone-too-far-Alexis-red-gold-and-green-cruise-missiles-are-the-guarantors-of-peace-we-begin-bombing-in-five-minutes-just-rejoice-at-that-news-you're-about-as-easy-as-a-nuclear-war-isn't-Princess-Di-pretty eighties.

It was a difficult decade for idealists, and not only because crassness and shoulder pads were all the rage. Margaret Thatcher's constant tuneless refrain "No Alternative" was the biggest-selling single of the decade. The crushing weight of mainstream stupid-ity was becoming increasingly impossible to resist with marginal eccentricity, quaint lyricism, and a sketchy knowledge of the works of Pierre-Joseph Proudhon. In bitter hindsight, it's possible to see that the eighties were nothing less than a glacier, composed of icy common sense and hard commercial realities, that smoothed and ground the culture flat and featureless, ready for the Nothing nineties.

But before that glacier did its terrible work, there were still quite a few young people who dared to be different, to dream, to be . . . well, *prats*. Even punk's nihilism had been based on an essentially idealistic belief in the sacred role of youth—young people's divine right to rebel, reject, purify, and generally behave like a bunch of total wankers.

The postpunk early eighties may have been a period of increasing disillusionment and cynicism, but it still boasted the last generation of young people who were naive enough to believe that there was an alternative—and that a pop-star prophet would come and save them from dowdy darkness and take them to the lacy light via his fey ways and magic, spangly codpiece. This was the last generation to actually listen to pop records; all those who came after would merely shuffle tracks. And I mean really, really listen, in a way that young people today would, quite rightly, consider merely "sad."

This intensity was partly due to the fact that young people in the early eighties had nothing better to do (Ecstasy had not yet been added to potato crisps, and watching your parents' homemade pornography on the Internet was not a common teenage hobby back then) and partly because they really did believe that if they listened hard enough and often enough, they would hear the Answer.

It was the measure of both his genius and his dangerousness that Morrissey, the latest and last—and most preeminent—in a long line of pop wrecks turned pied pipers, wrote lyrics that finally justified this kind of hopeless attention, right at the very moment when pop as a whole was descending into pointless gibberish. The situationist, anarchic stunts and poses of punk had long run out of steam; the glamorous, postmodern sashays and simpering strategies of the New Romantics had been shown to be ultimately empty if rather gorgeous attention-seeking; while the initially exciting urgency and icy aestheticism of electropop would soon descend into a disco inferno.

Morrissey saved pop not by just making it lyrical and melodic again (with help from Marr's sacred guitars) but by making it intellectual, by making it literary—even Bowie's "cut-up" lyrics had been merely artful where Morrissey's were inspired; coldly contrived where Morrissey's were wittily, deadly accurate. Ironically, or perhaps inevitably, making pop music intellectual. Morrissey succeeded in provoking some of the most passionately emotional responses to pop music ever. As a final proof of his destructive creative genius, Mozzer, the greatest enemy of the eighties and everything it represented, would ultimately come to be remembered as its greatest artist.

Morrissey was a pop antichrist in the way in which a contemporary controversy-merchant like Marilyn Manson cannot hope to be, no matter how many gallons of eye shadow he sprays on each morning. Manson offers only a grotesque pantomime and travesty of everything that a pop-rock star is supposed to be—a reductio ad absurdum in which all the drama of rock music is externalized, which may be ironic and, frankly, fucking hilarious, but is no more inspiring or subversive for that. Morrissey, on the other hand, was the actual, fleshly (though maybe not that fleshly) antithesis of everything that pop and rock had come to stand for. He was bookish; he wore NHS spectacles and a hearing aid onstage; he was celibate. Worst of all, he was sincere. He said what he meant and passionately meant what he said. Especially when he was joking. Some thought him an arch ironist and stylist, a sultan of insincerity, like his Wildean role model, but they weren't quite right. Even though hyperbole was his idea of a healthy balance, Morrissey wasn't making it up as he went along.

In assaulting nostrums and clichés of pop and remaking it in his own image, Morrissey made the genre about the one thing both parents and pop music had been united against: intelligence. Forget drugs, forget promiscuity, forget green hair and safety pins, and certainly forget androgynous silver bodysuits. As Morrissey himself demonstrated incontrovertibly, Thinking Too Much was undoubtedly the most degenerate, most antisocial habit any teenager ever picked up.

This was the vengeful virus of Moz Pop: He made pop music that was so intoxicatingly melancholic, so dangerously thoughtful, so seductively funny that it lured its listeners, most of whom were not really damned, just slightly cursed, into a relationship with him and his music instead of the world. The Pop Pied Piper knows that life doesn't imitate great art, it is destroyed by it.

IT CERTAINLY DID mine. I was the barely living proof that whether or not an unexamined life is not worth living, an overexamined one simply isn't lived. During my Manchester embalmment, I forswore the corruption of the world in the form of meat and lived on a diet of curried lentils (which didn't help the condensation problem) and heady books (which didn't help the alienation problem). There was a limited number of reasons for actually leaving my room. Shopping for food wasn't really necessary, as a large bag of lentils lasts approximately fifteen years.

I would, however, visit secondhand clothing shops or Manchester's Central Library, both mortuaries of dead people's fancies. There were hours of bleak fun to be had sifting through the detritus of loves, hates, and passions just like mine. Wearing clothes worn by people now perished and reading books written by hands now melted weren't simply economic necessities, oh no. They were symbolic protests against the Way of the World and a championing of the dejected and downtrodden in a decade in which shopping and superficiality were rapidly becoming the national religion.

Like much of early-eighties youth, in other words, I was unemployed.

Difficult to believe, but back then, unemployment and a certain kind of poverty were actually fashionable, so much so that even Southern career girls Wham! noticed, and one of their early singles, "Wham! Rap," extolled the benefits of a life on benefits and the hipness of the DHSS (the government department that then paid them). All of which was quite fortunate, really, given that 3 million people were on the dole, most of whom lived in the North and most, unlike me, not through choice.

But the great thing about being unemployed in the early eighties was that you could devote yourself to the noble, sacred, artistic pursuit of Being Yourself. And Being Yourself was undoubtedly a full-time occupation: England owed us all a living and the fortnightly welfare check was really an Arts Council grant. Certainly being surplus to capitalism gave you plenty of time to practice your chords and stage moves. Or at least to think about practicing them. Finding a real job rather than planning your pop career was considered a compromise at best, collaboration at worst. After all, being a pop star was the only way you would get paid more than Supplementary Benefit for Being Yourself (though as the history of pop shows, making it as a pop star is actually about Becoming Someone Else—or in Morrissey's case, Becoming the Person You Were Meant to Be).

I discovered an amazing fact while on the dole: If you just

ate lentils and porridge, walked everywhere, wore secondhand plastic shoes, and nursed a half-pint of beer all evening on the only night you went out all week, you could in fact save money. It was, I suppose, another way of cheating the System. It was also very Northern.

Essentially, the trick to saving money on the dole was to minimize your life functions until they could barely be measured. This meant staying in bed for most of the day while wearing two layers of clothes, with your overcoat over the bed, to save fuel. In other words, you had to actually die in an economical, if not a clinical, sense. (Hence, it seems very likely that Morrissey was rather good at saving money during all those years he was on the dole).

My mate Herman, so dubbed because he looked a bit like Herman Munster, was another expert at saving money on the dole. Perhaps this was because he'd been on the dole for longer than anyone else I had known. Herman was a few years older than me and had been on the dole since the seventies, which seemed to me like another century. There wasn't anything Herman didn't know about minimizing your life functions. People used to come to him from as far afield as Stockport for tips on how to avoid eating for three months without going into a coma, something that would actually have been a very desirable condition if it hadn't meant that you would miss signing on and therefore would have your dole stopped. After all, Herman had managed to buy equipment for his band, the Suffering Ducks, from the money he'd saved on the dole. It had taken him about five years in bed.

The only activity that Herman actually recommended when one was trying to save money on the dole, other than staying in bed all day and holding your breath, was visiting the dentist. This was because dental care was free for the unemployed. "We may be starving," Herman would grin, proudly showing off a set of gleaming pearlies that made his vitamin-B12-deficient skin look even grayer than it was, "but we got perfect teeth!" A Wildean sentiment that no doubt Morrissey would have endorsed.

MANCHESTER ITSELF WAS somewhat malnourished in the early eighties: A vicious economic recession engineered by Morrissey's loved-hated Margaret Thatcher and designed to get rid of the troublesome working class and turn Britain into a postindustrial service economy based on finance, property, and hairdressing had hit the North harder than anywhere else.

Its front teeth weren't in good shape, either. Apart from the occasional tatty pub and job center, as well as a confusing number of bus and railway stations whose purpose seemed to be to evacuate people from the center rather than to bring them in, its heart seemed to be mostly a collection of boarded-up warehouses and abandoned Victorian office buildings—glazed red-brick neo-Gothic edifices that were once full of people working for life-insurance companies but whose sightless windows now bore testament to a society that had given up on the future. Most commercial life seemed to retreat into the climate-controlled, windowless refuge of the Day-Glo-orange shopping-center hell known as the Arndale, a structure clearly based on a prototype model for *Space: 1999*'s Moonbase Alpha, one discarded because it didn't look convincing enough (mercifully, it was bombed by the IRA the following decade).

Manchester—the Los Angeles of the nineteenth century, the British city to which the world once looked as the Future, the hub of industry and enterprise where Engels lived so as to study capitalism at its most dynamic—was at its lowest ebb, deprived of a future by its own past. The perfect *Diamond Dogs*–ian backdrop, in other words, for the arrival of Morrissey, a prophet of doom drunk on nostalgia.

But then, from the perverse pop view of things, which weaves joy out of misery, beauty out of boredom, this was Manchester's golden age, one that had begun in the late seventies with the Buzzcocks, Joy Division, the Fall, and the presiding mad genius of Tony Wilson's Factory Records and would last at least another ten years. If English pop was essentially Northern, and it was, of course (just like Englishness itself), Manchester in its doldrums had become England's pop capital. The Smiths weren't the only band that formed in the unemployed early eighties: James and baggy stalwarts of the early-nineties Manchester scene the Stone Roses and Happy Mondays also decided to take on the world at this time. If you have nothing, then it's easier to demand everything.

Twenty years later, those warehouses are million-pound loft apartments, and those abandoned redbrick neo-Gothic buildings are designer bars, cafés, and hotels. Brand-spanking-new buildings sheeted with green glass that look like giant top-of-the-line Swedish stereo systems shoot up overnight. Manchester, thanks to the IRA and an explosion of design terrorism, has been improved out of all recognition and, quite possibly, existence and is now a place where a London hairdresser can happily live. And many do. Manchester City Centre these days looks like a place that has everything.

But perhaps it also has nothing. Pop music is, of course, over. It isn't needed any more. What is the point of an aesthetic rebellion against the world if the world has been aestheticized? How can you deploy your youth to refuse the world—or demand it—when the world is much better-looking than you could ever hope to be? Manchester, so much to answer for, has upstaged its inhabitants.

AS FOR ME, well, I'm not sure I ever made it out of the early eighties, thanks to you-know-who. I did, however, make it out of Manchester. Sort of. After a few months in Levenshulme, I decided that there was more to life than lying in bed all day farting, sold my stereo and *The Smiths,* and started eating meat again. For good measure, I ran away to sea, working as a deckhand on sailing yachts in the Mediterranean, hoping that nature would make me a man, or at least tan me.

But when I returned to Blighty some months later, bronzed and braver, *Hatful of Hollow* had been released. I took to my mattress for a fortnight. I was right back where I started, though this time in a squat in South London.

I tried going cold turkey and living in the real world rather than a shell. I took a succession of jobs, including: TV deliveryman, bouncer, cocktail waiter, warehouseman, double-glazing salesman, gym instructor, housepainter, chauffeur, and photo-love-novel model (the horror!), all of which came to an abrupt end after I asked myself foolish questions about the wisdom of smiling at people instead of spitting at them.

I only need to mention the fatal names—*Meat Is Murder; The Queen Is Dead; The World Won't Listen; Strangeways, Here We Come*—and you'll know what happened to the rest of my mid-eighties. When the Smiths split in 1987, I was elated: I thought I might have a chance now, that I might be finally rid of this guy and his terrible illness. But then he released *Viva Hate* and some of the highest-charting, most intoxicating singles of his career. In the early nineties, desperate now, aware that my youth was already slipping out of sight like a boat on the Manchester Ship Canal, I tried running away again, this time to the West Coast of the U.S., where I thought I'd be safe. And I was doing okay, really I was, until someone put on a copy of *Louder Than Bombs.* The cloudless California sky immediately turned leaden, and I was back in the U.K. inside a week.

On my return, I drove five hours nonstop and flat out in a borrowed ten-year-old Renault 5 automatic, shredding the transmission on the Pennines, just to get to see him perform in Glasgow. I had to see my dealer. Of course, the bastard stood me up. The concert was canceled due to "ill health." A bitter Morrisseyan joke.

When I got to hear *Kill Uncle,* things began to look up. I felt optimistic about the future at last. I thought that we were finally through, that I was over him, that he'd finally returned the ring. But then in 1992, he made *Your Arsenal.* And followed it up in 1994 with *Vauxhall and I.*

I abandoned all hope. And of course did what anyone would do in such circumstances: I became a writer.

Then, just when I'd reconciled myself both to the fact that I'd never be rid of him and the incurable, terminal nature of the dose of melanalgia he'd given me back in 1983, Morrissey moved to the West Coast in the late nineties, and it looked as if he was on the verge of retirement. His "difficult" 1995 album, *Southpaw Grammar,* and the lackluster 1997 album *Maladjusted* were poorly received, and he was promptly dropped by his record company. In other words: Just when I'd begun to "come to terms" with him and what he'd done to me and I was finally willing to talk about it, the fucker had walked out on me!

To make matters worse, it looked as if he might actually be having *quite a nice time* in Los Angeles, that he might be *getting out and about,* and might actually be *having a life.*

This was intolerable. So I resolved to expose him. To write a book about him. Or, rather, to write a book about what he did to me and millions of others. With words. It was to be my revenge. Paragraphs taking on blank verse, prose assaulting bloody poetry. Pathetic and hopeless, I know, but satisfaction of a kind—the only kind available to me.

Inevitably, by the time I'd found a publisher willing to be an accessory to this vendetta, Morrissey was back in Britain with a record deal and on everyone's lips again. Now my revenge merely seems like tribute.

But then, just like the bitterness and sweetness, euphoria and nostalgia, melodiousness and melancholia of pop music—and Mozza's voice—there's maybe not so much between them.

A LITTLE BIT OF LOVE AND LUST

A person is not born a genius or normal. He becomes one or the other, according to the accidents of his history and to his own reaction to these accidents. I maintain that genius is . . . an outlet that a child discovers when he is suffocating.

— Jean-Paul Sartre, *Saint Genet*

I'd the upbringing a nun would envy. . . . Until I was fifteen I was more familiar with Africa than my own body.

— Joe Orton, *Entertaining Mr. Sloane*

3.

teven Patrick Morrissey was born in Manchester, England, on May 22, 1959. For most people, their birthday is a date they never forget. For Morrissey, it was a day he would never forgive.

Where and when were you happiest?
May 21, 1959.
　　—MORRISSEY

Angry, petulant children, unable to answer their parents' arguments as to why they should do or endure something they don't want to, often exclaim, "I didn't ask to be born!" Steven Morrissey may or may not have used this complaint when he was a child, but he would spend the rest of his life saying it over and over, in as many—or more—words.

Life, to paraphrase Shelagh Delaney, is thrust upon us without so much as a please or a thank-you, or even a light ale and bag of chips. A little bit of love, a little bit more lust, and there *you* are. The childish complaint "I didn't ask to be born!" is a futile attempt to tear up a contract that we had no part in drafting and that was in place long before we were slapped into life or were even a twinkle in someone's sty; an attempt to assert our uniqueness and our own authorship in the teeth of all the dreary, mundane evidence to the contrary. An attempt to establish our genius.

Life, much more than death (which is just the final sub-clause of life), is an implacable, immovable fact that we are supposed to get used to—or, to be more precise, abandon ourselves to. We are expected to "pull ourselves together" when it was not our idea or our pleasure that put us together in the first place. But not little Steven. Instead, he resolved, with all the fury, malice, resentment, and heroism of a small but very, very sharp child (which is rather a lot of fury, malice, resentment and heroism) that he would not resign himself. He would not forgive his parents, Nature, or Fate the outrageous demands they had made of him. He would not, in other words, grow up.

Most of us learn to stop making the complaint about our nonconsensual origins not because we change our minds and suddenly decide that life is a "great gift" (one, mysteriously, that you never find in Grattan's Xmas mail-order catalog), but simply because no one will listen to us. We discover very quickly that this whine does not get us what we want and try to forget about it; the lucky, "vital" ones among us succeed. An artist—especially one who craves fame—however, is someone who doesn't forget and instead persuades people to listen to his "childish" complaints for the rest of their lives. That is *his* gift and, of course, his ultimate curse. The artistic disposition is little more than an extreme form of sulking. And Steven Morrissey was destined to sulk for England.

It is no coincidence that Steven was born into a working-class, immigrant, Irish-Catholic family during the Feast of Humility, a celebration of the "life" of a thirteenth-century nun who voluntarily entombed herself, sleeping on her knees with her head resting on the wall of her bricked-up cell, consuming nothing but bread, water, and the occasional bunch of parsley. She was sulking for Jesus. Catholicism—the Mother Church—

has a masochistic relationship to the world that turns moaning into singing and keys into this basic human complaint about our origins. What else could the meaning of *original sin* be? Of course, original sin is seen by non-Catholics as a cruel, sick trick to play on innocent, pink-skinned, chuckley babies, but they miss the point. Infantile indoctrination is not the beginning of an unfair burden—conception is. *"In the midst of life we are in debt, et cetera."*

Catholicism celebrates the lives of those who resist the way of the world, the temptations and corruptions of the flesh, those who martyr themselves for the One True Faith and deny themselves mortal pleasures and safety for the promise of immortal bliss and protection. In this fatal cosmology, where the veil of flesh we are born into is our prison guard, our torturer, and our executioner, we are all spawned as monsters.

Those revered as saints are usually very peculiar chaps and chapesses who succeeded in refusing life just short of actually killing themselves (which is considered cheating and takes you straight to purgatory) or who arranged for someone else to kill them, preferably in some theatrically gruesome manner such as slow suffocation on a wooden cross or being torn apart by wild animals in the Colosseum. (Morrissey, in his relationship with the press and in his stage performances, was to reenact both scenarios repeatedly.)

Oddly enough, this life-denying strand of (Irish) Catholicism is highly compatible with the Puritan Protestant tradition of English culture, which is distrustful of pleasure, hostile to success, suspicious of riches, and always expects to be punished for any happiness—a tradition otherwise known as Northernness. Manchester, the dank, damp, melancholy town of Morrissey's birth, was this tradition turned into anxious narrow streets, resentful leaden skies, and gloomy terraced houses stained by soot from coal burned generations ago in other people's grates.

People always ask me if I'm religious, I don't know why.
Well, you were born into a Catholic household, weren't you?
Quite vividly Catholic. Then it became vaguely Catholic.
   —*NME, 1985*

Little Steven, however, was not destined to sulk for Jesus, despite his family's initial devoutness and his attendance at schools named after Catholic saints (Winifred and Mary), where he learned about hellfire and damnation. This was, after all, the sixties, and the Catholic Church was in decline, rapidly losing its authority to science and secularism and its flock to the Sodom and Gomorrah of consumer culture. The Mother Church's incense-and-bells version of show business couldn't compete with the new freedoms, sensations, and escapisms proferred by the neon-lit, stereophonic Cities of the Plain (and laughable as it may sound, Manchester to an immigrant from fifties Ireland was Sodom and Gomorrah with knobs on). Nevertheless, while the Morrisseys, like many of their immigrant generation, lost their respect for the Mother Church, they somehow managed to cling to their repression—it was, after all, what they knew, rather more tangible than God's love, and what they had in common with the natives.

There was no such thing as strong language or nudity. Un-
fortunately, I was raised with the notion that excitement
and exuberance were something other people did and were
not for me.
   —*DETAILS, 1994*

Steven, for his part, found a route to passion and apostasy through the dizzyingly sacrilegious, concentric grooves impregnated into the vinyl of a pop record. When he was just six, he bought his first 45, "Come and Stay with Me" by Marianne

Faithfull, a spooky, mysterious, enchanting record in which Marianne's neurotic yet strangely pure and soothing voice promises the listener anything he wishes and pledges, in a divinely passive-aggressive fashion, to negate all her own needs if he will only come and live with her. Steven didn't need to play his records backwards to hear satanic messages. Marianne spoke to him directly and personally and uniquely. Pop music's wicked apostasy, its false consolations and illusions, proved irresistible to young Steven, and he went to stay with Marianne and never came back.

> I lost myself to music at a very early age, and I remained there. . . . I did fall in love with the voices I heard, whether they were male or female. I loved those people. I really, really did love those people. For what it was worth, I gave them my life . . . my youth. Beyond the perimeter of pop music, there was a drop at the edge of the world.
> —SELECT, JULY 1991

Pop music was to be the vinyl heart in a heartless world, the catchy sigh of the oppressed. It became a place to which Steven Morrissey escaped as his home life deteriorated and closed in on him like a trap. His natural sulkiness was proved disastrously correct and was permanently reinforced when his parents' marriage, in a sign of their modernity and apostasy, began to fall dramatically apart, and he became not only someone who hadn't asked to be born, someone whose story had been written before he was conceived, but someone whose story was now being erased around him in the most brutal and frightening way. He was being turned into that most modern and common of jokes: the child whose reasons for existing, such as they were, had ceased to exist. Pulled apart by those who had put him together.

It's nothing unique. Millions upon millions of people come from "damaged backgrounds," shall we say. Mine wasn't so much damaged as merely nothing at all.
　　—*DETAILS,* 1994

If Morrissey's disappointments were entirely modern, so was his remedy. Unlike the Virgin Mary's, Marianne Faithfull's voice and love were palpable and always there, as were Cilla's, Twinkle's, and Sandie's, waiting in the grooves of the record. Visions appeared to order, without fasting and scourging. All that was needed to summon them and prove their fidelity was the devilish needle that he held in his hand in the besieged privacy of his room. These were disembodied voices, spiritual not fleshly, constant not fickle, beautiful not hateful, undemanding and existing entirely for him. In Steven's life, as in more and more young people's lives (though perhaps none quite so much as his), pop culture stood in for missing or congealed human relationships. In other words, Steven was turning into the prototypical nerd, a young man with a religious, fetishistic dedication to images and sounds—to the iconography of pop—and a superstitious, self-abusing aversion to people. In the eighties, he would be transported to world fame on the dandified back of his dysfunction, becoming the symbol of what turned out to be an increasingly single society trying to fill the love-shaped hole in their lives where Nietzsche would once have tickled a God-shaped one.

　　In Manchester's Stretford of the sixties, however, there was no such thing as a "nerd" and dandies were an endangered species. Morrissey was simply a freak. And he was about to discover the terrible truth of Wilde's assertion that while society often forgives the criminal, it never forgives the dreamer.

There's a famous quote which goes something like, "You are what you are, having secretly become what you wanted to be." Maybe there's some truth to that. We like to think that society shapes us, but I don't think that that's the way it happens.
—*SELECT*, 1991

Unfortunately for Steven, his graduation from the relative innocence of primary school to the Edenic exile of secondary school coincided with the deterioration of his parents' marriage. Secondary school, which might have rescued him from himself by offering human contact and interaction beyond the tragic histrionics of the kitchen-sink drama of his home life, turned out to be the source of even more despair, instilling in him as it did every day his separation from the human race. School was also where Morrissey learned the meaning of his class: *no prospects*. Sent to a secondary modern meat grinder designed to produce semiskilled, semiliterate, semiconscious fodder for Manchester's factories, he experienced a daily crushing of the human spirit, which was certainly not unusual for the time. But he felt it more intimately than most, precisely because he understood more than most the sadistic trick that society was playing on him.

Education is derived from the Latin verb *educo,* meaning "led out." But in Manchester in the sixties, this education was available only for middle-class kids and the handful of working-class kids smart enough or sad enough to determine whether the next symbol in the sequence should be a shaded triangle or a stripy square and thus make it to grammar school (public school for the lower middle classes) and escape their class sentence. For the rest, *education* meant simply "hem in," "stamp on," or "condition to expect nothing from life": *education in reverse.*

For a brilliant, extremely sensitive, and self-conscious young man who happened not to be very interested in symbolic algebra (he failed his 11-plus exam), this kind of "education" was little more than a daily visit to a slaughterhouse of the mind run by "belligerent ghouls." St. Mary's Secondary Modern was Morrissey's first collision with the world, and it almost destroyed him, confirming all his worst fears about the malignity of life. He discovered that if his parents had inflicted a narrative on him that he didn't want to feature in, then the world had even worse in store. It's a lesson that, as usual, he never forgot or forgave.

> My education in St. Mary's Secondary School in Manchester wasn't an education. It was all violence and brutality. As soon as you'd walk into the class at ten past nine, a minute later, someone would be viciously beaten. And everybody would just sit there in silence. It was so abysmal—and you may snigger, you may not, I'll chance it—that I've considered actually suing the Manchester Education Committee because the education I received was so basically evil and brutal. All I learned was to have no self-esteem and to feel ashamed without knowing why.
> —*THE IRISH TIMES*, 1999

Young Morrissey's experience of the horror of school life was mostly unmitigated by the usual childish alliances and shelters against the awfulness—friendships, gangs, games, and the loss of self in the crowd. He experienced it alone, apart, separate. Although his surprising prowess at athletics, an inheritance from his father that he was later to deliberately squander, meant that he wasn't bullied and saved him, perhaps, from becoming a dreary cliché, he was never popular or even noticed much. He glided through his school years like a ghost. A *snooty* ghost.

> I despised practically everyone. Which does somewhat limit your weekend activities.
> —*BLITZ*, 1988

Steven was already too much of a freak and secretly already too much in love with being a freak to connect with the other children. It would have meant lowering himself to their level. He would have had to be a phony. He would have had to pretend to be stupid. He would have had to pretend not to be an individual. In other words, he would have had to have wanted to be liked. Not perhaps such a great burden, since everyone wants to be liked, but Morrissey wanted to be liked so much that he couldn't bring himself to admit it. It would have meant risking everything, including what little peace and tranquility he had managed to scrape together from books and records and a haughty distance from the world. So, not for the last time, he resolved to set himself against his own desire and choose his own rejection.

> I think, yes, there was in some ways a willful isolation. It was like a volunteered redundancy, in a way. Most of the teenagers that surrounded me, and the things that pleased them and interested them, well, they bored me stiff. It was like saying, "Yes, I see that this is what all teenagers are supposed to do, but I don't want any part of this drudgery."
> —*MELODY MAKER*, 1984

Mummy, as is often the case (who would be a mother?), was to blame. Elizabeth, or "Betty," Morrissey, the librarian, had introduced her son to the literary vice and passed on her love of books in general and Oscar Wilde in particular. It was monstrous enough to have a brain but quite inexcusable to have a cultivated one. However, it is possible that Mrs. Morrissey had passed along something even more antisocial than an interest in words and ideas. Like many mothers unhappy with their marriage, which, back then, meant their lot in life, she may have passed on her aspirations, magnified through her own frustrations, and those aspirations had no place in a Manchester secondary modern sink school. A clue to Betty's aspirationalism, and a portent, perhaps, of her later "irreconcilable differences" with Steven's dad, appears on the infant's birth certificate: She gives her address as "17 Harper Street, Stretford"; Peter gives his address as "17 Harper Street, Old Trafford." They were inhabiting the same house but already living at different addresses (Old Trafford was the home of Manchester United Football Club and also a large, ugly industrial park; Stretford was a slightly more well-to-do, tidy, and respectable working-class area).

I was born in Manchester's Central Library—the crime section.
—*MELODY MAKER,* 1984

To her great credit and in stark contrast to Greater Manchester's school system, Betty had recognized little Steven's sensitivity, his brilliance, his enquiring mind, and his facility for words and had encouraged these traits. Morrissey was actually the "little genius" that many mothers like to think they have spawned when all they've really managed to produce is a failed candidate for *Countdown.* Steven was going to escape from the narrow life that she had had to lead and "make something of himself" (and Mrs. Morrissey was of a generation—perhaps the last one—that believed you "made something of yourself" by reading books). Steven and the world owe Betty Morrissey a great debt. But Betty may also owe Steven, because her ambitions and attentions, as always in these cases, had a price attached. They probably scuppered Steven as much as they made him, exacerbating his alienation from other children and setting him up for soul-destroying disappointment when he collided with Manchester schools' own idea of "education."

It is clear that Morrissey never quite got over his relationship with his mother. But then, most men never do. And Mrs. Morrissey was a mother who was more difficult to get over than most. She was pretty, she was intelligent, she was feisty, she was well informed. And she was devoted to her son. It seems reasonable to speculate that, in her heart, she had resigned herself to the failure of her marriage long before she and Peter finally divorced (when Steven was seventeen) and that she turned her spurned affections toward someone she could be more sure of, someone who needed them so much that he would never reject them.

If this is the emotional calculation that Mrs. Morrissey unconsciously made, then it would appear she got her sums right. Certainly, in a Freudian sense, her son has remained faithful to her: He has never married. Such an intense filial-maternal relationship is, of course, usually seen as pathological; Morrissey is probably imagined stalking his mother's house after dark in her nightie, clutching a carving knife à la Norman Bates. But perhaps it has to be pathologized precisely because such a relationship is so (un)easily understood. If your mother is attractive, intelligent, loving, and one of the few people you can have a decent conversation with, then why give up that attachment? Especially if Dad is out of the picture. Everything else is likely to be something of a disillusionment. More to the point, the insult "mummy's boy," one of the worst accusations in the English language, carries little or no sting if you are already an outsider and have, you believe, no care for the opinions of others.

> It's a national disgrace! We know there's a shame attached
> to it. If you're still living with your parents at nineteen,
> you're considered some clubfooted, bespectacled monster
> of repressed sexuality—which is in every case absolutely
> true!
>   —NME, 1986

An unusually close relationship between mother and son was the domestic dynamo that propelled some of the most creative talents in history. That good Jewish boy who loved his mummy, Freud, considered that when a son is sure of his mother's love, he is given a confidence that survives setbacks and can take on the world. Moreover, language is something that most sons learn from their mothers, and those fortunate enough to be born to interested mothers will also learn to read and appreciate the arts. Another famous Irish Englishman, Oscar Wilde, certainly did. The arts that Mum inculcates a passion for in her offspring can be the popular ones—Elvis Presley acquired his love of singing (and dressing up) from his mother, Gladys, and it was she, not Colonel Tom Parker and certainly not his loser father, who provided Elvis with his ambition and talent. Culture, if it is passed down, is usually passed down the maternal line, and that's no doubt the reason Judaism, which is also passed down the maternal line, is the oldest religion in the world. Catholicism— especially Irish Catholicism—built around the divine mother-child dyad, is also passed down the maternal line (along with guilt).

Why then is so much opprobrium and ridicule heaped on mummy's boys, especially within Protestant culture? Because the mother-son dyad is a bond to be feared and envied—separation from Mummy has to be enforced and compelled because otherwise it might never happen. It is the most enduring of all relationships (not for nothing do brave men dying on the battlefield call out for their mothers), and, at least during infancy, it is the strongest and purest of any love known, hence all other relationships can seem its mere shadow. Romantic love can be an eternal disappointment after true maternal love. An invincible "hand in glove" narcissistic energy in the mother-son romance is often reflected in the work of the artist touched by it. It is this energy that gives an artist, especially a performer, his "radiance" or "star quality," whether Elvis, John Lennon, George Michael, or the "quivering distillation of mother love" that was Liberace. The whole world recognizes it and is in awe of it. But *awe* is another word for *terror,* and in a Manchester secondary-modern school playground—even a Catholic one—this ageless relationship can provoke equally primal responses.

Of course, Oedipus has to pay a price. Perhaps not in the form of literal blindness, as in the myth, but certainly in a failure to be socialized, to be integrated into the world. This is often a source of resentment in adult life, when the cost becomes more apparent. For mummy's boys, the loss of the bright, massive center of their lives can be a trauma from which they never recover, never quite find their orbit again. Elvis famously never got over the loss of his beloved Gladys, and it was her death, not his entry into the army, that marked the decline of his talent. With Mum gone, the cherished, prized, spoiled son, protected so long from the harshness of life, is left alone in the world with his own mortality. And his "difference."

> *What did you want to be when you grew up?*
> Oh, I'm afraid I always wanted to be a librarian. To me that seemed like the perfect life: solitude; absolute silence; tall, dark libraries. But then they started to become very modern, you know, these little prefabs, and they had no romance whatsoever. So suddenly the idea had no fascination for me.
> —*STAR HITS,* 1985

Mummy's boys are thought to be feminine-identified, which until quite recently was considered the most terrible tragedy that could befall a boy (nowadays, of course, it lands you your own TV series). Indeed, young Steven appears to have made, at least for a while, a feminine identification himself. He stayed with his mother when his father moved out, and while he has often spoken of Betty, he hardly ever speaks of Peter (it seems likely his football-crazy dad was in some ways disappointed with his sensitive, bookish only son).

Not only did Steven want for a while to follow in his mother's professional footsteps, he also was an avid reader of feminist tracts that attacked masculinity and blamed men for the evils of the world. Even his famous decision, around the time of the formation of the Smiths, to drop his first name and to be known simply as the non–gender-specific "Morrissey" seems telling. A father often chooses the name of his first-born son, and "Steven" or "Steve" sounds like the sort of name and future an Irish working-class footballing father might choose for his son; it is certainly not the sort of name or future an Oscar Wilde–reading Cilla Black fan would choose for himself. He was, in other words, the son and heir of . . . *"nothing in particular."*

However, the filial-maternal family romance can be as suffocating as it is supporting. Certainly in Morrissey's lyrics there is often a close relationship between smothering death and motherhood: *"Oh, smother me Mother . . ."* ("Rubber Ring"); *"No, Mama, let me go!"* ("Shakespeare's Sister"); *"Oh Mother, I can feel the soil falling over my head"* ("I Know It's Over"). By saving her sensitive child from life, the overprotective mother runs the risk of making him fall half in love with easeful death and the tomb-womb. And the risk is even greater when the newspapers are full of extremely uneasy death.

I happened to live on the streets where, close by, some of the victims had been picked up. Within that community, news of the crimes totally dominated all attempts at conversation for quite a few years. It was like the worst thing that had ever happened, and I was very, very aware of

everything that occurred. Aware as a child who could have
been a victim. All the details . . .
  —*THE FACE,* 1985

Little Steven was just six when the "Moors Murderers" Ian
Brady and Myra Hindley were driving around the streets of mid-
sixties Manchester looking for their next child victim to whisk
away to the foggy moors, a brutal death, and a shallow, unmarked
grave. Being Morrissey, he didn't miss any of the significance of
these events just because he was so young. He understood them
all too well. He recognized completely that it could have been
him and had none of the cozy "it couldn't happen to me" psychological defenses that less-imaginative children have. He also
understood what these actions said about human nature, the
awful reality of deliberate human cruelty, in addition to the
unintentional variety he was becoming familiar with at home.
What had been dragged into the world against its will could be
dragged out again, just as pointlessly.

There was more than a little identification with the victims
on young Steven's part. This can be put down to his nascent
sense of drama, but it had as much to do with his precocious
knowledge of injustice. In a sense—the irrational, hyperbolic
sense of childhood hurt and resentment—he had been abducted,
tortured, deprived of his innocence and, ultimately, his life, and
dumped in a lonely shallow grave, not by Brady and Hindley,
not by physical assault, but by his experience of humdrum, dysfunctional, strangulated Manchester family life. "Suffer Little
Children," one of the first lyrics Morrissey wrote for Johnny
Marr, his Smiths songwriting partner, was about the Moors
Murders. A painfully evocative lyric, it begins with Morrissey
murmuring (bad) dreamily: *"Over the moor, take me to the moors."*
Which is as powerfully, dramatically direct an identification with

the fate of these children as anyone could make. Later, he gives the still-undiscovered victims of Brady and Hindley's evil a chance to rise and speak from where they lie buried: *"We may be dead . . . But we will be right by your side."*

This promise/curse seems to be addressed to Hindley and Brady, but it could also be Hindley and Brady's last words to their victims. It is also Morrissey's promise to the world in which he grew up, which had deprived him of his happiness and innocence. Morrissey is casting himself as the avenger of lost childhood, a role he was to play repeatedly in his work, well into a disgraceful middle age (though for Morrissey, of course, childhood is lost the day you are born). "Suffer" finishes with an eerie and ambiguous refrain that again blurs and smudges the bloody line between the murderers and adult society in general, and between Morrissey and the murderers' victims, implying that Morrissey sees himself, like the windswept sullen misty moors that loom over Manchester, forever separate, brooding, hostile, abandoned.

Brady and Hindley were, after all, the most terrible but also, perhaps because they were so terrible, the most glamorous thing that had ever happened to Manchester. Brady and Hindley's crimes were unspeakable, but no one could stop talking about them. Their cold-blooded, casual yet calculated destruction of other people's children struck at the very heart of Manchester society by assaulting the twin consoling myths of childhood innocence and the unassailable goodness of the family. They were like a film negative of what a couple should be: full of highly erotic, perverse passion for each other; reducing the population instead of adding to it; destroying other people's families instead of raising their own; *taking, not giving.* They represented passion, sadism, sex, rebellion—the spiciest elements of the popular culture that was luring more and more young people into its car and whisking them away from their families and familiar surroundings to an unknown fate. While the children were quickly forgotten by the media, Hindley ("society owes me a living") and Brady's arrogant black-and-white mug shots—especially Hindley's—stared out coolly from television sets and newspapers like the latest monarchs of the sixties' hit parade. (Even forty years on, Myra Hindley is still an icon: A giant reproduction of her mug shot, composed of the handprints of children, was the controversial centerpiece of the famous Britart exhibition in the late nineties).

Although Hindley hadn't carried out the actual physical torture or taken the children's lives, she was generally considered to be much guiltier than Brady. If Ian Brady was unfathomably sick, Myra, as the Christian-name familiarity suggests, stuck closer in the public mind and was decried as an obscene insult to her sex and to Nature herself. It was her fully complicit presence that made the abductions possible, her fatal reassurance to the young victims. With her natty clothes, with-it perm, and (initial) gritty determination to tough it out rather than resort to the evasions of the "weaker sex" ("Whatever Ian has done, I have done"), Myra was a very up-to-date young woman. She was monstrous but also modern in the sense that she rebelled against her anatomy, her class, and her social role. She was proudly hedonistic and shamelessly sexual; the sixties were, after all, the decade when abortion was legalized and the Pill became widely available. Four years before Gore Vidal's Ms. Breckinridge, Hindley was the monstrous, "murderous," "mannish" modern woman that all women guiltily feared might lurk inside them.

To young Steven, who increasingly felt himself to be something of a monster, oppressed and deformed by society's expectations and prejudices, Myra the Bad Mother, Myra the self-confessed harbinger of death and pain, Myra the malicious outsider must have been a terrifying but compelling figure. Especially to a boy more than usually dependent on his Good Mother.

Most of all, Myra showed him that in a world of wickedness, infamy was almost as good as fame.

You see it was all so evil: It was, if you can understand this, ungraspably evil. When something reaches that level it becomes almost . . . almost absurd really. I remember it at times like I was living in a soap opera.
—*THE FACE,* 1985

NORTHERN
WOMAN

The Northern Woman, she's like the Galapagos turtle. She's an entirely different species.

 —ALAN BENNETT

Morrissey is a woman trapped inside a man's body.

 —TONY WILSON

Tony Wilson is a man trapped inside a pig's body.

 —MORRISSEY

There isn't another man like me anywhere. I'm one on his own.

 —SHELAGH DELANEY, *A Taste of Honey*

4.

The most arresting thing about Morrissey's work, the thing that grabs you like a particularly overzealous store detective, is that voice. It's a voice that drives some to distraction and others to infatuation. Love it or loathe it, it is a voice on its own. In an industry full of stars who started out by imitating their predecessors so badly that they were mistaken for original talent, Morrissey's voice seems utterly, shockingly unique. Aurally *and* authorially.

That oddly affective/effective self-possessed wobbliness—which disgruntled parents, rightly worried that their daughter or son is listening to something deeply unhealthy and unhygienic, have described in irate letters to the star as the sound of a man "having his legs sawn off"—is the signature of someone who is determined to sing but at the same time is half reluctant, driven but self-doubting, inspired but repressed. A soft boy who has made some very tough choices—a choirboy who has chosen his own damnation. All underscored, comically, mockingly, by his understated but unmistakably hard, sharp Northern vowels and softly cynical-lyrical, almost Chaucerian consonants and vowels (*"And in the darkened unnderpasss / I thought, Oh Godd my channce has cum at lasst"* [phonetically typing, that is]), delivering that native black humor (*"and if a ten-ton truck / Kills the both of us"*); that self-promoting self-deprecation (*"Me without clothes? / A nation turns its back and gags"*); and that oddly naturalistic, poetic pop vernacular (*"Bruises big as dinner plates"*).

In fact, the reason so many people hate Morrissey's voice is precisely because it is so dramatically *personal,* confiding in their ear that he is not just another jobbing popster or busking entertainer, thank you very much. The forthrightness and candor of his voice impart an instantly recognizable challenge that its melodiousness merely makes more pronounced; his voice demands that you listen to it, really listen to it, instead of merely hearing it, and at the same time it conveys the impression that if you don't like it, well, you can bloody well lump it. If you happen to be too stupid or too Southern to get the joke it is always telling against itself, there is nothing more abrasive and offensive than Morrissey's voice.

In a (regional) sense, of course, Morrissey's "voice" is not really so unique. In fact, it's rather common—as common as you can get, according to some Southern snobs. Morrissey's voice, you see, is that of the Northern Woman.

However common the Northern Woman might be, she is still a very special creature, thriving only in damp, cool, slightly backward climes where people actually talk to one another at bus stops and checkout queues and where you're never more than a ten-minute walk from a good fish-and-chips shop. She has a certain intensity mixed with a certain breeziness, a certain desperation mixed with a lot of self-irony—perhaps the product of her awareness of her contradictions. She doesn't suffer fools gladly, but she doesn't always make sense herself. She is direct but frequently overdone. She is a survivor but strangely tragic. She is strong but touchingly vulnerable. She is all woman, but sometimes there seems to be more than a little man in her. She's a bit of a queer fish, the Northern Woman, and she is Morrissey.

I have a talent for eavesdropping and it's amazing what you learn while waiting to pay for your fruit juice.
—*MELODY MAKER,* 1987

Yes, of course, she's quite *camp,* too, though the word has been so abused of late that it seems almost worthless now. In this context, it might mean that she's "larger than life," but she's also larger than conventional ideas of femininity. The sharp-eyed social comedians Alan Bennett and Victoria Wood, from the Northern counties of Yorkshire and Lancashire, respectively—and much admired by Morrissey—made impressive careers in the eighties out of recognizing the comic potential of the Northern Woman and her lovable, minor monstrousness and modest madness (qualities that were taken to their hilarious extremes in the nineties and noughties in *The Mrs. Merton Show* and *The Royle Family* by working-class Mancunian comedian Caroline Aherne). Like Morrissey, Wood and Bennett are Northern artists who did something very few other writers bothered to do before them: They listened to the way Northern women talk. Morrissey's achievement, however, was the incorporation of that voice into eighties pop music, introducing the Northern Woman to millions of young people around the world who had never heard of her before. And even if they had, the last thing they expected was for her to speak to them through the skinny body of a bequiffed, bejeaned James Dean impersonator.

However, the Northern Woman had made it onto the British pop charts before, way back in the sixties. And Morrissey had bought all her records. He spent his childhood adoring Northern girls who had grabbed the limelight: women such as Cilla Black, the little Liverpool lass with the big voice, big ambition, big teeth, and even bigger nose, who sang in a Northern accent complete with workingmen's club cabaret (*"Sumthing tells me sumthing's gonna happen to-ni-i-i-i-i-i-ght"*). Or Lulu, the raucous redhead who exhorted, *"Everybody shout now!"* and was so Northern she was actually Scottish.

[Lulu's "Boat That I Row"] has nothing to do with a boat—
I'm sure you've guessed. She's more or less saying to the world,
"You're not going to change me. This is me, take me as I am."
There's always more to these things than meets the eye.
          —*BRIT GIRLS,* CHANNEL 4, 1997

Or Viv Nicholson, the Yorkshire lass from a mining town who
didn't cut a record but whose spectacular football-pools win in 1961
represented the same kind of disposable success as a Top Twenty hit—
and had the same giddily transforming effect. Viv bought her way
into a realm of bad taste so extreme that it took her back into penury
but gained her fame, turning her into a folk hero, immortalized in
her warts-and-all autobiography (now a West End stage show) *Spend
Spend Spend.* She was accorded the exceedingly rare and prestigious
honor of gracing not one but *two* Smiths record sleeves ("Heaven
Knows I'm Miserable Now" and "Barbarism Begins at Home").

The sixties in Britain was an era of social mobility, or at
least the promise of it. The rise of consumer culture was fueled
by wage increases to the working classes, which meant that for
the first time they could afford to buy some of the things they
made and that kids like Steven had pocket money to spend on
Cilla Black records and other faddish nonsense. This new spending power and the explosion of pop culture it provoked gave
working-class status a new sexiness and fashionability. It was seen
as an antidote to the stuffed-shirt, stiff-lipped (Southern) British
bourgeoisie. Culturally, bigheartedness was gaining the upper
hand over small-mindedness, and the common people were now
hip and in the charts. And in Britain, the most common people
were Northerners, which was precisely why they had been
derided and pitied for so long—and why the Northern voice
began to be heard loud enough to wake the deaf cow next door
in the British popular culture in the sixties.

Northerness in British culture has faint echoes of *blackness* in American culture. The sixties saw the first real advance of "coloreds" in the U.S.: "Vital," "soulful" black music from the booming "Motortown" of Detroit was crossing over into the mainstream—that is, white—market (and finding its way into the record collection of young Steven, who was a fan of Motown). Ironically, many working-class Northern British female singers in the sixties sang songs that had originally been written for stateside black artists whose blackness was considered uncommercial in Britain. Cilla *Black* (who was christened Priscilla White) for example, built her career on covering Dionne Warwick hits (much to Dionne's distress, apparently). Even her pals the Beatles, from Cilla's hometown of Liverpool and of mainly Irish-immigrant descent, began as Chuck Berry impersonators and later included on their records songs originally performed by black girl groups. In Britain, to be Northern, working-class, and Irish, as Steven Patrick Morrissey knew only too well, was the next-best worst thing to being a nigger. Not for nothing did his skinny spiritual antecedent, the Southern Anglo-Irish malcontent John Lydon, title his autobiography after a notice that was a common sight in the windows of London rooming houses in the fifties: NO IRISH, NO BLACKS, NO DOGS. (It wasn't necessary to add NO NORTHERNERS, as a strictly controlled internal passport system meant that until the sixties, Northerners weren't permitted south of Newport Pagnell.)

> *Is God alive?*
> I'm far too provincial to answer that question.
> —*ROLLING STONE,* 1999

Mind you, just as "blackness" turned out to be a quality not entirely exclusive to blacks, "Northernness" wasn't exclusive to the North of Britain. Since the Northern Woman was an archetype, she didn't actually have to be from the North geographically—just emotionally. For young Steven, London's Dusty Springfield, a.k.a. Mary O'Brien—with her soulful singing style, beehive, extravagant eye shadow, and not entirely convincing (overconvincing) femininity—qualified immediately.

But standing head and rather broad shoulders above them all was Sandie Shaw, née Sandra Goodrich, "the princess of Britpop," who hailed from Dagenham, a dour-but-doughty working-class motortown downwind and downriver from London. Steven fell swooningly in love with Sandie (eventually consummating his passion in 1984, when he persuaded and cajoled her out of retirement to cover his beloved "Hand in Glove," the song that Sandie had being trying to sing all her life).

> It's fantastic working with Sandie Shaw—it's like meeting myself in a former life.
> —MORRISSEY, 1984

Sandie was not just any old pop singer but a true star in the sense that she embodied all sorts of contradictions. Her voice was strong but soft, giving it unusual depth, and her big hit songs conveyed a happy melancholia, hinting at a psychological complexity beneath their apparent straightforwardness. Songs such as the poignant urban hymn "(There's) Always Something There to Remind Me" (probably responsible for Steven's later weakness for overlong single titles), the extravagantly bittersweet "Girl Don't Come," the clearly influential "Heaven Knows I'm Missing Him Now," and the paradoxically self-pitying "Stop Feeling Sorry for Yourself" (*"don't sit there on the shelf / Get out, stop feeling sorry for yourself today"*), a song that dispenses wise advice but somehow only encourages you to ignore it, which was obviously written specially for Steven. Even her exuberant smash hit "Long Live Love" (*"Venus must have heard my plea / She has sent someone along for me"*) seems to have a kind of implicit ironic pessimism to its very naivety. The dark side even makes itself felt in her 1967 Eurovision winner "Puppet on a String," which for all the lyric's grating shallowness and the mechanical Euro-oompah-pah orchestration, Sandie manages to somehow suggest it might be a reference to a toy execution.

> I liked "(There's) Always Something There to Remind Me" because it sounded as if she'd just walked in off the street and begun to sing, and strolled back home and bought some chips. Good old Essex.
> —*BRIT GIRLS,* CHANNEL 4, 1997

Nor was Sandie an unambiguous figure herself. Tall, big-boned, she was not exactly the shape that a girl was supposed to be. Worse, she had a reputation for being somewhat strong-headed and didn't appear much bothered with pretending to be ladylike. She also had ideas that a girl wasn't supposed to have, taking an interest in left-wing politics and feminism—probably part of the reason she came to loathe "Puppet," with its vacuously submissive if not downright masochistic refrain.

> We don't talk about that ["Puppet on a String"]. Not round here.
> —*BRIT GIRLS,* CHANNEL 4, 1997

Through the alchemy of sixties pop music and thanks to the rising tide of androgyny, Sandie became loved, prized, beautiful; she became a star. And, apparently, on her own terms. Shucking her shoes off on *Ready, Steady, Go!* was a sexy gesture of liberation from restrictive definitions of femininity, which Steven recognized completely (and more substantively, perhaps, behind the scenes, she also retained tight artistic control and was producer of most of her music, a fact that went publicly unacknowledged for more than twenty years). Although her songs were often sad and about suffering at the hands of men, Sandie, by dint of her personality and that belting voice, came to represent a new feminine independence and optimism.

There were other, more native Northern Women who made it onto Steven's TV screen in the sixties. Granada TV's *Coronation Street,* Britain's first soap opera, was full of them. Set on a cobbled street of terraced houses in Manchester and centered around the corner pub, the Rover's Return, *Coronation Street* managed to capture (and fetishize) working-class life at the very moment that it was changing forever as a result of the rise of the consumer and pop cultures that the show itself symbolized (i.e., it was paid for by advertising).

Coronation Street was first broadcast in 1960 on ITV, Britain's only commercial channel at the time, and rapidly became a big hit nationwide; the show still dominates the ratings today and is an institution of Manchester life. The characters—and they really were *characters*—soon took on lives of their own, and *Corrors,* as it was known locally, became more Manchester than Manchester, something that Mancunians had to watch or else miss out on what it meant to be Mancunian. *Corrors* gave the residents of this "backward" Northern mill town, including young Steven Morrissey, some early lessons in postmodernism and irony—and how life can be made to imitate art.

Usually North Country people are shown as gormless, whereas in actual fact they are very alive and cynical.
   —SHELAGH DELANEY

Like most soap operas, *Coronation Street* was aimed largely at women and tended to portray them as very much in control and tough, wise and self-reliant but also vulnerable, and often as tragi-comic creatures forever being let down by the fickleness of foolish men whenever they made the fatal mistake of failing to treat them like aberrant little boys or mental retards—men whose masculinity always proved sadly lacking next to their own. As the eighties character Susie, a young, dodgy strumpet type bestowed with great psychological insight, memorably remarked, "Men! They're all limp lettuces, aren't they, Gail?" This was partly flattery to the show's core audience and partly social verity—the North is a devoutly matriarchal culture. However, the *Corrors* girls' battery of caustic put-downs, tart common sense, and fondness for gallows humor barely disguised a deeply romantic worldview, one that had been disappointed time and time again in its contact with the world in general and men in particular, but one that often took a perverse, I-told-me-so consolation from the disappointment. The credo of pop culture, in other words—or at least of the kind of pop culture Steven was devoted to.

To Steven, *Coronation Street* was not a TV program so much as Utopia in a cathode ray tube. It featured characters that were entirely familiar to him—were him, to some degree, and were certainly family—but the like of which had never been seen or even acknowledged before on television (with the possible exception of afternoon reruns of Bette Davis movies, America's own, aristocratic version of the especially impossible Northern Woman). For a boy rapidly retreating into the wasteland of his head, it was a world that he could be part of from the comfort and safety of his own (matriarchal) home. Most enticingly of all, *Corrors* offered Steven some hope: If *Coronation Street* could be a hit, then perhaps there might be a place in the world of pop culture for a mummy's boy from the streets of Stretford. He bombarded Granada TV with scripts and story lines, all of which were politely declined, perhaps because the producers suspected that Steven was pitching for more than a writer's credit—perhaps he was really asking to be allowed to live on Coronation Street, probably with Elsie Tanner, played by that "force of nature" Pat Phoenix (who would later be officially canonized by her appearance on the sleeve of "Shakespeare's Sister").

> Oh, she [Pat Phoenix] was simply a blizzard of professionalism—of goodwill, of warmth—she was like a hurricane. She just simply exploded into the room and I was quite taken aback by this. You simply wanted to rush toward her bosom, and—you know—remain there forever.
> —*RECORD MIRROR*, 1985

FORTUNATELY, STEVEN DIDN'T go to live with Elsie Tanner (or disappear into her bosom). Instead, he went to live with a dreamy, gawky girl called Jo, in her dilapidated bedsit in Salford. Jo was the creation of Shelagh Delaney, from her winsome play *A Taste of Honey,* written in 1958, made into a film in 1961 by Tony Richardson, and now seen as one of the best examples of the short-lived New Realism movement in British cinema, before the escapism, materialism—and commercial success—of U.S.-targeted Bond movies sidelined kitchen-sink drama to the small screen. Morrissey's voice may be that of the Northern Woman, but it is supremely the voice of one Northern Woman in particular: Shelagh. Such was the influence of this one—in some ways rather slight, in other ways extraordinary—play on Morrissey that references to it run through his entire oeuvre like the lettering in a stick of Blackpool rock. Sandie may have been the love of his preteen years, but Shelagh was the love of his adolescence, reaching him in a way that no one else had done before, emotionally *and* intellectually.

JO: You've got terrible tendencies, haven't you?
GEOF: How do you mean?
JO: You like everything to be just that little bit out of date,
don't you? Clothes, books, women.
    —SHELAGH DELANEY, *A TASTE OF HONEY*

Shelagh was swallowed whole by a ravenously lonely boy
and eagerly incorporated into his world. In fact, *A Taste of
Honey* became his world in much the same way that, years later,
Morrissey's own work would provide an alternative, symbolically
rich landscape for millions of other lonely kids to inhabit/moon
about in. Just as his words were to provide a generation with its
inspiration, so Shelagh's provided him with his own.

Shelagh isn't the only writer whose words have been taken
on loan by Morrissey—the big-nosed roll of honor includes
Dorothy Parker, Elizabeth Smart, Joe Orton, Dame Edith Sitwell,
Leonard Cohen, James Dean, Oscar Wilde, Noel Coward, Richard
Allen, and Jack Kerouac, to name just a privileged few. However,
none of these, not even Oscar Wilde, provided Morrissey with the
lyrical "inspiration" that Shelagh did. The list of cribs from *A Taste
of Honey* alone is so impressive it is worth setting out (more or less)
in full:

"Hand in Glove": *And I'll probably never see you again*
    ("I'll probably never see you again. I know it!")
You're the bee's knees / But so am I
    ("You're the bee's knees, but so am I.")
"Shoplifters of the World Unite": *Six months is a long time*
    ("It's a long time, six months.")
"I Don't Owe You Anything":
    ("I don't owe you anything.")
"Alma Matters": *It's my life / To ruin / My own way*
    ("Anyway, it's your life, ruin it your own way.")

"This Night Has Opened My Eyes," an exquisitely mournful track even by Morrissey's moody standard, from the second Smiths album, *Hatful of Hollow,* in which his voice hovers behind Marr's lilting, stone-kicking, shoulder-shrugging riffs like a persistent painful-pleasurable memory, is an intense, distilled, three-and-a-half-minute version of the play, where the "lifts" come thick and fast: *"Wrap her up in the News of the World / Dump her on a doorstep, girl"* ("You can't just wrap it up in a bundle of newspaper . . . and dump it on a doorstep"). Characteristically, Morrissey improves the line by changing "newspaper" to *News of the World,* a Sunday scandal sheet otherwise known as *News of the Screws*—an ironic comment on an unwanted baby's first contact with the harsh realities of life. *"In a river the color of lead"* ("That river, it's the colour of lead"), and most famously, *"The dream has gone / But the baby is real"* ("Oh, well, the dream's gone, but the baby's real enough").

Even I—even I—went a bit too far with *A Taste of Honey.*
—Q, 1994

YEARS LATER, MORRISSEY was to accuse Suede's Brett Anderson, someone who has clearly assembled himself from left-over bits of seventies David Bowie frocks and spare Morrissey lyrics, of having reference points so close together that there was no space between them. An unkind and unenlightened person might have said the same about Morrissey's early work. But these are more than simple cribs. As the man himself is fond of quoting: "Talent borrows; genius steals." Morrissey was no petty thief; he was much more professional than that. He turned up in a removal van outside Shelagh Delaney's house in broad daylight, instinctively knowing which potted plant she'd hidden her keys under, and brazenly emptied her house of its contents. (The neighbors didn't call the police because he looked the sort that Shelagh would hang around with.)

Morrissey took much more than mere words from *A Taste of Honey;* he took its world, its language, and its voice, making them his own and in the process fashioning something new and yet timeless.

> You're nothing to me. I'm everything to myself.
> —SHELAGH DELANEY, *A TASTE OF HONEY*

It isn't too difficult to see why *A Taste of Honey* would have such an impact on a teenage Steven, buried (half alive) in his bedroom, hunched alternately over a book or the manual type-writer his mother had bought him, trying to master the world through words. Written by Anglo-Irish Shelagh when she was just eighteen and set in her hometown of Manchester, it is the bittersweet story of Jo (played in the film by a captivatingly goggle-eyed, slightly boyish Rita Tushingham), a misfit, bastard teenage girl struggling not to be a victim of fate, whether in the form of her sex, her class, or her origins. She is the unwanted but not unloved product of her sluttish mother's "little love affair that lasted five minutes" with a "retarded" man Jo never met. (Jo's "brass" mother is played by the redoubtable Dora Bryan in an oddly affecting semicomedic performance that is one of the great supporting roles of British cinema.) Exemplifying the awful injustice of original sin, Jo's own birth ended her mother's mar-riage, ensuring she would never have a father and distancing her from her mother, and, to boot, may also have bestowed upon her a genetic predisposition to madness, a concern that preoccupies her throughout the play. Like all of us to some degree, and Morrissey more than most, Jo is an embarrassed, neurotic prod-uct of dissipated passion. It just so happens that the passion that had produced her dissipated sooner than usual in polite society.

I'm afraid that they [the British sixties New Realism films
he loves] probably remind me of my childhood because I
lived in lots of those circumstances and I also think
that ... I gaze upon them fondly because it was the first
time in the entire history of film when regional dialects
were allowed to come to the fore and people were allowed
to talk about squalor and general depression and it wasn't
necessarily a shameful thing. It was quite positive. . . .
People were allowed to be real instead of being glamorous
and Hollywoodian, if that is a word, and I sincerely hope it
isn't.

—MORRISSEY ON AUSTRALIAN RADIO, 1985

In an attempt to break away from her mother's well-meaning
if dissolute and distracted influence and to taste what little sweetness life has to offer, Jo has an affair with a black sailor, another
outsider in fifties Manchester. He asks if she's worried about being
seen with him; she replies that she "doesn't care." "You mean it,
too," he says, impressed. "You're the first girl I've met who really
didn't care." Jo, like our Steven, is already outside society, so she
really doesn't care; she has nothing to lose (*"And if the people stare
then the people stare / I really don't know and I really don't care"*).
However, she knows—and perhaps half hopes—that despite the
ring he's given her and the way he is dreaming big dreams and
planning big plans, "I'll probably never see you again." She's proved
right and discovers that she, like her mother and a billion other
women before her, is pregnant with spent affection: "The dream
has gone, but the baby is real enough."

Having, half-gratifyingly, discovered love to be just a miserable lie and reconciled herself to a single life, Jo embarks on a
platonic romance, unlike any other love, with an effeminate
homosexual art student who wants to mother her (and practically give birth to her baby himself) while she wears the

trousers—two misfit bastards (Geof, as "one of them," is illegitimate by default), victims of and rebels against Nature, clinging
hand-in-glove together, refusing to be downtrodden, the sun
shining out of their behinds. There is a slight, eerie premonition
of Myra and Brady in this odd, outsider relationship, but with
pathos instead of bloodlust, impossible desire instead of evil.

> I'll bash its brains out. I'll kill it. I don't want his baby,
> Geof. I don't want to be a mother. I don't want to be a
> woman.
>
> —SHELAGH DELANEY, *A TASTE OF HONEY*

Taste is arrestingly realistic and matter-of-fact yet has a
dreamlike quality to it, something more pronounced in the film,
which, even in 1961, seems to be already nostalgic for a disap-
pearing Manchester; the black-and-white cinematography of
cobbled streets and factory chimneys, together with the poignant
use of light and dark, sunshine and gloom, lends an aesthetic
reverie to the gritty documentary feel, especially when backed
by the strangely bittersweet sound of children laughing and playing in the streets and continuously, endlessly, effortlessly singing
hypnotic nursery rhymes (lyrically underscoring the pre–pop
music context of Jo's world, but also an echo of Morrissey's own
solitary investment in singing to himself, something he spent
much of his childhood doing).

There's even a day trip for Jo and Geof to the moors outside Manchester, affording a distant, aerial view of the narrow
streets (a sunlit, carefree visit now inevitably contrasted with the
"sullen misty" moors of Myra and Ian). Most of all, the film is
steeped in the sense of disappointed desire, of happiness just out
of reach, forever slipping away in plain view, like Jo's sailor smiling and waving to her from the deck of his boat as he disappears
down the Manchester Ship Canal, off on the "alley-alley-o," tak-

ing his lying promise with him. In other words, *Taste* is the landscape, the mother country, the heart of much of Morrissey's work, especially his Smiths period; it is a lyrical play whose affecting but plainspoken poetry proceeds from ordinary people showing their extraordinary side, the ordinariness of extraordinariness. Likewise, it exists narcissistically in a world of its own, where it is everything to itself: The drama and all the characters seem to proceed from Jo's adolescent imagination; they are merely aspects of her own predicament, conversations between her emotions. This is not so much a weakness as a strength and the source of the play's—and Morrissey's—mesmerizing charm.

> Women never have young minds. They are born three
> thousand years old.
> —SHELAGH DELANEY, *A TASTE OF HONEY*

Unlike the other works by fifties (usually Northern) working-class authors that were turned into films in the early sixties, such as *Saturday Night and Sunday Morning, Billy Liar,* and *Room at the Top, Taste* was written from a female perspective, or, rather, *intro*-spective. Unashamedly self-absorbed, it manages to be genuinely "shocking" and contemporary in its subject matter: adultery, promiscuity, teenage pregnancy, maternal irresponsibility, abortion, miscegenation, homosexuality, congenital madness ... (if this list reads like an episode of *Brookside,* perhaps this is why, in the late eighties, Morrissey made an appearance in a spin-off of that show called *South*). However, *Taste* managed to cover all these themes without being sensationalist, refusing to hide behind pompous gestures and pseudo politics. It isn't a play about an angry young man, but a vaguely anxious young girl—a much more "universal" subject, since most of us are vaguely anxious young girls at some point in our lives. And all of these characteristics—poetic naturalism, shocking without sensationalism, refusal of pompous gestures, dreamy introspection, a freshly feminine perspective—were to be features of Morrissey's own work.

It has been pointed out that the Sheila in the Smiths' infectiously exuberant single "Sheila Take a Bow" is probably Shelagh Delaney. The song certainly sounds like a tribute, but one that recognizes the trap of self-sufficiency and isolation that lures those unruly boys and unruly girls who will not settle down—a trap that Morrissey can't escape from. Like Jo, he's speaking-singing to himself as much as anyone else, telling himself not to stay at home (not that he's going to pay any heed, mind): *"Is it wrong to want to live on your own?"*

Sheila/Shelagh/Jo/Morrissey/the listener is invited to take a bow and assert her independence, her strength, her purity, but at the same time, in typical push-me-pull-me fashion, she's told to come out and find the one that she loves and loves her back, which is in practice, as we all know, the ultimate compromise.

Morrissey is the one doing the singing, and it is he who tends to choose "sad" words, yet in a sense, it is Shelagh's voice in which he sings. Taking his identification with the Northern Woman to its ultimate conclusion, and tallying with the picture of Candy Darling—the Warhol transsexual and inspiration for Lou Reed's "Walk on the Wild Side"—on the single's sleeve, Morrissey is clearly also the Sheila of the song (perhaps this is partly why Sheila is bowing rather than curtsying). In this way he's just being true to Delaney's message. The gender roles within Geof and Jo's relationship in *Taste* are very mixed-up and unclear; it's what makes the odd affair of two single people being single together seem so exciting, liberating, fresh—and ultimately doomed. It's what makes it seem so genuinely touching in places where you haven't been touched before. Hence, in "Sheila," the identity and gender of the narrator, as in so many of Morrissey's songs, is not so much unclear as *transcended,* providing both the male and the female listener with multiple points of identification, which is the key to the subtle, fecund richness of so many of Morrissey's lyrics; even subject and object naughtily refuse to follow convention and switch positions frequently, sometimes playing top, sometimes bottom.

A little later, both the song's and Morrissey's deliberately, exuberantly confused "transsexuality" is spelled out in an invigoratingly casual fashion. It's the childish, infectious, taunting, carelessness—wordlessness—of the single-syllable finale that stays with the listener, haunting him long after the last chord dies away, like the sound of the children playing happily in the streets in *A Taste of Honey*. It's a lyrical raspberry blown to the world, and the destiny that it decrees is anatomy, a brazen, laughing, giggling, brawling challenge to convention and normality—a challenge that Morrissey, hand in hand with his inner Sheila, from "Girl Afraid" to "Alma Matters," would continue to deliver like an insult wrapped in a kiss for the rest of his career.

> *Did you hear t.A.T.u.'s version of "How Soon Is Now?"*
> Yes, it was magnificent. Absolutely. Again, I don't know much about them.
> *They're the teenage Russian lesbians.*
> Well, aren't we all?
> —*WORD*, 2003

Jo should have been a pop star, but she appears to live in a world where pop music hasn't been invented yet—at least for girls like her. Her "madness" is the protest of someone suffocating, gasping, drowning—a child born prematurely but somehow still alive.

Morrissey would change all that. Morrissey, the ultimate if highly unnatural evolution of the Northern Woman, made his masculine body the instrument of Jo's frustrated, premature aspirations. He took her tough vulnerability, her girlish resolve, her proud awkwardness, her endearing neuroses, her dreamy realism, her Lancastrian scorn, and, hand in hand with his own perversity, he strode off with them into posterity, far surpassing the artistic achievements of all the Northern Woman pop stars of the sixties whom he adored.

But all this was to come later. In the meantime, teenage Steven was to be abducted by a transsexuality much more overt and extreme than anything Delaney had ever come up with.

It was called the seventies.

PADDY IN PLATFORM'S

To be natural is such a very difficult pose to keep up.

—Oscar Wilde

All truly beautiful things are a mixture of masculine and feminine.

—Susan Sontag

Beauty is nothing else but a promise of happiness.

—Stendhal

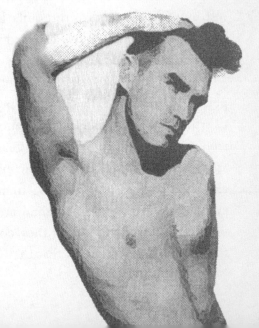

5.

lam rock saved Morrissey, at the same time damning him forever.

In 1971, Steven attended a T. Rex gig at Manchester's Apollo Theatre. He was just twelve years old. Like his attendance at a gig by the Sex Pistols when he was sweet sixteen, it was a rendezvous with fate. His tickets to these events were delivered to him by Lucifer himself. In fact, it could almost be said that glam and punk only happened so that nice boy Steven could be exposed to them and be led gloriously astray. If these cacophonous movements hadn't produced a single record worth listening to thirty years on, they would still have proved themselves more than worthwhile just by what they did to this quiet little Sandie Shaw fan. Steven was directly and intimately exposed to the most corrupting influences of the decade. Fortunately, he took copious notes.

Glam rock was the crowning glory of pop, and it was perched on Marc Bolan's pretty, perm-curled head. Glam rock was the strutting, preening realization of the transformative, terrifying potential of pop culture. Glam rock was a second chance at the fifties for the British, who had been too strangulated by class and convention (and the memory of rationing) to really enjoy that decade the first time around. Glam rock told those who once had nothing that they could now have everything. If sixties pop had told them that they could have fun and sex, and maybe even be rich (one day), then the seventies were telling them that they could be something much more valuable: that they could be beautiful. That they could be noticed. That they could be loved . . . and more than a little feared. Glam rock said that proletarians were the new aristocracy.

Such captivating creatures that they could become the center of their own universe, sufficient unto themselves, not beholden to parents, convention, class, or even gender. The glam-rock pop star was the symbol of pop culture's supremacy, living out the fantasies of his frustrated fans with increasingly psychotic determination. As a badge worn proudly, arrogantly, on school blazer lapels at the time announced, half ironically, half threateningly, MARC BOLAN RULES, OK!

A ruthless, willful, seductive, and entirely self-conscious childishness was at the irresponsible, glittery heart of glam. Freud once mockingly dubbed the infant tyrant who has no interest in anything except the immediate satisfaction of his own needs "His Majesty the Baby." In the age of vulgar aristocracy that glam heralded, His Majesty the Baby was not to be mocked but emulated. Infantilism was the very essence of "star quality"—a calculating wonderment and fierce innocence. "Nothing more resembles what we call inspiration than the delight with which a child absorbs form and colour," wrote Baudelaire. "Genius is nothing more or less than childhood recovered at will." And just as it is difficult to imagine childhood or royalty without the luxury and sensation of color, so it is difficult to imagine glam rock without *color television,* which, typically, arrived in Britain much later than in the U.S., not reaching working-class homes until the early seventies. Pretty much the whole of the "swinging" sixties had been witnessed by Brits in monochrome in their front rooms.

Then, suddenly, in the early seventies, thanks to the "white heat of technology" and installment plans, *Top of the Pops* was a Technicolor dream, a Land of Oz where the twister of pop music could snatch away any young person trapped in one of those gray, ugly new houses in the suburbs.

> To me, popular music is still the voice of the working class, collective rage in a way, though seldom angst-ridden. But it does really seem like the one sole opportunity for someone from a working-class background to step forward and have their say. It's really the last refuge for articulate but penniless humans.
>
> —*NME*, 1984

> Really, if the lower orders don't set us a good example, what on earth is the use of them?
>
> —OSCAR WILDE, *THE IMPORTANCE OF BEING EARNEST*, 1895

However, the rising aspirations of consumer culture only turned up the contrast on the monochrome reality of British working-class life in the early seventies. Since there was little or no chance, postsixties, of changing the world, the only option was to conduct your own personal coup d'état and aestheticize yourself: The "children of the revolution" weren't fools, but they didn't mind dressing like gorgeous ones. The instruments of vibrant transformation were within the reach of everyone: tubes of glitter, satin, itchy man-made fibers, platform shoes, and, most important of all, cheap hair dye. Millions of kids undertook this solemn bathroom ritual, often with disastrous results—and not just for their mums' best towels and the bathroom carpet. Horrifically, their hair frequently turned a peasant, muddy green color instead of the divine gold they were aiming for. Bathroom-sink dramas hit both Steven and that other sharp-tongued second-generation Anglo-Irish dandy misanthrope, John Lydon. John, who was also moping around his parents' council home (in

Finsbury Park, North London, a couple of hundred miles south of Steven), nursing a grudge against life, would have his own moment of revenge on the world seven years before Morrissey, in a movement whose hairstyles seem to have been inspired by those earlier glam bathroom-sink disasters and that was, in many ways, glam with the lining turned inside out: *"We're so pretty, oh-so pretty . . . and we don't care!"*

> I was born into a working class family in Manchester at the right time. I was overwhelmed by British pop culture as it was conquering the world. And I started to get involved when punk music arrived. So that was perfect. It would have been a fate worse than death if I was born in 1974. But I would also have hated to be born in 1930 . . . and believe me, I have spent much time thinking about this dilemma.
>
> —*POP,* 1998

The exasperating reality of working-class life in the seventies and the frustrated creativity of the vandalism wreaked by bored, angry kids, which made the landscape to which they were condemned only more depressing, was captured most evocatively —so evocatively that it sounded defiantly beautiful—by new-wave mod band the Jam in "That's Entertainment": urban boredom and frustration, the "smash of glass and a rumble of boots," vandalized phone booths, watching television, and "thinking about your holidays." Appropriately enough, the track was later covered by Morrissey himself (sounding, to paraphrase David Bowie commenting on a Moz cover of one of his records, like Morrissey doing Paul Weller doing Morrissey). Glam rock was not Entertainment. Glam rock was the end of Entertainment. Glam rock refused the adult division of the world into work and play, pleasure and pain, a life ordered around bells, factory hooters, electric-train schedules, and regimented bank holidays. Instead of industry, it advanced idleness; instead of repression, it advanced . . . a better-dressed kind of repression. Glam rock called for, and for a brief moment seemed to actually offer, escape from the humdrum by becoming your own special creation. It was a glamorous glue giving off fumes of excitement, adrenaline, fear; it was life as funfair. A call, orchestrated through the apparatus of pop music, for the childish mob nationwide to rise up, mobilize, take to the streets in an ominous clatter of platform shoes and flutter of fake silk scarves, and demand, right here and now . . . beauty.

According to Johnny Marr, "Panic" (one of the Smiths' biggest chart successes, reaching No. 10 in 1986) was written at a time when Morrissey was especially obsessed with Marc Bolan, and he exhorted Marr to copy the chugging rhythm of Bolan's "Metal Guru" to the point that they were "almost the same song." "Panic" was officially an attack on the pap-pop music of eighties BBC Radio 1 (which banned Smiths songs), prompted by the station's most popular and most loathsome DJ, who also happened to be the most implacable enemy of the Smiths, playing, completely unsullied by any irony whatsoever, Wham!'s vacuously sunny "I'm Your Man" after a news item that reported the explosion at the Chernobyl nuclear reactor. But even here, in one of the Smith's more overtly "political" songs, one ostensibly concerned with Morrissey's pet cause of environmentalism, the Chernobyl explosion ends up being really just a faint and somewhat delayed echo of the emotional explosion from his childhood, with which Morrissey is much more fascinated (with an admixture of Morrissey's own apocalyptic fantasies). "Panic" captures perfectly the danger, hysteria, and revolt of a youth cult like glam, and how, like nuclear fallout, there was no escape from it once it was in the air, causing panic on the streets of regional cities.

Not for nothing does the list of provincial towns in uproar sound like a list of tour dates; Morrissey saw the Smiths as seditionaries, spreading aesthetic, lyrical rebellion across the glummest, most despairing—and yet for all that, the most oddly attractive—parts of England. "Panic" builds and builds into a repeated, catchy refrain that sounds like an amalgamation of a football chant, a revolutionary slogan, and a nursery rhyme—just like glam, in other words. One that makes explicit, albeit ironically, the threat of political violence in glam: *"HANG THE DJ, HANG THE DJ, HANG THE DJ."*

As much, if not more, as it is about crass indifference to environmental disaster, "Panic" is about Morrissey's vengeful hopes of a day of reckoning for the collaborators with blandness who have betrayed the incomparable legacy of British youth culture and bowdlerized its only hope—pop music. The masterly touch of children's voices backing the baying for blood recalls both the radical childishness of glam and the purity and naturalness of its hatred (and also the street kids of *A Taste of Honey*).

It's difficult to appreciate the wickedness of glam unless you understand something about the nature of the British class system. Until the mass deindustrialization and unemployment followed by the lifestyle consumerism of the eighties and nineties (a poor, stunted descendent of glam) effectively destroyed it, working-class identity was based entirely on the idea of work. What you did was who you were, even if it was the most boring, mindless work imaginable. If you didn't work, then you were literally no one. A waster. A bum. Invisible. Idleness was unthinkable; chosen idleness, unimaginable.

My mother always supported me in an artistic sense, when many people around her said she was entirely insane for allowing me to stay in and write. It's this working-class idea that one is born simply to work, so if you don't, you must be of no value to the human race. Because I didn't work, it was a cardinal sin.

—*THE FACE,* 1984

Working-class men in particular were supposed to make themselves *useful;* they were to work with their hands, not manicure them. Thus the sissy, effeminate, or simply unmanly boy was an embarrassment in most working-class families, at least to his father. Fairy boys—for that's what they were, regardless of their sexual orientation—were worse than useless, and frequently less loved than runt puppies. Their only hope was to run away to London and become hairdressers. Or pop stars. "Nature's cruelest trick" was to put a sensitive, dreamy boy in the body of a working-class lad. And nature played its trick on Morrissey as cruelly as she could.

Above all, the working-class man was supposed to work on something, usually something that belonged to someone else. This was his lot in life, and he was supposed to lump it; whining was definitely not permitted. His labor, his feelings, and ultimately his life were alienated from him before he was even born. Glam opposed that. Glam said you were your own boss and encouraged working-class boys to work on something they did own—themselves. It proved to be the only job that Steven was qualified for.

I remember buying David Bowie's "Starman" when it was No. 42 in the charts and that was a truly extraordinary time for me. I was falling in love with the potency of the pop moment. That's why I'm here. That's why I'm involved in music, because the pop moment in my life was the only thing that ever spoke to me.

—*THE IRISH TIMES,* 1999

Steven was taken to the mountaintop by the Men Who Fell to Earth—Marc, David, and Bryan (the Geordie coal miner's son turned cool miner)—and shown the kingdom of an alternative, lazy kind of world, a world where people like him would be revered as royalty instead of treated like freaks, followed as leaders rather than chased down the street. But the world turned, and Lucifer, the brightest evening star, began to wax, wane, and set over the horizon. Marc faltered, Ziggy returned to Mars, and Bryan went to L.A. Steven was forced to look to the New World to keep the faith.

IN 1973, HE saw a kooky, anarchic underground U.S. glam band called the New York Dolls on a late-night TV rock program and quickly became their biggest U.K. fan—more devoted even than he had been to Marc. Bolan had been too commonly adored, too successful, while the obscure, foreign, self-destructing Dolls were all Steven's. Throughout the seventies, he held up a lone lighter flame for them in the auditorium of pop fandom, until his gas ran out, editing a breathless fanzine/scrapbook about them and penning fervid letters to music papers and even TV producers extolling the East Village junkies' limitless merits and damning their critics to eternal perdition (though there weren't too many critics—most were simply oblivious). Characteristically, Steven had chosen to worship a pop band that wasn't very popular, ensuring that there was little chance of finding himself in a social milieu as a result of his new obsession. His fascination with pop culture wasn't to give him something to chat about down at the pub; it was a way of making himself even more inaccessible. His pop interests led him not out of his bedroom into a world of laughing, smiling, dancing, drunken young people, but farther into the recesses of his own unhealthy mind. Glam rock and rebellion were all very well, but you mustn't let them become too *democratic*.

I don't know where the New York Dolls obsession came
from. . . . I went to all the right gigs in Manchester in the
seventies. I was there at the age of twelve, I was there at the
age of fifteen. I may have gone to these events totally alone,
but I stood there and I saw everybody, so cross-breeding
this with understanding words and enjoying Joyce Grenfell
is . . . well, what is it? It's made me what I am today.
      —*NME*, 1989

In choosing to support the Dolls, Steven had, as always,
demonstrated impeccable taste. But the point of taste is to distin-
guish yourself from the hoi polloi—especially when it is the culture of the hoi polloi you are consuming and enthusing about.
When, around 1976, Steven began to realize that his only
hope—in fact, his only option—lay in somehow turning himself
into one of those professionally idle creatures known as pop stars,
he began advertising in the music press for other band members.
Of course, he stipulated that they must be "New York Dolls/Patti
Smith fans" (the strung-out, stormy, tortured New York songwriter and poet was the kind of woman on the inside that the
Dolls tried to be on the outside; she may even have provided the
patronymic for Morrissey and Marr's "marriage"). There were no
replies. But that must have been saddening and gratifying all at
once. As was often to be the case in Steven's life, disappointment
was its own consolation.

However, young Steven wasn't quite the only person in the
U.K. to see the potential of the New York Dolls. The London-
based, Manchester Poly–educated fashion designer, situationist
spiv, and Fagin-wannabe Malcolm McLaren was also a fan of the
band accorded the singular honor of being voted the Best and
also the Worst Band of 1973 by U.S. magazine *Creem*. Hence
the Dolls ended up being the strumpet American progenitors of
that other seventies pop revolution, a transatlantic bridge of pink

panty hose between glam and punk over which Malcolm McLaren, who "managed" the New York Dolls for a mad moment before they finally imploded (a sticky end he hastened by dressing them in red patent leather and hanging a hammer and sickle behind them onstage), was eventually to lead John Lydon and the swaying Sex Pistols, a group that took the "street" and "hustler" parts of the Dolls' street-trannie-on-the-game look but discarded the rest. (Steven was to complain vociferously in letters to the British music press about the Pistols' bad clothes.)

For their part, the Dolls seemed to base their striking look, and quite a bit of their driving sound, on the Rolling Stones circa their 1966 hit single "Have You Seen Your Mother, Baby, Standing in the Shadows?"; in the promotional film, the Stones dressed in disturbingly sexy forties drag.

Arthur Kane, on bass for the Dolls, wore tights and black sequined hot pants; guitarist Johnny Thunders wore leather pants and a miniskirt; Sylvain Sylvain (such a good name, such a pretty name, he used it twice) and Jerry Nolan sported big, teased perms; and David Johansen wore little more than a pair of pouting lips. Theirs was a glam look crazily cranked up (literally—the Dolls had a reputation for serious drug abuse) until it was precariously close to out-and-out drag.

However, what made the New York Dolls special, and what endeared them so much to a certain fourteen-year-old increasingly obsessed with the tyranny of gender roles, was the fact that their "drag" was not terribly authentic; instead, it was terribly, provocatively "half-cocked." It was neither one thing nor t'other—neither Arthur nor Martha. Moreover, their playing style was extremely tough, aggressive, and hard. They were androgynous but they weren't eunuchs. These were rowdy trannies, the kind that were more likely to roll you in the alleyway than to kiss you. If all beautiful things really are a mixture of masculine and feminine, then perhaps it's also true that all truly terrifying things are also a mixture of masculine and feminine.

The crossed cross-dressing of the New York Dolls, which was probably basically heterosexual (whatever that might mean), had parallels with the "rad-drag" of gay-liberationist street activists who were very visible in Manhattan's Village in the early seventies (before gay lib was taken over by the disco-dancing Marlboro Man). In an attempt to theatricalize and expose what they saw as the absurdity of gender conformity in general, and masculinity in particular, these street activists would take *cross-dressing* at its word: wearing female clothes but being careful not to shave; or shaving and wearing fussy wigs and pancake makeup but pulling on a pair of men's trousers and not bothering with underwear. The effect was intended to frighten the horses, and frequently did.

The fuck-you gender fuck of the New York Dolls, years before the antics of Kiss and other metalheads rendered them a cliché (and, it goes without saying, massively popular in a way that the Dolls had never been), was troubling and transgressive precisely because it wasn't neatly explained in either a commercial or a political sense. The Dolls dressed the way they did because they wanted to. It was by drawing on the spirit of this almost forgotten tradition, rather than on the obvious campy panto drag of the New Romantics, that Morrissey's understated, casual androgyny of women's shirts, men's jeans, and cheap plastic jewelry seemed so fresh when it arrived on the pop scene in 1983, rendering the gender benders' "outrageous" frocks passé overnight (with the honorable exception of Pete Burns, of course, who was practically the sixth, Scouse member of the New York Dolls; not so much gender *bender* as gender *mugger*).

Gender bending/gender fucking was already well under way in Western culture in the seventies, and both glam rock and gay lib were as much expressions of this as causes of it. The rise of

feminism in the seventies, which Steven was to support as
fiercely as he had supported glam, and the arrival of women in
public life and the workplace had already messed around with
gender roles and flipped male supremacy the bird (quite literally,
in the case of a leathered-up, feisty female glam rocker like Suzi
Quatro). Militancy was "in," and slogans such as "The personal is
political" and "Our bodies, ourselves" filled the air. Glam interpreted these currents in its own vain, selfish, largely male fashion.
Although glam rock didn't see itself as part of an assault on
"patriarchy," even in its bruising, bricklaying Sweet/Slade incarnation, it represented the most blatant expression so far of the
unspoken but universal wish among young men on which pop
(and rock) music was built: *Please, God, don't let me grow up to be
like my dad.* If long hair pissed dads off in the sixties, platform
shoes and makeup were bound to give long-haired dads in the
seventies a stroke—an outcome that a fourteen-year-old Steven,
trying (not very hard) to negotiate his Oedipus complex and his
father's indifference/absence, must have found not entirely unappealing.

Self-invention as a mantra, androgyny as evangelism, sexual
ambiguousness as a style, narcissism as a religion, self-cultivation
as a way of life—this was the credo of glam rock that Steven
Morrissey enthusiastically intoned, confirming those elements of
his own personality that he had already developed as a strategy of
psychic self-preservation (and, ultimately, retribution). Of course,
practically speaking, they weren't the best lessons an unpopular,
sensitive boy trying to survive a sinkhole Manchester secondary
modern in the seventies could learn. Dyeing your hair, wearing
eyeliner, and carrying a handbag made from the seat of a pair of
old jeans was not going to make you Captain of Games.
Fortunately, Steven, despite his sporting prowess, wasn't terribly
interested in being Captain of Games (even if he may have
sometimes enjoyed watching him from the sideline).

He told himself that he wasn't interested in being popular, either—and ended up almost believing it. And for the first time in his life, he was being noticed—or looked at twice. Steven was beginning to openly advertise his uniqueness; he didn't want his appearance to declare anything but his genius.

JIMMY DEAN
ON THE DOLE

I had a very small bedroom and I remember going through periods when I was eighteen and nineteen where I literally would not leave it for three to four weeks. . . . I'd be sitting there in near darkness alone with the typewriter and surrounded by masses of paper. The walls were totally bespattered with James Dean, almost to the point of claustrophobia, and I remember little bits of paper pinned everywhere with profound comments . . . newspaper clippings like FISH EATS MAN. Probably the most important quote was from Goethe: "Art and Life are different, that's why one is called Art and one is called Life."

—MORRISSEY

It is through Art, and through Art only, that we can realize our perfection; through Art, and through Art only, that we can shield ourselves from the sordid perils of actual existence.

—OSCAR WILDE

6.

Life for Steven failed to begin when he left school at age sixteen, armed with three O levels, in English literature, sociology, and the general paper. All fairly useless qualifications in the worldly scheme of things, but quite sufficient for someone destined to be only the greatest lyricist and pop star of his generation.

In fact, apart from the occasional call of nature and plate of baked beans on toast, he now had no reason to leave his bedroom at all. He did make some brief, half-hearted attempts at living in what passes for the real world, working as a clerk for the civil service and later for the Inland Revenue—typical bureaucratic government jobs for a literate secondary-modern-school leaver in the pre–information technology and Mrs. T. seventies; "It's secure and has prospects," the school careers officer would say, trying to accentuate the positive aspects of being buried alive, completely wrongly as it turned out. But by the time he was eighteen, Steven found himself bored before he had even begun, and so drew the curtains on the world, signed on the dole and off the human race, and spent the rest of his adolescence living in a shell. Like all dreamers, Steven mistook disenchantment for truth.

I was never young. This idea of fun: cars, girls, Saturday night, bottle of wine . . . to me, those things are morbid. I

was always attracted to people with the same problems as me. It doesn't help when most of them are dead.
—*IN HIS OWN WORDS,* MORRISSEY

Life may not have begun when he left school, but at least his education did. While his contemporaries were satisfying themselves of their own identity and destiny by exploring oral cavities other than their own and taking their clothes off in company, Steven set out to discover himself and his future through reading forgotten books and watching old movies. While others practiced the tricky business of walking down the street arm in arm, Steven was courting famous corpses such as Oscar Wilde and James Dean. While others heavy-petted in the park, he was conducting a spot of cultural grave-robbing to further his fiendish experiments in self-invention. While they worried about unwanted pregnancies and whether it really was safe to shag a girl standing up, he was feverishly fathering himself in the form of the literary-inseminated monster Morrissey.

I read so much that I tried to give it up because I wasn't actually living. I was just creased up in a chair twenty hours of every single day. . . . I tried to be a journalist but failed miserably. I used to write songs but with only nebulous tunes, because I couldn't play an instrument.
—AUSTRALIAN RADIO, 1985

STEVEN WAS DETERMINED to make something of himself by way of the most difficult route imaginable: mastering those impotent, worthless, fickle things called words. The desperate pathetic fool was determined to become that most absurd of creatures, *a writer.* He lived for the written word, and people came second or possibly third. The very intellectualism, the very self-reflexiveness, the very illness that had ravaged and ruined his life and set him apart from the human race was, he thought, going to set him free. He was determined to make sense of himself, the world, and his place in it by . . . typing. It was, needless to say, a ridiculous enough project in itself. Yet Steven's nuttiness went further. He harbored the loony, laughable notion that words might one day help him to conquer something as defiantly illiterate as pop music.

Of all the silly scribblers that Steven cavorted with in his bedroom, Wilde was quite the silliest, and hence the one who aroused him most. His style was irredeemable and his way with words quite fatal. Wilde, of course, was a poet of foolishness, a spinner of oddly convincing sophistry who managed to bring the world to its knees before it came to its senses instead and sent him to rot in Reading Gaol.

> I've read practically everything (by and about him) and I
> have a vast collection of first editions. Although he was the
> most intelligent, he simplified everything, therefore
> practically anybody could read Oscar Wilde and
> understand. He wasn't complicated, yet he still left you
> lying on the bed panting because it was so real and
> truthful.
> —*NME,* 1988

A piece of pop trivia that would have appeared anything but trivial to Steven: The New York Dolls gave a performance in 1972 at the Mercer Arts Center in New York in a room named after the effeminate Irish dandy who entertained, anatomized, shocked, and finally provoked respectable British society to strike him down. It was an entirely apt venue—as has been pointed out, Oscar Wilde was, after all, the leader of the nineteenth-century glam-rock movement (though back then it was known as the Aesthetic Movement). This relatively vulgar upstart full of gentle rage set about assaulting English bourgeois mores with relentless zeal, but more important—and this was something that both disarmed and embittered the English—with wit. No wonder Steven was obsessed with Oscar.

Moreover, Oscar was that very rare kind of writer, one who appealed to the heart and the head simultaneously (an even rarer gift among lyricists until Morrissey). By sheer force of will and the meticulous cultivation of his personality, Oscar succeeded in making himself a pop star without learning to play an instrument, forming a band, or signing to a record label long before pop music had even been invented. His epigrams were 45-rpm singles *avant la lettre:* beautiful, poisonous, brilliant little flashes of lyrical egotism and vanity that proved instantly catchy, zooming to the top of the social hit parade and getting played over and over again at parties.

Wilde was entirely artificial, but he frequently succeeded in being more direct and honest than anyone else. He was a creature of culture but managed to appear completely natural. His style allowed him to step outside of himself and social expectations and into something much more truthful and fearless than any man had a right to.

Oscar's whole life was a work of art, which is to say that he was entirely doomed. He was both enthusiastically perverse and a keen invert, which means he gleefully turned conventional wisdom upside down and knavishly assaulted traditional attitudes, something any star worth his twinkle would want to do.

What do you consider the most overrated virtue?
Common sense.
　　　—*KILL UNCLE* TOUR BOOK, 1991

These were reasons enough for Steven to want Oscar as his spiritual father. But there were more. Oscar was a mummy's boy, but like many overtalented mummy's boys, including Steven, he was the author of his own personality; more his own man than any daddy's boy could ever be, or would want to be. Oscar was Irish, but like many other Irish émigrés to England, he became more English than the English. Oscar became more aristocratic than the aristocracy, which were already beginning the undignified scramble to become middle class. Despite this, or perhaps because of this, he succeeded in appealing to all social classes, even Americans. Best of all, he embodied and lived his own creative contradictions: He championed idleness but was at least intermittently prolific; he was an idealist and the Queen of Cynics; he was a romantic yet frighteningly realistic; he was a moralist yet completely dissolute. (Morrissey, of course, is an immoralist who is scandalously virtuous.)

> Do you want to know the great drama of my life? It's that I have put my genius into my life; all I've put into my works is my talent.
>
> —WILDE, QUOTED IN ANDRE GIDE'S *OSCAR WILDE*

Oscar's life was of a piece with his work and ended up transcending his art. Sexual scandal involving rent boys made this aesthete and all that he stood for synonymous with the "filthiest" and "ugliest" of crimes, provoking national disgust, anger, and hysteria on such a scale that it lasted well into the next century; the merest mention of his accursed name was sufficient to drive some men into apoplexy. However, by the sixties and seventies, it was precisely his indecent acts and scandalous reputation that had made him the hippest dead poet in town. The symbol of aberration had become a symbol of liberation. In 1967, in the wake of one of their drug scandals (by this time, drugs were the new degenerate threat to British life), the Rolling Stones single "We Love You" was promoted with a short film in which they reenacted Oscar's trial. Mick Jagger, of course, was the poet in the dock, complete with green carnation, symbol of the Aesthetic Movement. It was a slightly impertinent gesture: After all, despite what might be described as Mr. Jagger's "cocksucking lips," a claim to Wilde's corrupting-inspiring mantle by a pop star wasn't fully justified until two decades later, when Morrissey covered the stage and his audience with flowers and petal-jism during a performance of "This Charming Man."

> I hope you have not been leading a double life, pretending to be wicked and being really good all the time. That would be hypocrisy.
>
> —OSCAR WILDE, *THE IMPORTANCE OF BEING EARNEST*

Today, in a world that has been conquered by rock and pop, or at least by its most vulgar representatives, and where everything has been aestheticized and made-over, the rehabilitation of Oscar Wilde is horribly complete. He is now the Queen Mother of New Labour, loved by everyone, a threat to no one. Tacky statues to him are unveiled by government ministers and glossy feature films are made portraying him as a harmless poof with some good one-liners and tasty waistcoats, the hapless victim of other people's nasty, outdated, unfashionable, chintzy bigotry. In fact, today Wilde's greatest misfortune, you might be forgiven for thinking, was that he was born too soon to be a presenter on *Changing Rooms*. Wilde, who once existed outside of society to bring it to account, now exists for it, to tell us how with-it we are, how tolerant, how groovy, how good-humored, how tasteful, how *relaxed*.

GERALD: I suppose society is wonderfully delightful!
LORD ILLINGWORTH: To be in it is merely a bore. But to be
out of it, simply a tragedy.
—OSCAR WILDE, *A WOMAN OF NO IMPORTANCE*

To be sure, the real Wilde was an outsider who wanted to
be an insider, but only the better to spike the city's drinking
water. Oscar has been done to death by his fans, even more than
Reading Gaol.

Of course, this assimilated, emasculated, populist Wilde
bears no relation to the wicked Wilde that Steven worshipped,
emulated, and relentlessly rehearsed in his bedroom. There were
probably always two Wildes: Steven's Wilde and Stephen's *Wilde*.
But just as Morrissey's skinny, malcontent Wilde is the only version worth remembering and imitating, it's perhaps inevitable
that Fry's flabby, social-climbing *Wilde* is the one the world
would ultimately take to its bosom. (It is equally inevitable that
even before the first clod of earth hits his coffin, Morrissey will
himself be rehabilitated, too—miraculously cured of his scorn
and self-destructiveness, he will be remembered as a lovable
"eccentric," a singing Grinch with a touching tendency to
become mildly distracted at the plight of small furry animals and
small furry orphans; in his biopic, he will be played by Gareth
Gates wearing a hearing aid.)

Mind you, the worship of a fan like Steven is a very dangerous thing; much more dangerous than the worship of a Stephen.
While most who emulate their heroes (quite deliberately) never
come close to matching their achievements, let alone surpassing
them, Steven was to match Wilde's achievements and quickly
overhaul them. After all, how many times was Oscar hugged and
kissed onstage? How many times did he throw his sweat-
drenched silk shirt into the crowd and witness it torn to shreds?
How many times did he get on *Top of the Pops?* How many

millions of adolescent bedrooms was he entertained in? Oscar
may have scandalized and corrupted nineteenth-century polite
English society (and a few rent boys who didn't exactly need
much corrupting), but Steven was to corrupt a whole generation—in their parents' homes. And pay *him* for it.

Young Steven wasn't entirely monogamous in his affections,
however. He kept in his room another famously cool corpse, one
younger and fitter than Wilde but even more pernicious. If Wilde
had tainted the golden age of English bourgeois culture, this one
had almost single-handedly spoiled the American fifties, depriving it of its innocence and white-picket-fence mom-and-pop
blandness. Even better, he had died before his twenty-fifth birthday, just at the moment when his corrupting influence on
American/Western youth was about to provoke an unstoppable
chain reaction and just before the world could exact its usual
price for his fame. By impaling his young body on his Porsche
Spyder's steering wheel, he reneged on his Faustian deal and
managed to cheat the world of its revenge; he didn't end up in
Reading Gaol or Bel-Air. He didn't just leave behind a beautiful,
if somewhat worse-for-the-wear, corpse; he left behind a reputation unscathed.

> I would like to go to Indiana and mess with his soil, but so
> many others have done it. They've taken away the
> monument, they've taken away the stone, and they've taken
> away the grass. People have been so greedy. What's left for
> me?
> —*NME*, 1985

His name, of course, was James Byron Dean. And his image
covered the walls of Steven's adolescent bedroom prison, as if he
wanted to replace the dreary limits of his Manchester existence
with Dean's beauty. And why not? Jimmy symbolized success,

fame, glamor, originality, integrity, and immortality. *Handsomeness;*
such heartbreaking, hurtful handsomeness.

> He had that strange quality that he could look good
> anywhere, in anything.
> —*THE HOT PRESS,* 1984

Dean was the epitome of Steven's lifelong obsession with
men whose looks bring them popularity, smooth their passage
through life, and appear, rightly or wrongly, to be an index of
their ease in their bodies and the world. Their happiness. Like
many outsiders, Steven felt himself to be essentially unlovable. To
feel simply ugly would have been a relief; instead, he felt *monstrous.* Like most who stand apart, Steven had exiled himself with
his own inferiority-superiority complex. Learning that Dean was
also insecure and unhappy only made the actor's handsomeness
all the more astonishing and alluring.

> Send me anything that Jimmy touched.
> —*JAMES DEAN IS NOT DEAD,* 1983

By pasting his bedroom walls with countless images of
Jimmy, he turned his prison tower into a fantasy mirror in which
he saw himself reflected back as he would have liked to have seen
himself: a creature who may be tortured and full of self-doubt
but always manages to look comfortable in his skin and radiate
an animal magnetism. Steven may have wanted Wilde's mind, but
he wanted Dean's body. In an attempt to get under Dean's skin
and to combine two of his obsessions—words and beauty—he
wrote an essay about Dean in which he described himself as a
"James Dean fan and devotee." Essentially, it was an act of literary
resurrection; reading it, you can feel Steven trying to breathe life
into Dean's broken body with his feverish words. Called "James

Dean Is Not Dead," the subtitle might have been: "He's Just Sleeping Under My Bed."

> You can look into a mirror and wonder—where have I
> seen that person before? And then you remember. It was at
> a neighbor's funeral, and it was the corpse.
> —*BLITZ*, APRIL 1988

Steven's identification with Jimmy was intense, possibly sexual, and certainly sick and ill—but then, so was the interest that most young men had in Jimmy. Steven's peculiar perversion was to apply his intellect to what was, essentially, a splendidly stupid phenomenon. But to lonely, misanthropic Steven, hiding from the world in his bedroom in his mother's council house in Manchester, it must have appeared perfectly natural—or the least unnatural thing in his life. Jimmy was, after all, the most hopeful dead body Steven had in his bedroom—an unpopular loner who achieved world fame and worship from teenagers of both sexes on a scale never seen before. He was a mummy's boy who was masculine. He had been rejected by his father, but he had become his own man. He was masochistic but fearless. He was a complete twat, but he was cool. He was bisexual but all-American. He was that most cosseted of creatures, a Hollywood actor, but he took terrible risks. He was a total fuckup but achieved astounding success. He was famous but—and this is a trick that few mortals ever manage to pull off (today's generation of pliant young Hollywood stars don't even bother to try)—*on his own terms.*

Above all, he was a freak, *but he was desirable.* James Dean was the latter-day Narcissus, in love with the reflection of himself on the silver screen. Jimmy had given a face and a name to a romantically depraved male vanity and made it not just acceptable, but hip. Steven wanted that face. Fortunately for him, it was for sale.

If Wilde was "the first pop star," then Jimmy was the first pop star you'd want to shag (Frank or Bing sans cardigan and slacks, anyone?), the first pop star whose body, whose desirability, was completely commodified. The public queued up, in a (strange) manner of speaking, to sniff his underwear. This was the nature of the pervy deal that pop culture offered. In exchange for your dough, you were given the chance to possess a commodity that was a fetish, or Holy Relic, standing in for the star: the film (the residue of his aura); the poster (the imprint of his halo); the blue jeans (the nearest thing to his skin—and talent); and above all, the single (the magical piece of vinyl that captured his soul). But, of course, there weren't any singles, since Dean happened to be a pop star who didn't make records, just movies (it would take Colonel Tom Parker to work out what the world needed, producing a singing hillbilly Dean).

I gotta know who I am. I gotta know!
—JAMES DEAN IN *EAST OF EDEN*

Perhaps this was why, after Dean's death at the age of twenty-four, in 1955, the very year that the pop star and pop music were definitively brought together in the person of Elvis—who actually wanted to be a film star like Dean—the teenage public went crazy for Jimmy. Now that Dean was gone, they couldn't get enough.

Death was undoubtedly more than half hinted at in Dean's self-absorption, particularly in *Rebel Without a Cause*, eerily released after he was already six feet under and food for worms, but death at *high speed* (in his own "chicken run" with a black-and-white sedan driven by a rustically oblivious Mr. Turnupseed on Highway 46) was the perfect ending for Dean. It contained the elements of both activity and passivity, which marked his on-screen persona and made him so desirable (and which

Morrissey was to incorporate into his own persona). Death rendered Dean entirely prone, subject to complete possession by his audience, and as commodified as the hamburger and the ice-cream cone, which his hometown of Fairmount, Indiana, also bequeathed to a lip-smacking world. But the manner of his death, its impetuousness, preserved his dangerously boyish masculinity and at the same time guaranteed that he would "never be a man"—or become Dad. Hence, Jimmy was the first pop star to live forever.

Steven, whose own fame would not begin until he was the age at which Dean died, was awed by Jimmy's Oedipal Houdini act but resolved that he would improve on Dean's achievement by pulling off this feat of famous frozen adolescence without having to resort to the inconvenience of actually dying (much of his carefully assembled iconography and album covers have the whiff of holy relics about them).

As Steven described breathlessly in "James Dean Is Not Dead," 2,000 letters arrived at Dean's studio every week addressed to a man who was famously deceased (obviously the letter writers thought Hollywood would have a forwarding address for him, or else thought Hollywood was actually Heaven). Others bought rings that claimed to contain chips from his tombstone, or paid to sit in the Porsche Spyder, next to the buckled steering wheel that tore open his chest, and touch his dried blood. *East of Eden* director Elia Kazan pointed out that James Dean was a "sick kid"—but pop culture was far sicker. Morrissey himself would later be accused of having a morbid and unnatural interest in death and suicide and fetishism, of which charge he is entirely guilty. But the James Dean cult taught him that death, suicide, and morbid fetishism are what pop culture is all about—lessons that ensured he would end up a pop star adored as much by his fans alive as Dean was after his death. (A point ironically underlined by the scene in the promotional video for the 1988 single "Suedehead" in which he "messes with the soil" of James Dean's grave in Fairmount—an act of homage and also perhaps a kind of desecration: *"Why do you come here when you know it makes things hard for me?"*)

But there was something more to Dean's fatal narcissism, something more unyielding and lasting than all the diamonds that Hollywood pay-packets could buy, something with which Steven passionately identified: Dean was a Beautiful Bastard. A traitor not just to his father and friends but to his trade, he was determined to betray all its values and transgress all its fond nostrums and proud traditions for the sake of a much higher cause: *himself.*

Acting is just interpretation. I want to create myself.
—JAMES DEAN

In contrast to Brando and Clift, the actors with whom Dean is usually compared and who were consummate professionals, able to immerse themselves chameleonlike in their roles, Dean was never very interested in his characters or what he could tell us about them. He was interested in them only in terms of what they could tell him about himself and what he could tell us about himself through them. Dean had little or no technique, only style. Like Wilde, he pursued a more authentic version of himself through artifice—his style was the truest expression of himself. He habitually changed lines, dropped them, or omitted whole speeches, and he frequently eased himself into the director's chair (Nicholas Ray allowed Dean unprecedented input during the making of *Rebel*). He abused his profession in the most appalling fashion, had no respect for it or for the film industry or, for that matter, for the fifties, and consequently transformed it beyond recognition and assured his greatness. This was the pattern that Morrissey was to repeat faithfully in his own career.

It's not his acting, actually I think he was a bit of a ham. I get quite embarrassed when I see those films. But I'm fascinated by the way he seemed to represent his time and his generation.

—*HOT PRESS*, 1984

In his single-minded, selfish, slightly psychotic self-creation through pop culture, Dean the Beautiful Bastard became an inspiration for millions of young malcontents who, like Steven, were unhappy with the role or script that their agent, Dame Fate, had landed them. He was to become an inspirational Oedipus for the illegitimate children of junk culture, a boy determined not so much to kill his father as to cut him off from his destiny by simply refusing to reproduce him, instead choosing his own antecedents taken from pop culture (Dean hero-worshipped Brando as much and as embarrassingly as Steven later worshipped Dean).

In *Rebel,* his compromising, complacent, uncool father—who attempts to ingratiate policemen by offering them cigars, allows himself to be henpecked by his harridan wife, and can never say what he thinks or feels—is clearly not worthy of being Jim Stark/James Dean's father (though in deference to fifties gender politics and a fashionable paranoia about momism, Jim Stark is portrayed as being driven to rebellion by his pinny-wearing father's emasculation; by contrast, Steven and Jimmy's problem appears to have been a conventionally masculine and distant fifties father who never wore a pinny). In *Rebel,* Jim's delinquency derives from a refusal to be a product of his parent's dysfunctional narrative, which deprives him of his own identity: *"You're tear-ring me a-part!"* He, on the other hand, is putting himself *together.* He wants to tell his story, not repeat theirs. The Beautiful Bastard is a rebel with a cause—a psychopathic determination to be unique.

Of course, there is another "bastard" in *Rebel,* one whom Steven probably recognized only too well. Plato, played by a brooding, sullen Sal Mineo, is from a broken home. Abandoned by his father, he lives with his overprotective mother. He has a soft-focus publicity picture of Alan Ladd, a potential Smiths cover star, pinned on the inside of his school locker where he should have a picture of Jayne Mansfield or a faceless baseball star. Clearly possessing an eye for the iconic, he dotes on Jim with big, black, upraised cow eyes almost from the moment he meets him (in the police station, appropriately enough). For a brief moment in the final reel, Plato becomes Dean's barely platonic, mildly incestuous "son" (Dean lets him wear his soon-to-be-famous and much-copied windbreaker, something that clearly causes Plato more than a frisson of pleasure), with Natalie Wood as his strangely indulgent mother, playing peculiar happy families in a condemned building.

Rebel was released six years before *A Taste of Honey,* another parable of an alternative family blooming and withering in a derelict landscape. Of course, Hollywood organized a much tidier and more humane ending than *Taste:* Where Geof mooches off into the night, Plato is helpfully gunned down by the cops (when Jim sees the dead body, he zips up the windbreaker Plato is still wearing, in a fetishistic gesture of consummation that millions of young men around the world were to repeat after Dean's own death.)

Not surprisingly, Steven didn't want to be Plato. Truth be told, this failed school-leaver and wannabe delinquent was fed up with *being* Plato. He didn't want to be a victim. He wanted to be a new kind of hero. One with great hair. Steven was determined that the world would one day look up to him with the same wide, greedy eyes as Plato, and he would see reflected in them . . . Jim Stark.

The problem was he had no idea how he was going to bring this about. And time was against him now.

BRILLIANT
BEHIND'S

I just opened the door one day and there he was, exactly
how he found me he hasn't made clear. He just appeared at
my door one day. It sounds really fanciful, but that's
exactly how it happened. He said, "Would you like to write,
and form a group?"

— MORRISSEY, "ASK ME, ASK ME, ASK ME," 1984

The lunatic, the lover, and the poet
Are of imagination all compact....
Such tricks hath strong imagination,
That, if it would but apprehend some joy,
It comprehends some bringer of that joy.

—WILLIAM SHAKESPEARE, *A MIDSUMMER NIGHT'S DREAM*

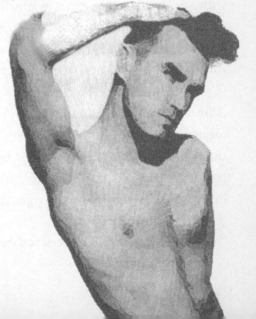

7.

fter "Morrissey," Johnny Marr was Steven's greatest inspiration. So no wonder he loved him.

Marr, like anyone meshed in the web of someone else's desire, like any beloved trapped in the amber of the lover's imagination, labored under the extravagant delusion that he was his *own* idea. He even thought that meeting Steven that fateful day in 1982 and proposing they form a band was something he had dreamed up himself. He was gravely mistaken. All these things came from Steven, and Steven's exceedingly uncharacteristic decision to answer the doorbell—if only because the idea of Morrissey, assembled in Steven's bedroom for more than a thousand years, was so intense and had a gravitational attraction so strong, so irresistible, so evil, that it was bound to make a satellite of anyone foolish enough to fly anywhere near him.

Marr the beloved had to love Morrissey back for reasons that no mortal could argue with: Because Morrissey wrote at the drop of a hat the kind of lines that other lyricists strive for over a lifetime. Because he sang to Marr's music like his life depended on it (which, of course, it did). Because Morrissey, for all his heinous faults and failure to mix at parties, had the most beautiful soul in the world (in the right light), which he proceeded to pour all over Marr.

It was perhaps understandable that Johnny should have

entertained such notions about his own authorship and agency. Even though he was, chronologically speaking, four years younger than Steven, he was the worldly-wise one. He was a ladies' man, a wide boy, a charmer, and a virtuoso guitarist whose riffs were the envy of his mates. Steven, on the other hand, was just a loser—a skinny, celibate vegetarian who couldn't play a note on a vibraphone and could barely even leave his room in his mother's house; Steven was seven going on seventy. He had no friends to speak of. He certainly had no lover. He had no job. He had no life. Johnny, of course, had everything, and anything he didn't have, he knew how to get. And Steven wanted to be tied to the back of his car.

> I lead a saintly life, he lives a devilish life. And the combination is wonderful. Perfect.
> —*NME*, 1983

In other words, Steven was a dreamer and Johnny was a man of the world. But men of the world and all their enviable practical qualities are invented by dreamers, because men of the world are necessary for dreamers to do what all dreamers want to do, what all dreamers have to do: inflict their dreams on the rest of us.

Naturally, the world and men of the world (and more often than not even the dreamers themselves) don't want to see it that way. They want to think that activity controls and shapes passivity, when, in fact, passivity always encloses activity, using it for its own ends.

> Johnny, Mike, and Andy played their instruments in a very aggressive way. The feeling of power was just like having a vacuum cleaner shoved up your blazer.
> —*NME*, 1990

According to the legend, Johnny was the gallant Prince Charming to Steven's sulking Beauty. Johnny's arrival on Steven's doorstep cut a swath through the enchanted forest that imprisoned Steven in Stretford; the romantic proposal to "write and form a band" was the awakening kiss that liberated him from his womb-tomb bedroom and let him loose on the world. However, the script and even the gender roles in this production were not what they appeared. As it said on the sleeves, the words were by Morrissey and the music was by Marr. Since it was written by Steven, the script was more *Rebel Without a Cause,* and Johnny Marr was more Natalie Wood than Jimmy Dean (certainly Johnny's unfortunate haircut on the sleeve of *Hatful of Hollow* bears this out). Jimmy was, after all, the tortured, introverted loner that Natalie—outgoing, popular, and a bit of a tomboy— introduces to "the kids." Jimmy, the passive/impassive boy, stands apart, as distinct and scornful as Steven's Deanian coif.

> Johnny had grasped the thread of all that was relevant and yet he was—and remains—a very happy-go-lucky, optimistic person who was interested in doing it now. Not tomorrow, but right now! Also, he appeared at a time when I was deeper than the depths, if you like. And he provided me with this massive energy boost. I could feel Johnny's energy just seething inside of me.
> —*THE FACE,* 1985

Perhaps Marr's decision five years later, in 1987, to break up the family and leave Morrissey and the Smiths was prompted by the realization that he was more Morrissey's fancy than his own man. A decision that may have devastated many fans, including, of course, Morrissey, and that may have been a mistake, professionally speaking—the world was at their feet in 1987—but one that no one, not even Morrissey, could really hold against Marr.

Johnny, in addition to being by all accounts a likable, modest guy, is a great, dazzlingly original, and bafflingly talented musician and composer who has been rightfully guaranteed a place in the pop pantheon. Nevertheless, Johnny the Charmer's greatest and most serious contribution to pop/criminal history was to galvanize Morrissey into action, to bring levity into a world of depression, and, most of all, to provide him with the means by which he could impose his wonderfully warped reality on the world—to be the catchy vector by which the Moz virus could infect and ruin millions of lives.

For Steven, as for any hermit prophet whose wish comes true and the mountain comes visiting, meeting Marr was literally fatal. Just as he had hoped and willed and dreamed and prayed, (chaste—the only kind, really) love and salvation came to him through the medium of pop music. He had been vindicated in his misanthropy and malcontentedness. Now that he was actually going to become a pop star and was, moreover, to have company along the way, there was no need to ever become socialized, no need to grow up, no need to ever enter into the world of people or compromise. *No need to ever become a human being.*

> Oscar Wilde had a few words to say, of which you should take careful note: "When the Gods wish to punish us, they answer our prayers."
> —*THE FACE,* 1984

> We had no row during the entire existence of the Smiths. For a long time, Johnny and I were intertwined—and that's unusual in pop music—in his life and certainly in mine.
> —*THE GUARDIAN,* 1997

This was an odd, fateful marriage between Beautiful Bastards; it was Jimmy and Natalie, Jo and Geof together against the world (though, like Jo, Steven was already pregnant before he met Marr). Together they set up their own alternative family called the Smiths, a name that, like most of the Mancunian misanthrope's art, is both a deliberate parody of average normality and a wistful homage to it. The family that emerged from the derelict, condemned postindustrial landscape of early-eighties Manchester included not only the lost boys Mike Joyce on drums and Andy Rourke on bass, but later all their fans—an extended family of Beautiful Bastards. And, like a traditional girl getting married and starting a family, Steven changed his name. Steven, the poor child, was gone, banished. Now there was only the iconic "Morrissey."

The wedding music was not traditional, however. The first single, "Hand in Glove," released in May 1983, an ominous day in the history of pop music, contains lyrics that appear to be as much a declaration of Morrissey's love for Marr as they are a declaration of the Smiths' manifesto, since the two declarations are, of course, one. It is, simply put, a declaration of war on the world. This is, in fact, the hidden agenda of all great love affairs, including Antony and Cleopatra, Romeo and Juliet, Alexander and Hephaestion, Wilde and Bosie, and Jo and Geof. All lovers are haters, haters of all that is unfortunate enough to be not them.

> GEOF: We're unique!
> JO: Young.
> GEOF: Unrivaled!
> JO: Smashing!
> —SHELAGH DELANEY, *A TASTE OF HONEY*

The adolescent arrogance of this love affair, its impish mooning at the world, is somehow all the more poignant for its ancient-as-the-hills irony: *"No, it's not like any other love."* Like any love worth mentioning, this love's greatest strength and its greatest delusion is its pathological self-sufficiency.

This is a love-hate so strong that it will succeed in sweeping away the empty-headed glamor and shoulder-padded power worship of the early eighties and, in fact, the eighties themselves. The "Hand in Glove" lovers may be in rags, reviled and mocked by the Good People, but they possess something priceless and unique. That "something" is integrity. Honesty. Intelligence. Wit. Total fanaticism. Genius. Scary stage movements. Otherwise known as Morrissey. Hand in glove he stakes his claim.

These are the words of a man taking on the world and relishing it. Marr couldn't have been listening too closely, otherwise he would have split much sooner. What Morrissey was promising was the loneliest of musical partnerships (well, lonely for Marr; for Morrissey it was positively crowded compared to his adolescent exile). The Smiths was to be a vast, noble, windswept mountain on top of which Morrissey and Marr would live alone, breathing in thin, cold air and surviving on a diet of lichen and snow, Joyce and Rourke biding their time thousands of feet below them at base camp. From their glassy aerie, Morrissey and Marr would cast down their bouquets and bolts of lightning and watch them awe and stun the ants below. No manager, no record label, no business or professional imperatives—no reality—would be allowed to touch a hair on the head of the Smiths. Morrissey did not see Marr and the Smiths as a way to open a door onto the world, but a way of *kicking in* the door of the world. Like all lovers, dangerous idealists, and teenagers, Morrissey would brook no compromise; he wanted nothing less than the imposition of his reality on the world. He wanted revenge, and he wanted it NOW.

I won't rest until that song is in the heart of everything. It was so URGENT—to me, it was a complete cry in every direction. It really was a landmark. There is every grain of emotion—that has to be injected into all the songs and it

worked perfectly with "Hand in Glove." It was as if these
four people had to play that song—it was so essential.
Those words had to be sung.

    —*JAMMING*, 1984

Listening to this first single, Morrissey's brilliant, barmy
agenda is all too apparent, and Morrissey's voice and vision stand
out. While Joyce on rhythm is crashing around like his punk
idols, Rourke the disco fan is funking on bass guitar, and Marr is
indulging in a nearly embarrassing spot of Beatles "Love Me Do"
homage-hubris on his harmonica. But Morrissey already sounds
completely confident, fully formed, and utterly, terrifyingly original. Yes, his sources are worn on his sleeve, but his conjunction
of them is truly inspired. After all, a bloke who looks like an
anorexic James Dean singing words steeped in Shelagh Delaney
and Oscar Wilde in the style of Sandie Shaw crossed with the
New York Dolls in a Mancunian accent is original enough for
anyone.

    In fact, Morrissey sounds like nothing ever heard before, yet
entirely familiar, all at once. Unearthly yet disarmingly real, a voice
beyond tears and laughter, he sounds assured that this is it, this is
his chance for a taste of the honey, and no one and—after all these
years of hiding in his room and not answering the doorbell—no
inhibition, no care for what society or *Jukebox Jury* thinks, is going
to stop him. "Hand in Glove" is pop songness distilled so strongly
and sweetly that it threatens to make any that come after it sound
weak, foolish, secondhand, and second-rate. There's an urgency
and directness in Morrissey's voice that will brook no delay, no
argument, no excuse. When he growls and groans between lines,
like a wounded animal with perfect pitch, or (as in later songs,
such as "Barbarism Begins at Home," "The Boy with a Thorn in
His Side," and "Last of the Famous International Playboys") allows
his words to sublimate themselves into a divine, demented yodel-

ing, he transmits a passion that is all the more eloquent in its wordlessness, coming as it does from someone so supernaturally articulate.

In "Hand," Morrissey sounds exactly like what he is: a Northern librarian with a frightening but spellbindingly beautiful grudge against the world let out of the damaged-books storeroom, where he's been locked up for a month of endless Sundays, yet sounding disarmingly fresh where he should be dusty. It's a grudge enacted through words but distilled into something much more dangerous and debilitating through the heat of his own passion—into something truly melodious. It's a grudge, in other words, the listener can't resist, can't help but end up sharing. However, like Jo, Morrissey is aware that this union will be fleeting: *"And I'll probably never see you again."*

There is something in the third repeat of that last line and its drawn-out delivery that is sad and pensive but also celebratory: *"I'll prob-ly ne-ver see you-ou a-gain."* It's partly the bitter wisdom of inexperience, something that you can collect duffel bags of if you spend your teenage years indoors reading too many books, but it's also a sentimental greediness, an inability to resist savoring the sadness of something gained and then lost before it's lost, or even just slightly misplaced. That this is the closing line of the song, providing a pessimistic counterpoint to the insolent opening optimism, makes it quite clear that the prospect of losing what has been gained is already preoccupying Morrissey. In turn, this implies that the whole point of possessing someone in the first place is so that you can lose him.

This is perhaps the very essence of pop: something that at its best and most powerful is a kind of masturbatory melancholia, a kind of crying to oneself. Even when it isn't explicitly about loss and pain, appearing instead to be about the "upside" of love going right rather than the dark downside of love going wrong, pop music is still about loss and pain. The "Ooh, I really love you baby" lyric is frequently implicitly about a perspective gained in contemplation after losing "baby." Pop is a murmuring, sighing attempt to master the experience of loss by making it something you control, making it something that makes you feel ooh-so-good-it-hurts, but also something you secretly wished for yourself and therefore imagine now that you *brought about yourself.* It's a childish game that we all play from the earliest of ages to try and master our own basic unhappiness and inability to control the world and the people around us. Morrissey understands better than any other performer—no, Morrissey *exemplifies* the fact—that at its happy-sad heart, the magic of pop music, its dreamy narcotic effect, is precisely this bittersweet-sweeter blend of hope and despair; the sweetness of happiness and the even sweeter sadness that lies behind the happiness.

For Marr, alas, it is also proof that even during the triumph of their very first single—a triumph singularly unhampered, it has to be said, by chart success—Morrissey already had the idea of Marr leaving the Smiths for him.

It is Morrissey's hand in the glove.

HAND'SOME DEVIL'S

I repeat, the only thing to be in 1983 is handsome!

—MORRISSEY

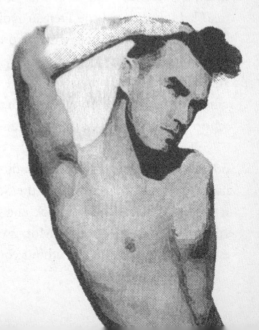

8.

n 1987, a distressed young man in Denver, Colorado, held his local radio station hostage, insisting, at gunpoint, that it play nothing but Smiths records. This they did—for four hours—inflicting Morrissey on the good Christian people of Colorado, who up until that point had been for the most part blissfully unaware of his existence. Eventually, the police besieging the building persuaded the unhappy young man to give himself up.

This was both an unhinged, impotent romantic gesture and a dangerous, revolutionary act. If any music ever had a chance of changing the world, or at least giving it some seriously bad dreams, it was the music of the Smiths. The fervent zeal of this mad lad who forced the Denver radio station to saturate the airwaves of his hometown with records by this obscure, depraved British band was, in its own casualty-free way, more "murderous" and ambitious than the rage of the two young shallow nihilists who went on a shooting spree many years later in their high school in Littleton, also in Colorado.

The Smiths were relentlessly opposed to the world as no other band had been before, including even those priceless sneering antiheroes of the seventies, the Sex Pistols. Unlike the Pistols, who often bluffed it, or struck antagonistic poses for their own sake, the Smiths—or rather, Morrissey—really did appear to hate everything, or at least, everything young people were force-fed as "normal." His lyrics assaulted the education system, the family, marriage, adulthood, gender, the Church, meat eating, money, governments, royalty, discos, fame, relationships, the music business, and, in fact, the whole of the eighties. Morrissey was the real mad lad holding the world hostage at the point of a pop single.

When did it dawn on you it would work?
Instantly, really . . . because it did happen very quickly, even if we're just talking about the first few Smiths gigs. It was more than I expected. There were lots and lots of people ready to identify with what I was feeling. Hatred! Hating everything but not being offensively hateful. It was like hate from quite gentle people.
—MORRISSEY

When, after the frustrating failure of "Hand in Glove," the Smiths' second single "This Charming Man" charted in the top thirty in November 1983 and they were finally invited on BBC TV's *Top of the Pops,* the excitement of Rourke, Joyce, and Marr put together did not even equal the excitement of the plastic beads around Morrissey's neck. *Top of the Pops,* the loved-and-hated tacky TV chart-show institution where he had seen so many of his heroes: Sandie, Bowie, Bolan, Sparks. The hopeless, helpless fan(atic) had finally become a *star.* His strange whooping, whirling, lunging movements on the BBC stage that evening, which so alarmed the schoolgirls bused in from Basingstoke, may have formed the dance of the damned, but of the damned who knew they were not going to hell alone anymore. Like a genie released from a bottle with no intention of granting any wishes except his own (after all, he had released himself), he taunted the world that had stoppered him up for so long. He was going to make sure that people not only noticed him but *experienced* him. Like the romantic terrorist in Colorado, he was committing the most violent, most terrifying act of all: *making people feel what he felt.*

> The Smiths do tease people, making them laugh, then making them cry—operating at opposite ends of the emotional scale. What we're ultimately hoping to do is make them laugh and cry at the same time.
> —*MELODY MAKER,* 1986

Perhaps because it was sincere, Morrissey's hatred was *sensual.* Unlike the oddly asexual Rotten persona, which understandably eschewed romantic lyrics, Morrissey's aura of hatred was openly corporeal. It was a decidedly *handsome* hatred. Instead of theatrical violence, he offered a poisonously sensitive lyricism; instead of gesture politics, he traded in the most powerful and distilled language of hate—love. Instead of nihilism, he offered romanticism. In order achieve these ends, he committed the supreme act of terrorism: He tried to reinvent sex.

> Every song is about sex. I'm very interested in gender. I feel I'm a kind of a prophet for the fourth sex. The third sex, even that has been done and it's failed. All that Marc Almond bit is pathetic. . . . I'm bored with men and I'm bored with women. All this sexual segregation that goes on, even in rock and roll, I really despise it.
> —*SOUNDS,* 1983

Morrissey, the self-styled "prophet of the fourth sex," was intimately committed to destroying the affective world that most people inhabited but from which he had been excluded, or from which he had excluded himself. His erotic terrorism consisted of nothing more than speaking the "truth" of desire—naked (if somewhat neurotic) lust unclothed by fond clichés about gender and warm prejudices about sexuality. In the sweaty handful of first Smiths singles, the seedy-chaste first album *The Smiths,* and its bountiful overspill *Hatful of Hollow,* Morrissey ejaculated a completely careless desire into the face of the world. A desire that was outside—outside of marriage, outside of the family, outside of convention, outside of romance, outside of sexuality. As the definitive outsider, excommunicated from even the brief satisfaction of frustration and alienation offered by "normal" or even conventionally "abnormal" sex, Morrissey understood perfectly that desire is always outside—outside the institutions with which society tries to civilize desire and force it to speak in more hopeful, house-trained, certain terms than it can or should. A desire that is, finally, outside of *us,* and, therefore, ultimately unknowable. Love may well be Natural and Real, but never for *us.*

True to his doomed devotion to the revolutionary truth of desire, sex in Morrissey's work is almost always anticipated, frustrated, averted, or disappointed rather than consummated: *"I doused another venture / with a gesture / that was . . . absolutely vile"* ("I Started Something I Couldn't Finish"). When sex actually does manage to raise its sorry head, it is almost always in lonely public places—literally outside: *"Under the iron bridge we kissed"* ("Still Ill"); *"But I don't want a lover / I just want to be tied to the back of your car"* ("You've Got Everything Now"); *"I know a place where we can go / Where we are not known"* ("These Things Take Time"); *"If you ever need self-validation / Just meet me in the alley"* ("I Want the One I Can't Have"); *"And I know a place / Where no one is likely to pass"* ("Jack the Ripper").

Morrissey's devotion to the undomesticable truth of desire has nothing in common with the mainstream tendency of pop to validate "sex" as good in and of itself, exemplified in its relentless empty pursuit of "sexiness" (which, in any case, is just about selling—which is not actually very sexy at all). Morrissey's vision of desire is utterly pessimistic, but it's strangely liberating for that.

Pick five words that describe yourself.
Loving, lovable, lovely, lovelorn, loveless.
    —Q, 1995

This outsider "love," which represented a rejection of everything society called "decent," (in other words, what everyone knows is false), is the very heart not only of Morrissey's rebelliousness but also his directness. The unpretentiousness of the Smiths, their plain name, appearance, lack of marketing, and sweetly simple guitar arrangements was not only a reaction to the pomposity of New Romantic excess but also a way of driving home the naked truth of Morrissey's words; a constant reminder that the Smiths were not about show business, they were not about entertainment, they were not about packaged escapism, they were not about cheap shock tactics. They were not, in other words, about pop music or sex in ways that most people understood these things. Instead, Morrissey sang sincerely and frankly from his own bitter experience of frustration in such a way that neither pop music—nor sex—could ever be the same again.

While the early Morrissey cultivated a certain understated androgyny in his appearance, sometimes looking like a lesbian attempting a half-hearted gesture at femininity for her visiting parents, it was so subtle, especially in the context of the strumpet world of early-eighties pop, that it represented a rejection of tired ideas about what was unconventional. Instead of the exterior androgyny of glam rock that had been resurrected by the New Romantics and gender benders, Morrissey was really offering an exploration of *interior* androgyny, where handsomeness supplanted glamorousness. In place of the explicit, sensationalist, yet oddly didactic lessons in "sexuality" offered by bands like Frankie Goes to Hollywood and Bronski Beat, Morrissey offered an implicit, innocent seediness—a depiction of desire that may be outside but is not Other, since we all know what it is to be born seedy and innocent, even those of us who are not fortunate enough to be Catholics. Marc Almond, who publicly proclaimed his "bisexuality," did offer a seediness that was more satisfying than most, but compared to Morrissey's it was rather suburban and, truth be told, *showbiz* (despite all the Jean Genet references he was to employ later in his career).

The famous ambiguity of Morrissey's lyrics is often cited as an example of his cleverness in appealing to as many people as possible and his ability to hide, or at least submerge, his own preferences behind a smokescreen of words. This is utterly mistaken. In his terms, Morrissey's lyrics are not in the least ambiguous and speak of desire entirely as he has experienced it. The songs may often be deliciously vague in terms of the gender of the subject and the object of desire, and Morrissey may love code and obliquity, but this is not an evasion or a cynical "confusion." This is actually in some senses a *clarification,* since desire, by its very arbitrary, capricious nature, tends to cause confusion—confusion of gender and subjectivity and identity in ways that our prudish social expectations won't allow us to articulate. When Morrissey does, it is explosively funny and poignant all at once: *"But she's too rough / and I'm too delicate"* ("Pretty Girls Make Graves").

Sex for Morrissey—and for anyone foolish enough to think about it—is an insoluble problem, which gender, viewed through either a hetero- or a homosexual lens—in fact, the lens of "sexuality"—doesn't come close to making sense of. The "transsexualism" of songs such as "Half a Person" (*"I booked myself in at the Y . . . WCA"*—itself an inverted play on the lines from Elvis Presley's "Guitar Man": *"I hitchhiked all the way down to Memphis / Got a room at the YMCA"*), "Sheila Take a Bow," and "Vicar in a Tutu" (*"The fabric of a tutu / Any man could get used to"*) are not about the desire to become a woman, but about the essential absurdity of gender itself—of "men" and "women." In "Girl

Afraid," Morrissey perfectly encapsulates—from a safe distance—
the preposterousness of "masculine" and "feminine" and the
social comedy these necessary fictions produce, in which a girl
"in the room downstairs" sits and stares, worrying about her
boyfriend's "intentions" and then whether he has any at all; while
he "sits and stares," worrying that "prudence never pays" and,
besides, "Everything she wants costs money." Comically, tragi-
cally, they both resolve, *"I'll never make that mistake again!"*

Despite being of "opposite" sexes and despite articulating
their frustrations according to the clichés of their respective gen-
ders, they end up in the same place but alone, the same "room
downstairs" (a typically tongue-in-cheek Morrisseyan suggestion
of genitalia and desire), but bereft, where they "sit and stare"—in
other words, the one thing men and women share and inhabit
together is the same despair.

The real joke is that most of us go on making that "mistake"
over and over again—most of us except Morrissey, that is, who is
having his celibate, bitter revenge. Again. Most people discover
themselves as freaks when confronted with the frightening and
alienating nature of their relationship to desire, especially the young,
who haven't yet learned to lie to themselves half-convincingly, in
the way that adults conveniently do. And that is precisely why
Morrissey's handsome terrorism immediately recruited so many
fanatical young followers, particularly among young men.

> *Do you consider yourself to be an ordinary or an extraordinary
> person?*
> I'm probably extraordinary.
> *And yet a lot of ordinary people can feel great affinity with things
> that you write.*
> That's because probably everybody's extraordinary and the
> minority of people in this world are very ordinary.
> —*MELODY MAKER,* 1985

In keeping with his campaign of handsome terrorism, he deployed images of naked male passivity, desirability, and flagrant narcissism—"deviant" masculine qualities that when added together denote "homoeroticism"—on the sleeves of the first vinyl salvos he fired at the world. Not because these qualities were shocking (though in early eighties, pre–Levi's Launderette male striptease Britain—where the male body existed only to make war, make it to the office/factory, or make women pregnant—they most decidedly were) but because the desire they spoke of was as real, as natural, and as commonplace as it was unspoken. Hence, when used in Smiths propaganda, they succeeded in making Morrissey's voice a thousand times louder.

The appeal of these images was also cross-gendered—young men responded to the freedom that the rebellious new sensuality promised them; young women, to the opportunity to escape airless conventions about desire that proclaimed femininity always mapped on to passivity. Anticipating and far exceeding the ways in which advertising in the eighties would later exploit these very same "inverted" male qualities to invoke mass desire for commodities much less durable and infinitely less valuable than Smiths songs, Morrissey inverted the usual rock-and-roll depiction of the female form and mined a vein of masculine longing that had actually informed pop culture since James Dean but that had never been properly acknowledged before, not even by Ziggy and the glam boys, who were perhaps too distracted by the glitter and tinsel (on the female groupies).

Hence, the soft porn of the "Hand in Glove" sleeve: a naked, smooth young man who could be straight out of a fifties *Athletic Model Guild,* glimpsed from behind as he's leaning against a wall and showing off his eye-catching arse in a pose that could be one of touching vulnerability or cunning calculation; hence the hustler chic of *The Smiths:* a still from Paul Morrissey's *Flesh* depicting the casually muscled torso of a naked Joe Dallesandro, head bowed in dopey submissiveness; hence the indecent narcissism of "This Charming Man": a prostrate and criminally handsome 1949 Jean Marais trying to embrace his own reflection in a pool of water. This was a trick Morrissey would try to pull off himself, arguably with greater success; first, in the countless lascivious *N(ew)M(orrissey)Express* covers he posed for—he sold more copies to its overwhelmingly (hetero) male readership than did any other cover star, male or female, especially when he had his blouse off—and then, after the demise of the Smiths, on his own record sleeves. Of course, his female cover stars, from Pat Phoenix to Viv Nicholson, tended to be as strong and feisty (if glamorous and tragic) as his male stars were vain and submissive (though brawny and "tasty" looking).

> The sexes have been too easily defined. People are so rigidly locked into these two little categories. I don't know anybody who is absolutely, exclusively heterosexual.
> —*MELODY MAKER,* 1987

Dr. Freud, who nowadays is accused daily of sexist/heterosexist crimes against humanity, would obviously have found Mr. Morrissey a fascinating case study—but also a stimulating colleague. Freud often commented that, wherever he went on his journeys into the human psyche, he discovered that poets had been there first. Moreover, in his own way, Dr. Freud, nominally a staunch defender of the family and normality, was in some ways the Morrissey of fin-de-siècle Vienna. He found *masculine* and *feminine* to be highly dubious terms (if indispensable) and took great pleasure in saying repeatedly that he hadn't come across a single "normal" person in whom homosexual attraction did not play as important a role as heterosexual attraction. In fact, by most people's standards, Dr. Freud did not really believe there was such a thing as a normal person at all (one of his biggest hits was a book with the Morrisseyan title *Psychopathology of Everyday Life*).

And in the sense that most people understand heterosexuality today, Freud, who is most associated with setting its normative psychological standards, simply did not believe in it. He was a lonely (and celibate) figure for much of his life, even though, or perhaps because, he was a married family man. He also conducted a passionate pen-pal romance with a rhinologist named Wilhelm Fliess. One of Freud's letters may even have begun: "Wilhelm, it was really nothing."

Back in the late twentieth century, however, neither the glam rockers' sequins nor the gender benders' frocks, neither Frankie's leather whips nor Marc Almond's mascara, had actually spoken the ordinary, prosaic, *universal* language of same-sex attraction. Precisely because it is so universal and perfectly understandable, it had to be presented as something bizarre and exclusive, the special sensibility of an odd, minority species, when, in fact, it was at the very heart of pop.

It was left to Morrissey to represent a "homoeroticism" that was not "camp," "cross-dressed," "congenital," or, for that matter, "homo." It was simply *handsome*. This was the supreme subversiveness of Morrissey's erotic project—to use ordinary language and feelings to convey what were supposed to be extraordinary conditions (after all, as he has pointed out, no one talks about "heteroeroticism"; instead, they talk about "eroticism"). It was also the key to his artistic masterstroke: Since (homo)eroticism was simultaneously universal but still beyond the pale, it offered Morrissey an entirely fresh, unadulterated, virginal vocabulary for his depictions of human desire—and weakness. When Morrissey sang about longing, it would sound as if he were the first person in the world to ever speak of it.

While the songs are steeped in "homoerotics" and connote all kinds of queerness, they never *denote* "gayness" and, therefore, never exclude those who have not made that identification—which, of course, is almost everyone. It is easy to collect a list of "incriminating" Morrissey lyrics: *"A shyness that is criminally vulgar"* ("How Soon Is Now?"); *"All men have secrets and here is mine"* ("What Difference Does It Make"); *"But I don't want a lover / I just want to be tied to the back of your car"* ("You've Got Everything Now"); *"How can you stay with a fat girl who'll say: 'Would you like to marry me? / And if you like, you can buy the ring'"* ("William, It Was Really Nothing"); *"How can they see the Love in our eyes / And still they don't believe us?"* ("The Boy with a Thorn in His Side"). Some might even be inclined to replace the *shop* in "Shoplifters of the World Unite" with *shirt*. (This 1987 single may have been partly provoked by the then Tory government's moves to make illegal any attempt by local authorities to engage in "the promotion of homosexuality" in schools or to present it as a "pretended family relationship," later known as Section 28. After all, not only was Morrissey, from certain people's perspective, "promoting homosexuality" to young people, but "pretended family relationships" were something he, with his Jimmy-Natalie, Jo-Geof fixation, appeared to want to replace the more usual variety with; the Smiths were the most gloriously pretended, usurping family relationship of all).

> I think that "This Charming Man" was the most
> revolutionary single in popular music in that area—I'm
> quite convinced of it, because it was all just completely
> natural, about male relationships; it was nice and natural,
> but it wasn't banal.
> —*SQUARE PEG*, 1984

However, such a project of "outing" Morrissey's lyrics is finally rather "fruitless"—and slightly misses the point. All Morrissey's lyrics and songs resolutely refuse a "sexuality"—that's what makes them heroically handsome. As "Hand in Glove" valiantly insists: *"No, it's not like any other love."* Morrissey adamantly and adeptly refuses the identity with which society would quarantine and enclose such "outside" love.

All the same, as the song "Handsome Devil" (the B side to 1983's "Hand in Glove") demonstrates to an alarming and hilarious degree, the handsomeness that Morrissey espouses is avowedly not platonic or bookish—it is very definitely *hand-some,* to the point of being rapacious. The streets are full of things keen *"to be held."*

In a characteristic Morrisseyan sleight of hand, "be held" is also the logical development of *beheld*—to be looked at. Male tartiness does rather imply that young men are "asking for it." Exhibitionism may just be exhibitionism, but Morrissey deliberately refuses to respect the "look don't touch" rule in this song, precisely because he follows it so obediently in his own life.

Once again, the subjectivity of the song is anything but clear-cut, which is to say conventional. In fact, the most disturbing and exciting thing about the song is its *flux,* something conveyed by Marr's rambunctiously fast guitar sound, like an overexcited pulse. The dirty joke in the line *"A boy in the bush is worth two in the hand,"* with the knowing suggestion of helping with "exams," seems to depend on the narrator being female, or at least having a "bush," while a following saucy line about swallowing implies that both parties have swallowable bits (i.e., external genitalia); but on the other "hand," Morrissey's women do tend to be sexually assertive, and we already know about his anxieties regarding female "voraciousness."

Explaining a Morrissey song, like explaining a joke, is probably the definition of self-defeating, but if we really want to, we can take this further. *"Your mammary glands"* also suggests that the "victim" is actually female—after all, *handsome* is not an adjective that is exclusive to males, especially given Morrissey's taste in ladies. And so on.

So much for the "gay" nature of Morrissey's lyrics. "Handsome Devil," which seems at first glance like one of the most "obvious" and "explicit" "gay" songs of Morrissey's oeuvre, has a subjectivity that would have most gays running for the hills.

There appears to be, it must be admitted here, an almost fetishistic interest in mostly male "hands" on the part of this singer from a working-class background: "Hand in Glove"; "The Hand That Rocks the Cradle"; his sweaty attachment to the word *handsome;* the strong interest he developed later in his career in men who live by the handy art of boxing. Then there are the manual-oriented lyrics to songs such as "Boy Racer," in which a lad at the urinal *"thinks he's got the whole world in his hands";* "Shoplifters of the World Unite," containing the refrain *"Hand it over,"* which leads us by the hand to his interest in being pushed and shoved in "Reel Around the Fountain."

For its part, the tabloid press took its prejudices in both hands and unambiguously denounced "Handsome Devil" as a song promoting (homosexual) pedophilia, giving the Smiths one of their first major pieces of—not very helpful—publicity. While it could be argued that the song does seem to be giving controversy the glad eye, if not actually rummaging around in its short trousers, it should be remembered that the subject of this song is a boy (or girl) who is at least old enough to sit his (or her) O levels but more probably his (or her) A levels or degree. After all, it is about someone who has mistaken books for life. Someone, in other words, like Morrissey. As much as it is about anything, "Handsome Devil" is about Morrissey's *own* desire as an adolescent to be grabbed by some lustful hands and saved from his scholarly room. (Of course, if the song had been unambiguously about a teenage schoo*lgirl,* the tabloids would probably have described the song as "raunchy" instead of "sick" and run a Page Three topless-schoolgirl "Handsome Devil" special).

What is not in doubt, however, is that pedophilia is outside—in fact, the most outside kind of desire of all (so outside that it can land you a long stretch *inside*). Despite Morrissey's own passionate personal abhorrence for child abuse, it is perhaps the ultimate metaphor for the collision of seediness and innocence, virtue and lust, purity and worldliness, which informs his artistic outlook—and which, in fact, informs the human experience.

Perhaps this is why there are no less than three songs that could be construed as touching on child abuse on the debut album: "Reel Around the Fountain" (*"you took a child / And you made him old"*), "Suffer Little Children," and "The Hand That Rocks the Cradle," a shiveringly, shudderingly beautiful song that almost seems to suggest, via a kind of regression by Marr-ish musical hypnosis, a nonspecific recovered lyrical memory/fantasy of paternal abuse. It appears to be a father singing a lullaby to his child, asking him not to cry because *"the ghost and the storm outside"* will not *"invade this sacred shrine."* But it's a lullaby that is as disturbing as it is soothing: The father seems to get carried away with the threatening images he invokes, even as he promises protection from them.

Morrissey uses alliteration that sounds inviting and alarming at the same time—and this is, in fact, exactly what the father is in this song. The *ize* of *tantalize* is a corrupted rhyme and spooky echo of the earlier *lie*. It is clear that Dad himself is the seductive bogeyman. (He goes on to summon up the image of a piano playing in an empty room and with a macabre assertion provides an extremely ambiguous reassurance. "Cradle" ends with a couple of lines from Jolson's 1928 tearjerker "Sonny Boy," a song in which a father, fighting back tears, struggles to express his love for his dying son. The lines are given new layers of meaning by Morrissey's extraordinarily empathetic, intimate voice, which promises-threatens so much with its ominous reassurances.

Despite his critiques of the family and normality, Morrissey is also very capable of understanding the irresistible pull of the family romance, the original and most powerful—and most dramatic—of all love affairs. After all, it pulled him into the world and then pulled him apart. The "abuse" that this bastardized boy is drawing attention to here, with his hints at a warped paternalism, is not the specific, exceptional abuse of pedophilia and incest but the "healthy" sexual abuse of bringing a child into the world (full of ghosts and storms and torment) for your own selfish reasons—which are, of course, the only kind of reasons that anyone has for having children. Morrissey's lyrics, backed by Marr's languidly caressing, swaying melody, deliberately smear the already indistinct line between legitimate paternal impulses and the illegitimate variety, between what is "inside" and what is "outside," in order to draw attention to the potential deviance of something considered so normal and good.

Morrissey is not content to point out the naturalness of the "unnatural," as in "This Charming Man" or "Hand in Glove"; in "The Hand That Rocks the Cradle," he also spotlights the "unnaturalness" of the natural—the "outside" love that is inside all of us, bound up inextricably with our origins, like original sin. By way of illustration, perhaps, there is even a lyrical echo of the "wrong" love of the first "Hand" song: he sings of words as "old as sin." "The Hand That Rocks the Cradle" is a song, like so many of Morrissey's songs, about the monstrousness of desire (the "bogeyman outside," who is, in fact, inside.) Especially the desire we think of as most familiar, fond, and homely (even down to "kitchen aromas" that, according to "Meat Is Murder," are really the "unholy stench of murder").

Nor is the family romance he invokes a one-way seamy street. "The Hand That Rocks the Cradle" also hints at the child's desire for the father at the exclusion of the mother (*"your mother . . . she never knew"*), the so-called negative Oedipus complex, which Dr. Freud identified as affecting male children as universally as the more familiar love for the mother and desire to kill the father (but which his prudish followers hastily brushed under the couch after his death). The hand that rocks the cradle may rule the world, but it isn't always Mummy's hand doing the rocking: *"There never need be longing in your eyes / As long as the hand that rocks the cradle is mine."*

Unlike that of the mother, the warm, protective, seductive promise of this paternal love is, of course, never properly realized—can never be realized—particularly not, we can be sure, in incest. All boys grow into men with the lonely knowledge of this disappointment. Some feel it rather more than others; many spend their adult lives pursuing its impossible satisfaction, either by having sons of their own (and, inevitably, repeating the pattern) or by hanging around leather bars (a refusal to repeat which, ironically, results in *constant* repetition). Or by becoming pop stars. Morrissey himself was sired and brought into the world by a father whose distance and then actual absence seem to have characterized much of his later ambivalent "longing."

It was precisely this wounded, lost-boy quality in Morrissey that appealed to the growing ranks of other wounded lost boys. By the early eighties, the breakup of the family, which meant, in fact, the increasing obsolescence of the institution of fatherhood, was well under way (particularly in working-class families). Since women almost always gain custody, divorce is effectively a ritualized, finalized elaboration of paternal disappointment and separation.

The extended family of Beautiful Bastards, which Morrissey had imagined in his room for all those years, had turned out to be palpably real. And with the shining eyes that Plato offered Jim in *Rebel,* they eagerly looked to Morrissey, a very alternative masculine role model, to rock their cradle. *"Where is the man you respect? / And where is the woman you love?"* The answer, of course, is Morrissey.

It is a measure of Morrissey's greatness and of his unhappiness that having reinvented/abolished sex, he managed to reproduce himself asexually through the narcissistic voodoo of pop music. Squinting out from the stage through the dazzling spotlights at his audience, he is greeted by the sight of thousands of young Moz clones, male and female, complete with dyed black quiffs and eyebrows, eagerly trying to catch the eye of their "pretended," "perverted" pop cultural "parent"—whom many probably wouldn't mind swallowing in their scholarly rooms.

> A lot of male followers are, as far as the eye can see, natural specimens who have very anguished and devilishly rabid desires in my direction. And I find that quite historic.
> —*DETAILS,* 1991

Like all great pop stars, from Wilde to Bowie, Dean to Bolan, Morrissey was clearly a flaunting "pervert" in the sense of (ostentatiously) straying from the "natural" course—that is, convention. Calling himself the prophet of the fourth sex was not just an extravagant claim that made good copy but also a sober acknowledgment of his historic role. The pop star is an ambitious outsider, a pied piper, luring young people away from their parents and their known destiny to a completely unknown one, if they're at all original. In other words, just like desire itself.

Though, of course, desire more often than not is something that is supposed to stitch us into a familiarly unfamiliar world of compulsorily shared values and repetition. The family has been called the cradle of fanaticism, a folie à deux into which the child is introduced and immediately abused by the alien, ever-so-slightly psychotic consciousness into which he or she has been unwittingly and unwillingly immersed. In other words, from birth, children are forced at parental gunpoint to listen endlessly to a playlist they did not choose until they mistake it for their own fave raves. Pop, a gasp for air amid the family's incestuous ideological smothering, is a product of fanaticism and a protest against it. At its best, it's a form of revenge and (self-)hatred as much as a statement of identity. The fans are always impelled by their handsome hatred of what they are and where they came from as much as they are by their murderous desire for the pop star who tells them *please don't cry,* but makes them cry rivers.

And no one understood or represented this sadistic law of desire better than the gawky fan Steven turned criminally handsome pop star Morrissey.

PROFIT OF THE FOURTH 'SEX'

You see, it's not the marrying love between us, thank God.

—SHELAGH DELANEY, *A Taste of Honey*

Morrissey's just an old closet queen.

—BOY GEORGE

Whatever people say I am, I'm not. God knows what I am.

—ALBERT FINNEY IN *Saturday Night and Sunday Morning*

9.

The early, frenzied brandishing of gladiolus aside, Morrissey is perhaps best known for not doing the nasty. His abstinence is seen as symbol, proof, and cause of his eccentricity. After all, in an age utterly obsessed with and possessed by SEX, such party-pooping is inconsiderate, antidemocratic, downright unhealthy, and, well, positively sinful. And in a pop star who hasn't been knighted and whose main audience isn't grandmothers, it's actually *heretical*.

As Oscar Wilde put it, celibacy is the only real perversion; and in Mozza's eyes, this was a good enough argument for practicing it. Like any form of utopianism, reinventing sex requires you to renounce the thing you want to reinvent. Paradoxically, although celibacy is perhaps the least innocent sexual option—renouncing sex makes everything sexual—publicly, it provided Morrissey with the innocence he needed to carry off his seductive-seditious project. Celibacy, like the gladiolus, is, after all, a sweet, delicate flower with a rather well-developed phallus at its heart.

In order to be above sexuality, the prophet of the fourth sex had to be above sex. And in a world that can only, on a good day, conceive of two and a half sexes, the prophet of the fourth had to "take the vows" (and marry not Jesus but himself) to avoid being enmeshed in a dreary, mundane, mind-numbing parochialism.

Whatever he did, whatever the mechanics and topography of his nakedness with another person and the all-important, all-consuming detail of whether their genitalia were internal or external, would be taken as the complete explanation of Morrissey himself—what he was, how he wore his hair, how he tied his shoelaces, and, of course, the rationale behind his whole oeuvre. He would, in other words, lose control of his own narrative, surrender his own authorship. He would cease to be his own special creation and become instead someone else's dirty joke.

What do you like in your music?
I can't forgive anybody a bad lyric, really. I like to think a singer is singing with a sense of immediate death. The Gallows Humor, la-di-da. That it's the last song I'll ever sing, quite literally. I like singers to sing with desperation.
Humor?
Well, you know, desperation, humor, what's the difference?
Sex?
Well, yes, humor; we've mentioned sex.
　　—*NME,* 1989

Celibacy massively enhanced Morrissey's stardom by turning him into a conundrum, a puzzle that had to be solved. As a highly sexual pop star who had renounced sex, he made himself the Rosetta stone of sex and found himself interrogated about his "sex life" like no other pop star had ever been before. (By way of contrast, Boy George's infamous "I prefer a cup of tea" remark was rather too eagerly believed.)

Where does the anguish and the hate come from?
As with most things, I'm still trying to find out.
Why can you fall in love so easily with images, but not with people?

I'm still trying to find out.
  —*BLITZ*, 1988

In an age fascinated with telling the secrets of sex over and over again, Morrissey had to be made to talk. In interview after interview, the celibate star would be pushed against the wall, bright lights shone into his eyes, and made to explain his alibi repeatedly in the hope of catching him out. Tricks mixed with threats mixed with wheedling pleadings in an attempt to get this most uncooperative of witnesses to turn Queen's Evidence.

You must get a few propositions these days . . .
Not many! The shock of the whole thing to me is that not many situations do arise. I thought literally queues upon queues would form, but it's not the case. After the end of a sizzling performance, where people are simply eating each other to get close to the stage, I find myself back at the hotel with Scrabble and an orange. It's all very curious.
  —*JAMMING*, 1984

What is your ideal sexual experience?
I don't have a vision of it at all. Why do people ask me questions like this?
Because you ask for it. You're the only person who can seriously be asked those questions.
Oh, come now.
Is there any sex in Morrissey?
None whatsoever. Which in itself is quite sexy.
  —*BLITZ*, 1988

Well, I don't believe you haven't ever gone out with anyone, Stephen [sic].

Well, I haven't, so put that in your Sony cassette
and . . . *[laughs sharply]* I really haven't.
But you're a human being.
You've no evidence of that. Artists aren't really people. And
I'm actually 40 percent papier-mâché.
　　—*MELODY MAKER,* 1997

One biographer even announced that he was writing a book about Morrissey's "love life," an exceptional if slightly disturbing accolade (though, oddly, years later, there's still no sign of it). Clearly, by making his private life a tabula rasa, Morrissey succeeded in provoking everyone to write all over it.

What is the greatest myth about fame?
That someone somewhere consequently wants to sleep with you.
　　—MORRISSEY

Interviewers frequently asked him point-blank if he was gay. When this got nowhere, in their terms, some would resort to cutting out the question altogether, just going straight to the answer they wanted. One who grilled him for an American rock magazine in the early eighties announced: "Morrissey is a man who says he's gay"—without providing any quotes to back up the statement. As a consequence, Morrissey and the Smiths were perceived almost from the beginning in the U.S. as a "gay act," something that did not exactly help them and, rather more important, simply wasn't true. This journalist was merely doing his job, however. He was just simplifying things for his readers, just filling in the gaps, just helping Morrissey "out"—as more and more people have been inclined to do as Morrissey's career has progressed. Since Morrissey was openly admitting, nay flaunting—in his work—

the fact that he wasn't "straight," he must therefore be "gay."
Stands to reason, dunnit?

What these very helpful, very kind people forgot, however,
is that the law "what isn't one thing must be the other,"
absolutely correct and inviolable as it is, is a law that *only applies
to stupid people.* And to journalists.

> *Are you gay?*
> I feel that I am quite vulnerable and that's quite good
> enough because I wouldn't want to be thought of as
> Tarzan or Jane. . . . I don't recognize such terms as
> *heterosexual, homosexual, bisexual,* and I think it's important
> that there's someone in pop music who's like that. These
> words do great damage, they confuse people, and they
> make people feel unhappy, so I want to do away with
> them.
> —*STAR HITS,* 1985

> *There was that quote in . . .*
> Here we go, here we go . . .
> *. . . that you were gay or something like that.*
> Yes, I know.
> *How do you view that?*
> Well, I just think it's all so untrue and I think it's so unfair. I
> mean, obviously, any kind of a tag I'll dodge. I'll really
> dodge any kind of a tag, whatever it is. . . . I'm not
> embarrassed about the word *gay,* but it's not in the least bit
> relevant. I'm beyond that, frankly.
> —AUSTRALIAN RADIO, 1985

> *You write a lot about the homosexual experience. . . .*
> Well . . . not a lot.

Okay, you write a lot about homosexual "longing."
I've always said I leave things very open and that I sing
about people. Without limitation. And I don't think that
automatically makes me a homosexual.
You've always taken offense at that word.
Because it's limiting and restrictive.
    —*THE FACE,* 1990

What about camp flirting?
I never do that.
You do!
I knew you'd stray. I knew as soon as I mentioned *camp*
you'd stray from the real meaning of the word. I knew
you'd suddenly think of feathers and things like that. No, I
don't flirt. You were there at Wolverhampton, you could see
the steam, there was aggression.
    —*NME,* 1989

Some have pointed to the fact that Morrissey has admitted to
both male and female (rather unsatisfactory) encounters in his life
and wondered why he didn't simply announce that he was bisexual. Well, perhaps because bisexuality isn't an escape from sexuality
at all; it's *two* sexualities. Moreover, it suggests twice the opportunity instead of merely twice the frustration. Yes, Morrissey's struggle to resist the iron law of sexuality that most of the rest of us have
to submit to was always flagrantly self-important and lofty. Teenage
even. But isn't that what artists and stars—rather than common, or
garden variety, celebrities—are for? Morrissey's ambition, his perversity, his *sensibility* was far too large, too talented, too vicious to
fit into this harmless, silly, precious, sequined little word *gay*. (He
would assert repeatedly that he had nothing against G people, but
then who could blame him if he did?)

Have you got a love life?
I'm not answering that question.
Why not?
Because you're just too nosy, you don't deserve to know.
        —ON THE *JANICE LONG SHOW* ON BBC RADIO 2, 2002

Throughout his career, the pressure on him to come out (with his hands up) increased. This capitulation was allegedly for Morrissey's "own good," a contemporary version of that line from old cop shows: "Make it easy on yourself, kid." The skinny specter of the camp *Carry On* star Kenneth Williams, who claimed not to be interested in sex but admired workmen's oiled bodies in his private diary, was invoked rather too facilely. Besides, it wasn't as if Kenneth Williams was someone whose existential problems and narcissistic erotic attachment to his own sexual repression and isolation would have been solved by an appearance on *Gaytime TV,* a cocktail kiss from Serena McKellen, and a bottle of poppers. (Well, maybe the poppers might have helped.) People nowadays seem to imagine that "sexual identity" is a place where people find themselves and true love, rather than the place where they lose all hope.

Is celibacy really a victory of guilt over lust?
I wish it was, I wouldn't feel so badly about it then. In fact, I wish it had any purpose whatsoever. It certainly wasn't something I ever tried to instill on the public at large—I never expected a massive movement of celibates storming down Whitehall—it was just something that slipped out, really. In a manner of speaking.
        —*MELODY MAKER,* 1987

By the late nineties, the fashion for coming out had reached a feverish pitch; people who had once been happy to hear as little as

possible about gayness began to outpace even gayists in their dog-
matic insistence on the need for "honesty." A married British MP
caught visiting a male pickup area was clapped in the stocks by the
press, both tabloid and "quality," not because of the homosexual
dimension, they claimed, but for his "hypocrisy" and "denial"
about his sexuality (he refused to "confess" that he was gay). Even
the president of the United States faced impeachment for not
coming out about his extramarital (non–penile-vaginal and therefore, under the law of many U.S. states, "sodomitical") "sex" life.
And in 1998, that other sexually ambiguous British pop performer, George Michael, whose shuttlecock-stuffed shrink-to-fit
perma-crotch was launched on the world about the same time as
Morrissey's shrub-stuffed baggy-arsed jeans, was caught "performing" in a public toilet—in a painful pincer movement involving
the British tabloid press and the Beverly Hills Police Department.

> Sex is a waste of batteries.
> —*MELODY MAKER,* 1986

The refusal, up until this time, of the "elusive" Mr. Michael
to make a public announcement about his private life (despite
having all but announced his orientation in his more recent
work and interviews) apparently amounted to a crime of global
proportions. Realizing the game was up and ever the consummate showman, he responded by giving the public what they
wanted: He out-tabbed the tabloids and confessed all in televised
interviews in the U.S. and the U.K. By cooperating fully with
the authorities—and the public—in regard to his sexuality, he
was able to avoid having to express any shame about the arrest;
instead, he was actually able to go on the offensive and allege he
was the victim of police entrapment. He even released a hilari-
ously vengeful single and video called "Outside," which turned
his arrest into a celebration of "sexuality" and "public sex."

Ironically, though, the brightly lit, out-and-proud, undeniably catchy "Outside" was so concerned with sunny self-justification and literally shameless self-promotion, it failed to capture anything "outside" at all and said much less about the real, shadowy nature of desire and compulsion than his "in-the-closet" songs such as "Fastlove" or "Spinning the Wheel." Or—it goes without saying— any of Morrissey's criminally ambiguous and evasive "outside" songs. In truth, "Outside" effectively marked the end of George Michael's career as a serious artist, not because coming out turned the straight world against him but because, paradoxically, it meant that he could no longer write about "inside" feelings honestly. He could only be a spokesperson.

Were you being slightly flippant when you said your love songs were written from total guesswork?
No, I was being absolutely serious. Which isn't really funny.
—*MELODY MAKER,* 1985

Perhaps, as many people appear to be convinced, Morrissey is simply lying. Perhaps, secretly, he is the life and soul of Elton John's hot-tub parties, has his own booth at Heaven nightclub, possesses Europe's largest collection of peaked caps, and has a live-in boyfriend who is Kylie Minogue's personal stylist and colonic-irrigationist. (Funnily enough, no one ever seems to think that Morrissey's "really" covering up a life of secret heterosexual bliss, even though being outed as straight, i.e., postseventies Bowie, would probably be much more embarrassing for him).

But if Morrissey is just fooling us, just "living a lie," how do you explain his *work?* How do you explain the obvious, undeniable, massive, throbbing sublimation not just of eros but of *life* into his songs? Why, in other words, would this pathologically, paralytically, criminally shy creature *bother* to get up on the stage and sing at all?

Despite an acknowledgment of sorts in 1997 that he had finally succumbed, albeit briefly, to some kind of relationship with a young Cockney boxer (and, in all honesty, who wouldn't?) and heavy hints that celibacy and he had parted company, Morrissey resolutely refused the blandishments of the press and refused to kiss and tell and show the home video—except in his "enigmatic" songs—and the gossip and speculation continued. Perhaps because he was not vulgarly famous enough to warrant the kind of media gang bang at gunpoint that Mr. Michael endured, perhaps because he was not quite as reckless or perhaps simply because he still didn't really have much of a "sex life" at all, Morrissey was able to continue protecting and preserving the virtue of his private life—such as it is.

Many of Morrissey's fans, however, recognize his celibacy as a saintly gesture and continue to believe in it, rather like Catholics believe in the virgin birth (which is to say: "I know very well that . . . nevertheless . . ."). For most of his career, it had proved the seriousness of his commitment, even if that commitment was to his own misery. He might perform before a crowd of thousands, he might be mobbed by ecstatic, sweating fans, male and female, eager to hug and kiss him until they were finally dragged away by bouncers, but he returned to an empty bed every night—the perfect vantage point from which to observe other people's messy love lives.

> I find that people who are knee-deep in emotion and physical commitment with human beings, I find they're often totally empty of any real passion. . . . I mean, if we look back on the history of literature, it's always these really creased, repressed hysterics, if you like, who are enchained in these squalor-ridden rooms, who say the most poetic things about the human race.
> —*MELODY MAKER*, 1984

Celibacy—which, as has been pointed out pedantically by others, actually means a refusal to get married—crystallized Morrissey's image as the loneliest man in the world and only enhanced his appeal to those proceeding through the loneliest time of life, adolescence. It is a period that is often—even in this day and age, when sex is more compulsory than taxes—excruciatingly characterized in the relationship department by lots of thought but little action; a peculiarly pleasurable pain that Morrissey has vocalized like no other. In publicly eschewing the consolations of couple-dom, perhaps the only remaining religious faith in the Western world, he once again displays his genius for turning a powerless, frustrating situation (rejection) into an extremely powerful and satisfying one (rejecting)—again, something that powerless, frustrated adolescents under an entirely inhuman pressure to couple/conform can relate to.

> I constantly spectate upon people who are entwined and, frankly, I'm looking upon souls in agony. I can't think of one relationship in the world which has been harmonious. It just doesn't happen.
>   —*NME*, 1984

Morrissey's refusal to cop off was not a cop-out but an extremely brave avowal of his understanding of human relations and the futility, as he saw it, of intimacy; his life was the theory and his work was the practice, not the other way round. Pop music was his exhibitionistic route to a virtual, ironic intimacy, which, in some ways, has turned out to be rather more successful, and certainly longer-lasting, than the usual, "real" variety. When, during a particularly extravagant performance of "William, It Was Really Nothing" on *Top of the Pops* in 1984, he tore off his shirt to show the family audience tucking into their tea the words MARRY ME scrawled in Magic Marker across his scrawny chest, he was making a proposition to everyone in general and no one in particular—or was it vice versa? Whatever, his proposal was accepted wholeheartedly by millions, many of whom, twenty years on, still remain faithful; countless actual living human beings have come and gone out of their lives and have been forgotten. But not Morrissey. Even those who think they're over him, who think they walked out on him or that he walked out on them years ago, know deep down, in those really squidgy bits they don't let anyone else see, that they'll never, ever be rid of him. The more they ignore him, the closer he gets.

> I've still yet to touch perfection. . . . I'll know it when I do it, and I think it will be totally enchanting to affect other people's lives with a form of perfection. It will be like marriage!
> —*BLITZ*, 1988

Crucially, Morrissey's terminal singleness meant that the fans could possess him through his work—which was full of him and his eroticism in a way that his life wasn't—reassured in the knowledge that there was no one else, no shameless groupie nor jammy live-in lover who could possess him more fully, more authentically, than they. Morrissey's work and his public performance was, in effect, his "private life." His songs offered an intimacy that most people wouldn't inflict on their lifelong lovers. Morrissey was a fan who had crossed the bedsit Rubicon and become a star, but he had somehow retained the fan's greatest defining feature: frustration. He did not act out his fans' unfulfilled fantasies so much as embody them. His famous celibacy told his fans that he was still one of them, still lying alone on the floor of his bedroom listening to records and moaning *mother me smother me*—just as they were, even and especially those clever swine who had grown up and gotten married.

I'm just simply inches away from a monastery and I feel that
perhaps if I wasn't doing this, that I probably would be in
one . . . which, of course, is a frightening thing to dwell upon.
—PICTURE DISC INTERVIEW, 1984

Morrissey will have no need of sex with people as long as he
continues to have it with his audience. Each stage performance is
so obviously a sexual release, one of the things that makes his concerts so memorable and so sublimely, indecently unprofessional. If
the yelps and yowls and the desperate, ecstatic falsettos on tracks
such as "This Charming Man," "Barbarism Begins at Home," or
"Maladjusted" hint powerfully at an orgasmic release, then onstage
they turn into a form of musical pole-dancing—a protruding,
curling, fleshy tongue; a salacious smile; a sadistic whipping of his
mike cable; a coquettish swing of those magnificently inhibited
hips; a tempting spasm of his shiftless body; a golden sparkly shirt
torn from his back and flung into an audience that pounces on it
and renders it into the tiniest, dampest, most fragrant fragments
while the curious love object himself lies on the stage, writhing in
ecstasy-agony, or on his back, legs akimbo, airborne or draped over
a monitor in an obliging gesture toward his audience. A Morrissey
gig is an extraordinary, epic, religious prick-tease. But then, this is
the self-conscious nature of his relationship with his audience:
"Tell me tell me that you love me / Oh, I know you don't mean it."

Do you ever go out dancing, stuff like that?
Heavens, no! I can only do that in front of four thousand
people. It's the answer to everything.
—MORRISSEY

Morrissey's celibacy is the symbol of his central contradiction. For all his bravura posturing as the loneliest monk, he can't

quite make up his mind whether he is rejected or rejecting, which is itself the basic and irresolvable problem of self-consciousness. He keeps people at a distance because he feels too good for the world and the people in it, and because he feels he isn't nearly good enough for the world or the people in it. "I Know It's Over," an emotionally exhausting, scourging track on *The Queen Is Dead,* begins with the immortal self-immolating line *"Oh, Mother, I can feel the soil falling over my head."* In the next line, climbing into an empty bed is compared, typically, to a kind of burial; at the same time, it expresses the worry that he might go from the womb to the tomb without ever encountering any other kind of intimacy.

> Desire is excruciating to me, and as far as I know, that's all there is. I can't imagine response, and I can't imagine being loved by somebody whom one loves.
> —*DETAILS*, 1992

The joke here, of course, is that for Morrissey, there never will be "enough said" about the matter, as the whining title of the track that immediately follows, "Never Had No One Ever," demonstrates. However, in "I Know It's Over," celibacy is portrayed essentially as a rejection of life—all his achievements, including his art, are just empty distractions and consolations that, in the end, even more sharply underline this basic failure. He taunts himself, asking, if you're so good-looking and entertaining, why, at the end of the day, do you find yourself alone?

The question *Why are you alone?* is the question that solitude asks itself repeatedly and that can never be satisfactorily answered, even, and especially, by someone who has actually chosen loneliness, or at least likes to think he has (when it suits him). It is a constant theme of Morrissey's work that he would dearly love to be normal, and sex, after all, is something that we hope will render us human.

Which song do you wish you had written?
"Loneliness Remembers What Happiness Forgets"
(Bacharach–David).
    —Q, 1995

Of course, Morrissey's wish to be normal can be expressed only because there is no chance of it ever being granted; it is another, equally constant theme of his work that he's glad he *isn't* normal. For a man who is a collection of celebrated, creative pathologies and dysfunctions, normality/cure would be a kind of erasure. Morrissey is much less interested in being normal than in the gap between himself and "normality," as it is this disunity that makes him special, defines his genius, and describes the walls of his confinement (and refuge). *They* may be in each other's arms, but Morrissey is hugging himself with the lonely but rather delicious knowledge of his difference.

What or who is the greatest love of your life?
Next door's cat.
    —*KILL UNCLE* TOUR BOOK, 1991

In "I Know It's Over," he goes on to isolate another contradiction of his celibacy—the perverse antifaith that a cynical person has in the institution of love, rather like the atheist has in God.

As the emphasis in the song on the way that love is supposed to be *Natural* and *Real* suggests, there is an irony bordering on sarcasm attached to the delivery of these words, but this is probably just a defense mechanism; the cynical, celibate idealist invests Naturalness and Realness with more substance than anyone else, since his whole sense of self (-pity) is defined by his separation from these things. Undoubtedly, Morrissey's appeal to his fans and repulsiveness to his much larger number of detractors consists of the fact that he has made a home out of his loneliness. It isn't that

Morrissey is happy to be alone but that he is ravishingly resigned to it. Worse, he has made a glamorous career out of telling and retelling the "secret" most people, quite rightly, do anything to avoid admitting to themselves: *"This story is old . . . but it goes on."*

> If I see a beautiful woman, I can be attracted like any man. But I find it very embarrassing. It's the same whether it's an attraction to a man or a woman. . . . Human relations don't work. . . . If I see someone I find attractive, then I flee in the other direction.
> —*LES INROCKUPTIBLES,* 1995

Like a latter-day Saint Sebastian, exposing his flesh perhaps a little too eagerly to the cruel arrows of outrageous fortune, Morrissey has chosen to represent in himself an unpalatable truth about the contemporary human condition: the impossibility of intimacy. Impossible, that is, except through the laughably false medium of pop music. In this way, he has become a symbol of the basic paradox of postmodern life and the terrible curse of self-reflexivity, a symbol that most people would rather not read because within Morrissey's own eternally adolescent self-dramatization is a story of their own unhappiness and separateness— a teenage unhappiness and separateness only partly submerged beneath their adult busyness and sophistication. For such people who are understandably—commendably—determined to get on with their lives and not acknowledge the sadness in it, Morrissey is an unappealing cross between Coleridge's albatross and A. A. Milne's donkey, Eeyore: "Oh, God, Morrissey . . . he's soooo depressing. Have you got any Cheeky Girls?"

For those damned or foolish enough to read, however, Morrissey achieves through his art what his lyrics say is unachievable in life: By symbolizing the impossibility of intimacy, he becomes the only person with whom his fans feel a pure and genuine, "natural" and "real" connection. This is the very heart of pop's evil-beautiful transcendence, how the pop star both rises above and stands in for life and love.

> *You broke all our hearts and never said sorry.*
> That's because I never was sorry.
> *Are you a bad man?*
> Only inwardly.
> —*MELODY MAKER*, 1997

Morrissey himself has few illusions about his condition. For all his determined avoidance of limiting categories and dodging of discourse, Morrissey, the hypochondriac's hypochondriac, has a keen sense of his own pathologies. Diagnosing oneself is all very well and can, in fact, be quite enjoyable, since it's a form of self-obsession; other people thinking they have the right to do so (or worse, write bleedin' psychobios about you) is quite intolerable. "Southpaw," the last track on *Southpaw Grammar* (1995), a wistful and regretful work even by Morrissey's standards, asserts that a sick boy "should be treated" because he's "so easily defeated," as it seems to speculate whether an attachment to "Ma," or at least a failure to engage with life, has cost him the kind of "normal" happiness and companionship that more conventionally robust boys appear to have achieved without even thinking (which is, of course, the only way to achieve anything vital and normal). The song ends lingeringly on a closing couplet that speaks of a missed date with normality, repeated over and over—like someone murmuring tunefully in his sleep, not sure whether he's having a wet or bad dream—until it finally dissolves into wordlessness and a neck-hair-bristling guitar outro.

> *Have you ever met the girl of your dreams?*
> No, I've rather met the girls of my nightmares.
> —*LES INROCKUPTIBLES*, 1995

MURDEROU's MEAT

As for me, I've chosen; I will be on the side of crime. And I'll help children not to gain entrance into your families, your factories, your laws, and holy sacraments, but to violate them.

—Jean Genet

Strike them all dead! What right have they to butcher me?

—Fagin in Charles Dickens's *Oliver Twist*

10.

"oes the body rule the mind, or does the mind rule the body?" "I dunno, an' I don't fookin' care," replies the ruffian, since he is naturally ruled by the body.

Or so we, and Morrissey, like to think. And this is why Morrissey loves him. To the man ruled by neurosis, this kind of brutish subjection actually represents a sort of release. The ruffian's violence is a spontaneous and authentic expression of emotion—an outlet Morrissey was deprived of at an early age by his fate, by his family, and by his intellect. His emotions had to be suffocated, suppressed, bundled up in old newspapers and carefully hidden away under the bed of his airless room.

Morrissey loves the ruffian because the ruffian, from the point of view of the honest intellectual rather than the disingenuously spiteful one who never got over being bullied at school for wearing glasses, is free. The ruffian is working class but escapes the class system (for a while) by being lawless. The ruffian is male but evades the responsibilities of his sex—marriage, fatherhood, family life, and a fat arse—by being delinquent. The ruffian is independent but gives loneliness the slip by belonging to the brotherhood of rogues everywhere and kicking with the fray.

To a boy brought up to be "nice," and then wrestling with

the consequences of "nice" people's terrible lies, the ruffian represented something pure, something unattainable, something completely undomesticated—something Mum would never have in her house. And therefore, something actually worthy of Morrissey's stoppered, stupendous desire. He wanted the one he couldn't have.

As a result, the ruffian and his unattainable state of grace is at the very heart of Morrissey's art—the hooligan is his masculine muse. In a sense, the whole point of becoming a pop star was to bring the ruffian, the Beautiful Bastard, into his life. Marr was a lovable lout. Rourke and Joyce could, from the back of the auditorium with the houselights down, be mistaken for footpads. Smiths fans were a gang of tender hooligans. His solo band members are rockabilly rascals. His cherished Jimmy Dean was a delinquent, on- and offscreen. His beloved New York Dolls, the ragtag protopunk hell-raising transvestites with whom he shared his bedroom for most of the seventies, were raffia ruffians, as was his eighties hero, the Dead or Alive frontman-and-a-half Pete Burns—a glorious docker in (rock-and-roll) drag, as scary as he was beautiful.

In order to bring the ruffian into his life and thus attempt to solve the central problem of his existence—how to express feelings directly and experience "natural emotions" (with or without jumping in the ocean)—Morrissey had to become, through the alchemy of pop music, something of a ruffian himself. Even in his supposedly pacific flower-power Smiths period, before he went all Ted on us in his later solo career, Morrissey's lyrics bleed and throb with violent images: double-decker bus collisions and suicide pacts ("There Is a Light That Never Goes Out"), girlfriends in mysterious comas, hatcheted ears and spattered remains ("Death at One's Elbow"), smashed teeth ("Bigmouth") and nuclear holocaust ("Everyday Is Like Sunday," "Ask").

In his interviews, he wields his wit like a switchblade, and his stage performances are as stylized and serious in their aggression as any blood sport, most obviously in the tempestuous, up-tempo interpretations of his more rocking numbers, during which he throws his body around the stage and mercilessly whips his imaginary enemies and his past—and himself—with his mike cord, like a demented ringmaster or a self-scourging penitent who decides he isn't so penitent after all and turns his knout on the world. Like sex, extreme emotion is something he expresses in his work so much more easily than in his life. Like his hair, his shyness is something that he has fashioned into an elegant weapon.

Less obviously "violent," and thus more threatening, are the subtly, slyly aggressive gestures for which he is famous. This, remember, is the man who liked to perform Smiths singles on the now-let's-pretend-this-is-live *Top of the Pops* without a microphone. This is the man who, during a breezy rendition of "Shoplifters of the World Unite," took smiling aim at the bovine *Top of The Pops* audience with his fists and pumped a clip of cheerful automatic venom into them. The man who, when performing "Panic," swung his mike cable like a noose while delivering the decidedly nonvegetarian exhortation, *"HANG THE DJ! HANG THE DJ!"*

Passive aggression is none the less aggressive for being passive: *"Sweetness, I was only joking / When I said . . ."* Being consumed with self-pity often means having none left for anyone else. At least if your name is Morrissey. In the end, however, it is to his personal cost and to our general gain that his emotions are never expressed directly, which is to say unselfconsciously—or inartistically. Morrissey's "violence" is always somewhat ironic, always something of a performance, always somewhat *neurotic*.

In a sense, I am delicate, but in another sense, I'm not, and I've never been anxious to be seen as Kenneth Williams's

"I was born in Manchester's Central Library—the crime section."

1984 (KERSTIN RODGERS)

"Beyond the perimeter of pop music there was
a drop at the edge of the world."

"I lead a saintly life, he lives a devilish life. And the combination is wonderful."

1985 (CORBIS)

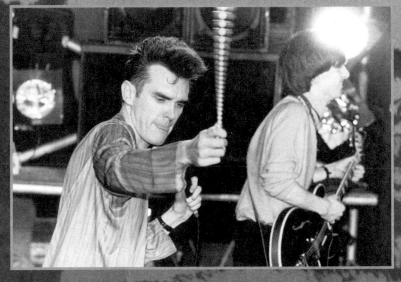

"There were lots and lots of people ready to relate to what I was feeling. Hatred! Hating everything!"

1984 (STEPHEN WRIGHT/REDFERNS)

"I repeat. The only thing to be in 1983 is handsome!"

1985 (STEPHEN WRIGHT/REDFERNS)

"I feel I'm a prophet for the fourth sex . . . the third sex has been tried and failed."

1988 (BBC PHOTO LIBRARY/REDFERNS)

"Sex is a waste of batteries."

1987 (ANDRE CSILLAG/REX FEATURES)

(RIGHT) "I think that everything there is to be lived
is hanging around the gutter somewhere."

1991 (BRIAN RASIC/REX FEATURES)

(LEFT) "The songs, and the album
title, and the sleeve, and whatever
else you might wish to investigate, are simply . . . me."

1992 (MICK HUTSON/REDFERNS)

"I am no longer strapped to the women's studies section of Waterstone's bookshop night and day."

"I do feel a one-off . . . It's a terrible, terrible curse. I wish I could just blend in."

"Admiring me,
shall we say, is
quite a task. If
you say you like
Morrissey you
have to explain
why."

2004 (BRIAN RASIC/
REX FEATURES)

"I was working class
and I was made to
feel like a peasant."

1998 (PHOTO NEWS
SERVICE/REX FEATURES)

"Does God exist? I'm far too provincial to answer that question."

2004 (BRIAN RASIC/REX FEATURES)

apprentice. Although that was daubed on my back door in heavy paint, which I didn't like at all. . . . So, yes, I played football a few weeks ago on Sunday morning and I scored four goals. I should add the game was against Brondesbury Park ladies.

—Q, 1994

When all's said and done, however, it's a mystery that anyone could ever have mistaken him for an unalloyed pacifist, as some of his drippier fans have. Even the third Smiths album, *Meat Is Murder*, which takes the injustice of violence as its theme, complete with an antiwar sleeve image, is a disturbingly violent work full of the satisfying sound of settling scores. In "The Headmaster Ritual," Morrissey subjects the belligerent fools who run Manchester's schools to a frenzied lyrical and vocal assault, which, if it were conducted with his hands, would have seen him sent down for a very long stretch indeed. As he spits in stabbing staccato sibilants, *"Spineless swine / Cemented minds,"* over Marr's bovver-boy guitar attack, it is just as if Morrissey had turned up at his old school with a gang of toughs to terrorize the staff. All we can do is cheer him on, since the violence of his revenge is as nothing compared to the stranded, lonely violence of school life as he paints it, with bully-boy teachers who thwack, knee, and elbow him, leaving bruises "bigger than dinner plates."

It doesn't matter whether the Bash Street Kids violence recalled here is literal or metaphorical; the sheer vividness of Morrissey's hatred makes the distinction superfluous—he clearly experienced it as assault. The violence that he is violently indicting in *Meat* is institutional violence, the lawful kind of violence practiced by society in the form of "education"; by the "meat industry" of the family in the form of its impossible existential demands where, according to "Barbarism Begins at Home," *"A crack on the head is what you get";* and by the British state in the form of the enforced, inborn inferiority and inequality it stands for: *"I'd like to drop my trousers to the Queen / Every sensible child will know what this means"* ("Nowhere Fast").

The eponymous title track of *Meat Is Murder,* complete with the whines of the doomed creatures, preaches vegetarianism, but more importantly and more powerfully, it conveys the author's identification with the raising, slaughter, and consumption of defenseless creatures by their "superiors"—no doubt as a result of his own experiences in the abattoirs of Manchester's education system, where domestically reared livestock had their brains fried and were processed into insensitive meat. The violence of meat-eating here is, as it often is for vegetarian anarchists, consciously or unconsciously, an unappetizing metaphor for the violence that human society wreaks: "This beautiful creature must die." Hence, the album sleeve depicting a young American soldier in Vietnam with MEAT IS MURDER written on his helmet by Morrissey—the military as another institution of civilized barbarism, another part of the meat industry.

Underlining the way in which a culture of meat makes brutes of us all as well as Morrissey's identification with the plight of defenseless creatures, the end of the vocal for "Barbarism Begins at Home," which concerns the violent abuse of children, breaks into an extraordinary rendition of helpless and baffled bestial-sounding groans and screams. Institutional violence makes vegetarian anarchists very bloodthirsty (his first solo album, *Viva Hate* (1988), featured the Gandhian track "Margaret on the Guillotine," which ends with the sound of the blade falling). Moreover, behind the outrage at the banal injustice of ending life merely for the satisfaction of selfish pleasure, there is often an even greater and prior anger at the "normal" and "natural" self-ishness that *starts* life for its own pleasure, and then thrusts that life helpless, baffled, and groaning into the world. Death for no reason, as Morrissey grimly intones, may be murder, but then so can life for no reason.

> *Are you more physical than it's assumed?*
> I think it's very obvious that I am. If you've seen any of the concerts . . . well, it isn't exactly the Incredible String Band.
> —*Q*, 1994

As if by way of confession that it is institutional violence that preoccupies him, the album that denounces the reduction of living things to insensitive meat with such spleen contains three consecutive songs extolling the tasty appeal of meaty delinquent boys: "Rusholme Ruffians," a tale of the dreamy-nightmarish but definitely sexy violence of the Manchester fairgrounds Steven couldn't stay away from in his youth; "I Want the One I Can't Have," a hilarious but all-too-convincing portrait of an obsession with *"a tough kid who sometimes swallows nails"* (director Howard Sachler described James Dean as "a tough kid who sometimes sleeps on nails"); and "What She Said," a song about a "girl" who thought her intellect put her above the physical world but soon found out otherwise: *"It took a tattooed boy from Birkenhead / To really, really open her eyes."*

> I feel very excited by Eric Cantona, as long as he doesn't say anything.
> —*Q*, 1995

"Rusholme Ruffians" is both confession and exposition of Morrissey's—and pop culture's—fascination with stalwart, lawless young men. Marr's music is based on a late-sixties hit, "(Marie's the Name) His Latest Flame," by the original pop ruffian, the rockin' hillbilly Elvis Presley, someone who was sold to the public by his ex–circus promoter manager as if he were a cross between a prizefighter and a fairground freak. Marr adds to his chugging and jaunty chords the essence of the fairground, the spirit of waltzers, cotton-candy machines, and drunken laughter. For his part, Morrissey's lyrics are a thieving homage to those of one of his idols, the northern comic Victoria Wood, in her song "Sixteen Again," but he transforms her wry whimsy into great art. Unlike her lighthearted recollection of the fairgrounds of her youth, Morrissey's account of "fun" fairs is decidedly dark, beginning with an act of casual violence, reported just as casually: *"The last night of the fair . . . a boy is stabbed."*

Far from disrupting the evening's festivities—or the song's reverie—we are simply told in the next line, *"And the air hangs heavy like a dulling wine."* Morrissey's fairground is a place of excitement and fear, life and death, hope and indifferent despair.

Which talent would you most like to have?
General lawlessness.
—*KILL UNCLE* TOUR BOOK, 1991

Everything is accepted at the fairground because everything is possible. The fairground was Steven Morrissey's most intense experience of popular culture's promise to the working class of escape from the narrow streets, from their repressions, from their *fate*—but also its captivating horror: Eden's dark side.

It's a macabre and very depressing fascination. Violence isn't a hobby to me. I'd rather it disappeared entirely from my life, even if I need it for my music. To me, violence is an everyday reality in human relations. People treat me as if I were abnormal, as if I weren't like them—and this is already a beginning of violence.
—*LES INROCKUPTIBLES,* 1995

The enormous energy required to power all this fun and recklessness is provided by sex and violence—the two life forces by which Morrissey seems to be repeatedly either sidelined or victimized. On the same album (if you have the U.S. version), he complains of leaving nightclubs alone and of a congenital *"shy-ness that is criminally vulgar"* ("How Soon Is Now?"), and vows elsewhere that if the day comes when he feels a "natural emotion" he'll likely collapse and die ("Nowhere Fast"). All the same, he doesn't see himself as an innocent. In "Rusholme Ruffians" and in *Meat* as a work, Morrissey is telling us that even though he did not "get involved" he is thoroughly implicated. The song juxtaposes falling in love and getting beaten up, since they are, of course, interchangeable, rather like his subjectivity.

Even as a voyeur/observer, Morrissey's senses are being dulled and corrupted. He is as drunk on sex and violence as he is addicted to them, as are the rest of us. It's in his blood. And besides, even from a distance, even viewed from the antiseptic loneliness of Planet Morrissey, he's far from safe from it himself.

> I remember being at a fair at Stretford Road; it was very early, about 5 P.M., and I was just standing by the speedway. And somebody just came over to me and head-butted me. He was much older than me, and much bigger. I was dazed for at least five minutes. What I find remarkable is the way you just accepted it. That was just the kind of thing that happened. I don't think it was even that I looked different in those days. There never needed to be a reason.
>
> —MORRISSEY

Given this lesson in the way that love and hate, sex and violence, death and life, blur into one intoxicating experience at the fairground, it's hardly surprising that the rough, tattooed types who worked the rides themselves become a promise of excitement. Perhaps this is why, five years later, post–Marr, Morrissey was to collect his own band of "speedway operators," rockabilly pinups who, with their slicked quiffs and tattoos—they were the greased-up boys of yesteryear who slouched on the sleeves of his later Smiths works brought to life—coolly handled the onstage, death-defying machinery of pleasure and pain at his concerts. (And perhaps part of the reason why his most passionate solo song, cowritten with Alain Whyte, the most fetching and talented of his crew of rockabilly lads, is called "Speedway.") "Rusholme Ruffians" ends on a poignant image of teenage love, a home-made tattoo declaring eternal fidelity, which contains within it its own bittersweet combination of pleasure and pain, hope and despair, love and loss.

Love and loss because, with the possible exception of Mum, the names of lovers engraved on a man's skin for all eternity almost always outlive to an embarrassing degree the affection that prompted them. Given their reckless defiance of the way of the world, it's no great surprise that tattoos often appear above the collar and beyond the cuff line in Morrissey's work, for example the single "Swallow on My Neck" (which may actually be a Morrisseyan term for *love bite*) and the rear of the sleeves for "The More You Ignore Me" and *Vauxhall and I*. And not just because tattoos are associated with roughness. Artistically speaking, Moz has always had L-O-V-E tattooed on one fist and H-A-T-E on the other. Tattoos, after all, are a passionate, usually doomed assertion of mastery of your own destiny, or at least a defiant embrace of one that you can't control; a self-branding of your "meat," reclaiming the body your parents and nature thrust upon you, which was beaten into shape by the family/school/the children's home/Borstal/prison/the army as your own. Aptly enough, tattoos have also become a sign of personal dedication on the part of the fans: During the U.S. leg of the 1997 *Maladjusted* tour, young men frequently asked the Moz to autograph their necks, returning the next day to show his signature immortalized/mortalized in india ink injected beneath their skin.

If the magnificently, wittily seditious single "Shoplifters of the World Unite" offered a glimpse of an alternative career choice for an outsider who can't actually cut it in the real world and is thus headed for a long stretch inside (the prison of his own head), then perhaps it isn't so surprising that the last Smiths album should have been called *Strangeways, Here We Come* (or his solo B-side compilation *My Early Burglary Years*). Strangeways is Manchester's notorious men's prison, opened in 1869 and is full of young ruffians with homemade tattoos in highly visible places. (The actual form of the title was probably inspired by a line from the sixties film *Billy Liar:* "Borstal, here we come.")

When Morrissey went solo, the romantic appeal of those boys who decided to go to hell in their own way, rather than wait to be sent there by some posh git in a wig and stockings, only increased. One of the first singles of his solo career, the instant classic "The Last of the Famous International Playboys" (1989), has more than a hint of penal flavor. It begins with a swaggering, rollicking bass intro that is definitely looking for trouble, followed by Morrissey's plaintiff voice penning a fan letter on prison notepaper. Ostensibly, "Playboys" tells the story of a young hooligan's crush on famous East End underworld bosses Ronnie and Reggie Kray, the brotherly smash-hit sixties gangster double act whose pop career ended when the terrible twins were sent down for life for the murder of Jack "The Hat" McVitie. Morrissey offers an explanation, of sorts, for the behavior of the young man, who claims emphatically that he is not "naturally evil," putting the world and its ways in the dock, suggesting that it was because the news world hands stardom to those who kill: *"And these are the ways / On which I was raised."*

Thankfully, Morrissey is doing much more here than offering a critique of "media irresponsibility." The bitter, relishing repetition of the lines *"And these are the ways / On which I was raised"* obviously suggests the repetition of the cycles of sin in the world, but they also refer back to Morrissey's childhood, offering an explanation of his own interest in violence and viciousness; after all, he was raised when the news world was handing the Moors Murderers stardom. He certainly isn't offering an apology, however. The young hoodlum (who, you may have guessed, is also Morrissey) may not be *naturally* evil, but that doesn't mean he isn't evil. When born into a world of unfreedom, choosing evil sometimes seems the nearest thing to freedom; the ineluctable concept of original sin requires that imaginative and ambitious children sin originally, or at least show initiative, even if they are somewhat derivative to begin with.

> The Last of the International Playboys are Bowie, Bolan,
> Devoto, and me.
> —*NME,* 1989

As with "Shoplifters," the glam, beefy beat, the rascally riffs, and the sing-along chorus of "Playboy" render (or simply admit) violence and rebellion perfectly understandable and more than a little sexy, an effect that is as much enhanced by the roguish humor of the song as ironized by it. This complements a strong suggestion of another kind of deviance to which violence and lawlessness often lead working-class boys when they're ultimately removed from female company. This subtle suggestion is turned into the lyrical equivalent of a hand on the knee at scoff time, or an arm dangled over the side of the top bunk at lights-out, by a heartfelt plea.

Violence and homoerotics, always courting one another in British working-class culture, finally come together in the institution of prison and in the formidable, glamorous per-

sonage of Ronnie Kray (and, of course, in Morrissey albeit
more . . . abstractly). Ronnie was doubly damned and doubly
romantic: The famously queer member of the terrible twin-
some reigned in two underworlds to Reggie's one. (Although
after his death, in 2001, it emerged that Reggie, for a long
time the great straight hope of many suburban gangster
groupies, had been having sex with both males and females
from an early age and that, for the last thirty years of his life,
courtesy of Her Majesty, he conducted cell-block romances
with an apparently inexhaustible supply of adoring young
male villains). The legend that Ronnie killed a man for calling
him a "fat poof" only adds to his aura—an extreme, almost
camp mixture of vanity and violence. Open about his interest
in young men, Ronnie was nevertheless determined in the
defense of his name.

> *Is it natural to hate?*
> Some people are very funny. Some people are athletic.
> Some people are very hateful. . . . It's whatever is in the
> blood.
> —*BLITZ*, 1988

Characteristics of the Kray twins read like a list of Morrissey
obsessions: sixties, East End working-class, violent, stylish, sadistic, famous, brutally attractive, mod mummy's boys. Much more
than their muscles, knuckle-dusters, and handguns, their twindom,
with the narcissistic and homoerotic undertones that twindom
connotes, combined with their intensely close relationship with a
mother whose aspirations and determination they had inherited,
gave them their strength, their independence, their untouchabil-
ity, their terror, their *glamor*. The sun shone out of their behinds,
they could go wherever they pleased, and everything depended
on how near they stood to each other.

> I think that everything there is to be lived is hanging round
> the gutter somewhere. I've always believed that and still do.
> —*THE OBSERVER*, 1995

Morrissey, like Wilde, may be in the gutter looking at the stars, but the stars he fixes his gaze on are decidedly not in the heavens (and, as we know, for all his elevated ideas, Wilde was not averse to a bit of rough, either). Despite the "this filthy song promotes kiddie fiddling!" scandal in the tabloids over "Handsome Devil," which plagued Morrissey's early days in the Smiths, "Piccadilly Palare" (1990), an upbeat, sing-along Moz song that lyrically grins from ear to ear, openly celebrates the attraction of being a teenage rent boy "on the game." Rent boys were young working-class males, often runaways from the North, who worked as street prostitutes (most notoriously in the sixties and seventies, Morrissey's favorite decades) around Piccadilly Circus in London, a giant roundabout with a statue of Eros in the center ("erected" in memory of, God's truth, the Earl of Shaftesbury), surrounded by neon signs advertising Coke and other tasty commodities. It was "the big wheel generator" to end all big wheel generators, the nearest thing the English had to a monument of desire that wasn't the outline of a man with a big club on the side of chalk hill. The pickup area in Piccadilly Circus, at one point outside the Wimpy burger bar, was known romantically to those in the trade as "the meat rack." (As if to remind them of their ultimate destination, the train terminus in Manchester that takes the young runaways to the bright lights and easy money of the Big Smoke fairground is also called Piccadilly).

These "playboys" were the subject of earnestly campaigning documentaries in the seventies, such as *Johnny Go Home,* and also prurient tabloid "exposés" that did their best to whip up a moral panic while wiping away the drool. Morrissey's treatment of the subject matter, however, is quite wickedly different.

Instead of portraying the boys as mere victims, needing pity, help, and a nice understanding girlfriend to get them back on the rails, he actually glamorizes their lifestyle. Or, rather, he merely refuses *not* to see the seedy glamour that is already there. Elbowing aside paternalistic concern and shrugging off moral outrage, Morrissey pushes his way to the front of the crowd and is so impressed by the boys' willful self-damnation that he joins them.

He goes on to declare himself with false modesty, *"a reasonably good buy"*; declaring that *"we plied an ancient trade / Where we threw all life's instructions away."* Throwing life's instructions away was something that Morrissey had been doing from the earliest age. Little wonder, then, that this easy nut-cutlet, who proclaims himself "a reasonably good buy," finds it natural to marry his subjectivity to that of a rent boy and enthuse about the camaraderie of the lost boys laughing at the world.

Palare's ancient roots probably lie with the nineteenth-century slang *parlyaree,* which was used by fairground and circus people as well as other despised outsider itinerants, such as prostitutes and thespians (this was before the Evening Standard Awards), and it also has connections with thieves' cant, Cockney rhyming slang, and sailors' argot. Of course, many of the lads who ended up plying the oldest trade were themselves from those marginal groups anyway. Palare is sometimes called "gay language," but this is inaccurate—"pre-gay language" would be closer to the mark, as it is an argot of desire and community outside convention and, in fact, "sexuality." It was not a language exclusive to queers; it just so happens they were probably the last group to use it (but quickly forgot it in the years of identity politics and then assimilation following decriminalization in England in 1968).

Palare, also known as *Polari,* allowed the "initiated" to express in public a desire, a perspective, a brotherhood that wasn't supposed to be expressed, that wasn't supposed to exist, and to mock society to its face without the "naffs" (straights/squares) "getting it." The Palare lines in the song translate to "So good looking . . . Your lovely face and your lovely hair" (*riah,* like many Palare words, is obviously back slang, further evidence of Palare's deliberate perversity, though in Morrissey's mouth, there's the added, piquant layer of irony that he seems to be saying "your lovely rear"). Like the appeal of the rent-boy life itself, conventional people just don't get it.

Nor, of course, do they understand Morrissey properly. The added deliberate irony here is that Morrissey's lyrical language is a kind of Palare, which can be read by anyone so inclined and glossed over by everyone else; it's a universal but secret code that speaks to outsiders and marginal types everywhere, to the boys and girls who have thrown "life's instructions away"—the Beautiful Bastards.

Despite the exceptional, often painful candor of his lyrics and their essential appeal to universal emotions, there is sometimes a level of intriguing obscurity to Moz's songs. As with Palare, the denotation may be overlooked by the naffs, who lack the intimate "underworld" knowledge to translate the references, even if they want to—but they aren't immune to the connotation. Palare acts like a distorting lens, not an impregnable cipher—an action that is very close to the mechanism of "deviant" desire itself. The sixties BBC Home Service radio comedy program *Round the Home,* a favorite of Morrissey's, in which *Carry On* star Kenneth Williams spouted Palare, was hugely popular not in spite of the fact that it was full of homosexual innuendo but because of it (and, in fact, some blame it for killing off Palare by blowing the gaffe). It was gibberish and knowing, naughty and innocent, silly and smart, outsider and insider all at once. In other words, essentially English.

As was the rent boy. For working-class boys who weren't

"good sons" keen to please their fathers and follow in their footsteps, male prostitution was a way out, and even a way to turn the tables on society. Paradoxically, by stepping outside the niceties of conventional morality and formalizing society's designation of them as "meat," they could (sometimes) literally hold the whip handle over toffs who otherwise wouldn't have given them the time of day, and get paid for it at hourly rates a lawyer might be envious of, all the while ignoring the inexorable toll of the school bell and the factory horn that were supposed to measure out their lives. And without ever becoming bourgeois. Rather like a career in pop music. (Even though, of course, today's pop artists as "celebs" are the new bourgeois role models.)

In fact, the first young British male pop stars of the fifties and early sixties were often little more than rent boys given a bath, a haircut, and a microphone and pimped out to the record companies and thence the public by some old queen or another (a process that continues to the present day, though in the case of some contemporary boy bands, apparently without the benefit of a bath). Punk rock in general, and in particular the Ramones, a Morrissey favorite, were very much associated with this tradition (*punk* being U.S. slang for a prison male prostitute, or the "receptive" partner—hence the holes in the knees of their jeans).

"Piccadilly Palare" archly plays on the pop-star/rent-boy connection in a very English fashion by including an Artful Dodger–style voice-over from Suggs, lead singer of eighties (very working-class) cheeky-chappie North London "Nutty Boys" band Madness, scolding in a chummy, worldly-wise elder-brother fashion: *"No, no. No. No. You can't get there that way. Follow me"* (and pickpocketing, after all, is not really so different from renting—both involve rummaging around in punters' trousers and relieving them of their wads).

As a former avid reader of feminist texts, Morrissey was perfectly aware that many boys on the game come from a background of domestic abuse, often running away from a tyrant/per-vert father, but being Morrissey, he doesn't appear to see any-thing remarkable in that. Instead of seeing their renting as abuse, or abuse as the cause of their renting, he sees their prostitution as merely a rational response to society's use of them—being "on the game," within the terms of this song, is neither sad nor bad; it actually makes a lot of sense.

As a parting shot, however, Morrissey speculates pessimisti-cally, if slightly tongue-in-cheek, on the fate of bad sons who have escaped their lot in life, who live each day as it comes, dependent on the fickle whims and peculiar tastes of complete strangers.

If you do it right, success in pop music—just as in renting your arse—is the "worst" thing that could happen to a boy. It means there is no escape, no way back home. The return ticket from Manchester Piccadilly to Piccadilly Circus is not open-ended.

MOST WORRYINGLY, SUCH a lost boy might end up making an album like the teasingly named *Your Arsenal* (1992)—the "bad" end that Morrissey's glam-rock pied piper tendencies had augured. *Your Arsenal,* which was critically well received, marks a break with Morrissey's more effete image of the eighties and early nineties. He finally "came out" . . . fighting, emerging as if not a bruiser, exactly, then certainly as something of a "tasty geezer." After the disaster of the previous year's anemic *Kill Uncle,* for which he received a richly deserved critical pasting, Stretford's rebel with a bookcase seemed to turn from an aesthete interested in rough lads into a rough lad interested in aestheti-cism (and rough lads). Musically, Morrissey emerged as the motorcycle-chain-swinging Ted that he always had been under those arched eyebrows and la-di-da affectations and that the original Wilde had always threatened to become, if he could have but raised himself from his chaise longue. *Your Arsenal* tri-umphantly fused the childish-threatening pop sensibility of glam with the coolness and greasy testosterone of rockabilly (glam rock was self-consciously fifties in its reference points anyway). Morrissey appears to acknowledge here that if pretty girls make graves, then pretty boys dig their own, and it's time to become, if not a *man* exactly, then something rather more than an aging boy.

The cover image for the album, taken by his lifelong friend and performance artist, sometime pop star, and art photographer Linder Sterling (who seems, judging by her handsomely andro-gyne appearance, to have been a member of Morrissey's private James Dean fan club), depicts a very different Morrissey from the dreamy dandy on the sleeves of *Kill Uncle, Bona Drag,* and *Viva Hate.* Onstage in flagrante delicto, tongue protruding, shirt torn open to reveal—gasp!—a muscular body (that paternal inheri-tance rediscovered), his microphone held teasingly between his legs, Morrissey is being somewhat *rock and roll.* His aggression, which no longer appears blocked, is positively broadcast. *Your Arsenal* is Morrissey's Mr. Hyde to the Dr. Jekyll of *Kill Uncle*—not the acquisition of a synthetic new pop "image" but the ecstatic liberation of something genuinely, thrillingly unpleasant that had always been there. With *Your Arsenal,* and squinting only a little, Morrissey appeared to have finally become the one he can't have, or at least his best mate, and it's written plainly all over his face.

Produced by Mick "Spiders from Mars" Ronson, cowritten with Alain Whyte, and Morrissey's first proper album with his band of rockabilly toughs, *Your Arsenal* is a work devoted almost entirely to the attraction of "lowlifes" and violent outsiders, albeit set very clearly, like its musical influence, in the rough-and-ready seventies of Morrissey's childhood. In addition to being a brawl-ingly boisterous LP, many of the track titles—"You're Gonna Need Someone on Your Side," "We'll Let You Know," "Certain

People I Know"—sound like snatches of overheard conversation in a particularly dodgy East End snooker hall. The lyrics for "Certain People I Know," in particular, seem to confirm that Morrissey has indeed been hanging around such unsavory places; he talks, tongue in cheek, about taking part in pool-room brawls and trusting *the views of certain people* who look at danger and *"LAUGH THEIR HEADS OFF."*

Naturally, "the views" here of certain people he knows are not so much views as instincts, the vital opposite of the intellectual and aesthetic standpoints adopted by the sort of people he was used to socializing with, hence the sarcastic delivery of the song in an affected drawing-room style. Morrissey is expressing a will-to-believe in the flawed nobility of those who express themselves spontaneously and directly, relying on their fists and fast friendships instead of insipid, faithless, fickle words (or laws) in the way that "nice" (i.e., lying) people do; this is the first Morrissey album not to feature a lyric sheet (tellingly, *Southpaw Grammar, Your Arsenal*'s younger, truant brother, is the only other Morrissey album not to sport a lyric sheet).

> I'm enormously attracted to people who can look after themselves. I'm obsessed by the physical, in the sense that it almost always works. It's a great power to be able to storm through life with swaying shoulders instead of creeping and just simply relying on your thesaurus. It doesn't work! I've had so many conversations with people, trying to convince them of a particular point, and although I find words central to my life . . . nothing shifts or stirs people like a slight underhand threat. They jump.
> —*MELODY MAKER,* 1988

Later in "Certain People I Know" our hero declares somewhat mischievously that he wouldn't want to be like certain people, knowing full well how "repellent" such thuggish, lumpen types are supposed to be to the decent dinner-party bourgeois and the decent, doorstep-scrubbing working class alike. In fact, *Your Arsenal* is full of discontented young men who, to quote the Jam, "smelt of pubs and Wormwood Scrubs and too many right-wing meetings." Morrissey isn't pretending otherwise. In "The National Front Disco," a song that would cause him more trouble than a lifetime of poolroom brawls, he sympathetically and humorously explores—instead of merely sanctimoniously denouncing—the alienation of a young loser-outsider who has turned his back on his parents, drifting into a netherworld of right-wing malcontents with grudges against a world they fantasize impotently about bringing to account—by going to a *disco* organized by the National Front, *"because you want the day to come sooner . . . when you settle the score."*

The National Front was an extreme right-wing party of the seventies that advocated the repatriation of nonwhite immigrants and, for a while, drew significant levels of support, especially from sections of the white working class, perhaps because, unlike the middle classes, their communities were in direct competition with immigrants for employment, housing, welfare, and status. The NF split and withered in the late seventies, after the Conservative leader Margaret Thatcher broke the cozy taboo on the subject within the mainstream political parties and talked about the dangers of being "swamped" by an "alien" culture, promising tougher immigration policies should she be elected. (She was, in 1979, by a landslide, with record working-class votes for a Tory—and she promptly set about to destroy the working class, whatever color.)

"The National Front Disco" is a savvy, stinging dissection of English social history in the form of a catchy pop song, and it's clearly anything but a recruiting anthem for racists—the title alone is a sad joke at the expense of their racially pure delusions.

Of course, pathetic nostalgia is a matter very close to Little

Englander Morrissey's heart, which is why "The National Front Disco" is such a powerful song and not another self-righteous lecture from a right-on whitey about the evils of racism. He is subtly but openly delineating the line between his own ironic nostalgia for a lost England and the cynical nostalgia proffered by racist parties—the line between his interest in rough "lost boys," and the interest that some rough lost boys have in reactionary politics—and exploring the possibility that such right-wing lost boys are not *necessarily* "monsters," that they might possibly be motivated by misguided love as much as misaimed hate.

Some might argue that this subtlety is "dangerous," because it is too artistic and not didactic (i.e., patronizing) enough, that its irony might be overlooked. And they'd be right. Morrissey's mocking, heavy-hearted irony *was* overlooked. Not so much by right-wing racists, however, but by knee-jerk leftists, who eagerly seized upon "The National Front Disco" as irrefutable "proof" of Morrissey's racism: "Of course Morrissey's racist!" they crowed. "He wrote a song called 'The National Front Disco'! He actually sang 'England for the English'!" Many of them even reheated the old chestnut "Panic" as further "proof" of his racism because it called for the burning of discos: "And disco is black music!" And *still* they didn't get the wry joke of the song title.

> The ones who listen to the entire song, the way I sing it, and my vocal expression know only too well that I'm no racist and glorifier of xenophobia. The phrase "England for the English" is in quotes, so those who call the song racist are not listening. The song tells of the sadness and regret that I feel for anyone joining such a movement.
> —*LES INROCKUPTIBLES*, 1993

Morrissey did, however, made things absurdly easy for the PC peasants coming after him with scythes and burning torches. In

1992, on a warm August afternoon in Finsbury Park, North London, he helpfully tied himself to the stake and covered himself in petrol when he appeared onstage at Madstock, a two-day music event organized around Madness. He appeared onstage in a glittery shirt (well, the transformation into a ruffian was never intended to be complete or unambiguous) with his rockabilly boys, performing songs from the recently released *Your Arsenal,* including "The National Front Disco," in front of a large backdrop depicting a classic photo of young suedeheads, a violent (mind, they were almost all violent) British youth cult from the late sixties and early seventies, whose look was that of grown-out skinheads. For good measure, he unfurled a Union Jack and wrapped himself in it.

IN HINDSIGHT, IT seems a shockingly reckless gesture—probably because it was. To Morrissey, however, it all made perfect sense. It was his usual form of total and merciless defiance, his fearless way of displaying artistic contempt for secondhand opinions and mealymouthed mores, his scorn for those half men who sought to blackmail him with their green-inked articles into apologizing for something he saw as, literally, the "best of British."

> Skinheads [are] an exclusively British invention. That the
> rest of the world around us looks upon skinheads as people
> who tattoo swastikas on their foreheads and throw fruit at
> innocent football supporters is a shame. Of course, I'm
> aware of the fact that there exists such "skinheads." But the
> original idea of skinheads was just about clothes and music.
> —*BLITZ,* 1992

Perhaps Morrissey also saw the Madness gig as an opportunity to escape the embrace of some of the paler fans he had attracted since his split with the Smiths and get back in closer contact with the more vital, working-class skinhead/bovver-boy audience—the kind of audience that the Nutty Boys had always attracted and in fact, the kind of lads they had once been themselves. A historic opportunity to forge a glam-rock revival, a last glorious stand of British youth cults, of "skinheads in nail varnish," against creeping Americanization *(people looking to Los Angeles for the language they use);* a chance to finally realize the delinquent dream that had corrupted young Steven back in the early seventies, at the hands of Bowie, Bolan, and the other "playboys" who had thrown life's instructions away.

But it wasn't to be. Instead, Madstock effectively marked the end of Morrissey's English pop dream and showed the limits of his alliance with laddism. Instead of a glam revival, he woke up to the dowdy reality that he had succeeded in offending just about everyone and had provoked an odd but perhaps not entirely unnatural alliance between the finger-wagging lefties and rabid right-wingers.

While a small but very vocal group of neo-Nazi skinheads in the Finsbury Park audience, unhappy with the reappropriation/liberation of "their" flag and "their" iconography by this guy in a glittery shirt, booed and bottled him off the stage (an exit not entirely mourned by many of the regular Madness fans turned skinhead taxi drivers present that day), some right-on sections of the music press did their best to bottle him off the music scene altogether.

The *NME,* the most powerful organ of the British music press and effectively pop music's Vatican, seemed to have decided that by flagrantly challenging its critics' authority as the self-anointed trendy vicars of pop morality, by refusing to pay any heed to the dire warnings, bulls, and threats they had already issued over "The National Front Disco," Morrissey was cruising for a bruising, and it was now their job to give him one (for the sake of the flock, you understand). The *NME* launched its marathon "MORRISSEY: IS HE A RACIST?" witch hunt, a latter-day equivalent of those duckings in which if the hapless defendant floats she is guilty, and if she sinks she is innocent.

Of course, Morrissey's guilt was confirmed by the fact that he wouldn't grant them the tearful, please–believe–me–I'm–not–a–racist–some–of–my–best–friends–are–beige MORRISSEY RECANTS! exclusive they had banked on. In the face of the most damaging allegations that such a newspaper could make against a pop star at the time, Morrissey simply ignored them and remained utterly, wickedly unbowed and apostate. In fact, the heretic excommunicated *Rome*. He would continue to snub the *NME* for the next ten years.

The real and serious charge against Morrissey, as ever, was daring to stand apart. Of course, this crime had once brought him adulation as well, but times change, and Morrissey was in the way of them.

One large headline famously denounced him as THIS ALARMING MAN—an unintended accolade from the "nice" boys in the (I)PC Tower, which revealed how little they'd understood him in the first place and also how much the "radical" music press had bought into the new bourgeois standard of respectability, otherwise known as political correctness. Morrissey was always alarming, and if in the past they hadn't seen beyond his charm, then more fool them.

> I am no longer strapped to the women's studies section of Waterstones on Kensington High Street night and day, as many people still seem to believe.
> —*SELECT*, 1994

There was also probably more than an element of jealousy here. Partly pent-up resentment at his unchallenged eight-year reign as the pop star of a music journalist's dreams and nightmares, the prophet who merely used the *NME* as a giant fax machine for his edicts and near-naked centerfolds, but mostly at what his new material suggested about his social life. Morrissey, "that big girl's blouse" with the fey ways and a good line in self-deprecating self-pity, the eccentric male feminist viewing masculinity and rough boys from a distance, twitching the net curtains of his mother's semidetached council house, was one thing. But a Morrissey dropping, or getting past, the feminism, apparently shortening that distance on working-class masculinity, and, worse, maybe actually getting out every now and again and *consorting* with "lowlife," was another, galling thing altogether. Much too much an insult for the ceremonial eunuchs of the music press to bear. "Who does he think he is?" they fulminated. Or rather, "Who does *she* think she is?!?"

Predictably, in this sticky explosion of journalistic jealousy, the first casualty was their tolerance of his sexual ambiguity. Doesn't he realize, complained one scandalized and deeply "betrayed" journalist at the end of yet another "why-oh-why-oh-why Morrissey?" article drunk on its own indignation, that the kind of people he's flirting with don't like homosexuals? Is he identifying with the oppressor? (Leftists are often perturbed when what they perceive to be their pet poofs turn out to have politics and penises of their own.)

Although Morrissey's artistic career is not directly equivalent to that of the French novelist and jailbird Jean Genet, not least in the matter of Genet's unambiguous, exclusive, and self-declared/self-imposed homosexuality (though it must be said that Genet's homosexuality was entirely at odds with what is now called "gay"), there is a parallel here with Genet's poetic perversity; his love for young toughs; his own challenge to the world to come and have a go if it thinks it's hard enough; and, above all, his compulsion to betray the narrative that others wanted to impose on him. When he was assigned by a leftist American magazine to report on police brutality at the Democratic National Convention in Chicago in 1968, he sent back copy that, instead of lambasting the "fascist pigs" as his commissioning editors eagerly anticipated, praised the "strong thighs" of Chicago's finest. Genet liked nothing more than "identifying with the oppressor," if he thought it would be fun—and cause Trouble.

Like Morrissey, Genet was an artist who willed his own destiny rather than simply accept the one bestowed on him and despised conventional, secondhand mores, whether of the left or the right (and also had an early interest in the phallic-romantic poetry of flowers). In other words, he was completely irresponsible—to everyone except himself. He also became, like Morrissey, by dint of an almost superhuman effort of will, both what he desired and what he wasn't, or wasn't supposed to be. According to one story, Genet fell so much in love with a young boxer that he taught himself the handy art of boxing to a standard that he could actually become the boy's trainer—which he subsequently did. (The boy, regardless of his own orientation, could hardly refuse or resist such a romantic and respectful gesture and became Genet's lover.)

Morrissey, who also developed a passion for boxers, did not need to become a trainer to pursue this fancy. He had, after all, spent a long time becoming something even more arduous, dedicated, and demanding—something, when done right, worthy of even more respect. A pop star.

And now, after Madstock, he was a pop star who was not just used to slogging it out alone, without even the benefit of a trainer to check his gum guard between rounds and whisper sweet nothings in his ear, but also no stranger to losing in front of his home crowd.

AS IF EXHAUSTED by his fight with his critics, and by fame itself—or simply because he had made his point—his next album,

Vauxhall and I, released in 1994 (to enormous critical and commercial success), when he had reached the ripe old age of thirty-four, and rumored to be his "retirement" album, was a much less aggressive and pugnacious effort than *Your Arsenal.* In fact, *Vauxhall* is permeated with a gorgeous sadness and resignation extraordinary even for Morrissey. Nevertheless, it carries within its introspective lyrics and (bad) dreamy, valiumesque music a tremendous strength and courage, a certain masculine assurance and presence—manhood even—as suggested by the picture on the sleeve of the brooding artist, unshaven and open-necked in a Ted frock coat. If *Your Arsenal* represents a late, delinquent adolescence for Morrissey, the boy who refused to grow up, then *Vauxhall and I* seems to represent a kind of (very) late maturity.

Even if you can't actually say that Morrissey has mellowed out, he appears to have achieved, or at least hopes to achieve, an accommodation of sorts with his past, as suggested in the religiously uplifting opening track, "Now My Heart Is Full," which, like the rest of the album, appears to be suffused with a mixture of mourning for the loss of the past and a kind of relief that it is indeed past and can finally be "let go" of—even if this means reassessing everything: speculating that *"a whole house will need rebuilding"* and that everyone he loves *"will recline on an analyst's couch quite soon."*

As suggested by the song's reference to and identification with characters from Graham Greene's novel about East End gangsters, perhaps this new outlook—and the rumors of retirement—had something to do with the fact that with *Vauxhall,* Morrissey seemed to finally really have the one that he couldn't have, in the form of a tattooed, thirty-year-old suedehead boxer called Jake, who tagged along on interviews, working as his driver and live-in general factotum, and may well have really, really opened Morrissey's eyes. The same Jake is credited with taking the picture on the rear of the *Vauxhall* sleeve, showing what looks like

Morrissey's paws on someone's muscular back with a swallow drawn on the right paw—a doodling habit, reportedly, of Jake's (hence, the single "Swallow on My Neck" is also probably a Jake-inspired work).

Jake's inked torso is also on the rear of the single from the album, "The More You Ignore Me," and he is offered "very special thanks" at the end of *Vauxhall*'s credits. It's even possible that the album title is a reference/tribute to Jake (and also perhaps the cult odd-couple 1986 Brit movie *Withnail & I*);Vauxhall is a historic working-class district of London, famous for its boxers and gangsters. In interviews, Morrissey reportedly referred to the name as the birthplace of "someone I know." In other words, the ruffian that Morrissey had been looking for, calling for, in his work all these years appeared to have finally materialized.

In keeping with the theme of analysis with which the album opened, Morrissey has some ideas about where his "sick ways" started. The sugary but deadly track "Used to Be a Sweet Boy" is a nostalgic parental lament about a child who used to *"make all our trials worthwhile"* before *"something went wrong"*— but also a head-in-the-sand parental refusal to take any responsibility: *"I can't be to blame"* says the distressed, bereft parent, more hopefully than seriously.

Parental nostalgia is one thing; Morrissey's, of course, is another. One of the most atmospheric tracks on the album is the quasi-erotically nostalgic "Spring-Heeled Jim," a song about a reckless and irresistible hoodlum who *"takes life at five times your / Average speed,"* which includes suggestive snippets of dialogue between lads discussing the exploits of various crims ("Smithy . . . 'e don't look 'ard, does 'e ?" "Nah, 'e looks a queer, don't 'e ?") from the famous 1958 documentary about working-class South London teenagers *We Are the Lambeth Boys,* directed by Karel Reisz (who also directed another Moz fetish, *Saturday Night and Sunday Morning,* two years later).

Morrissey repeatedly breaks into a heavyhearted "La, la, la, la-la, la," eerily reminiscent of the previous decade's "Sheila Take a Bow," but this time with a gliding gloominess instead of a glad-handed optimism, a contrast that makes "Sheila" and its ambition sound as if it had been written a hundred years ago, which, of course, it was. The last sound on the track, another sound bite from one of the fifties teenage tearaways, sounds like a comment on Morrissey's own career: "An' they catch 'im an' they say 'e's mental."

Vauxhall and I, cowritten, like *Your Arsenal,* with his Kentish Town Boys Boz Boorer and Alain Whyte and produced by Steve Lillywhite, is, quite simply, a masterpiece, comparable to almost any of the albums achieved during his partnership with the first ruffian in his life, J. Marr—an affair apparently paid "handsome" tribute to in the happy-sad track "Billy Budd" (the title is a refer-ence to Herman Melville's novel of male camaraderie and betrayal), which seems to be a kind of forlorn companion piece to *The Queen Is Dead*'s "The Boy With the Thorn in His Side" (*"And still they don't believe us? / And after all this time"*). It may be, as Morrissey sings, "12 years on" (they met in 1982), but when he took his job application into town, *"They turned me down."* Morrissey finishes the song mournfully implying that the demise of their partnership is something by which he still feels personally crippled. The track ends with a sample from David Lean's film *Oliver Twist* (1948): a very young Anthony Newley as the Artful Dodger implores in an echoing, reedy, Cockernee sparra voice, *"Don't leave us in the dark!"*

THE FINAL TRACK, "Speedway," a shiveringly beautiful let-he-who-is-without-sin rebuke to his accusers who *"slam down the hammer,"* which begins with what sounds like a chain saw revving (eat your heart out, Slim Shady—come—lately) and continues almost a capella over the rolling, ominous sound of drums, also offers a show-stopping confession about the rumors that have dogged his career.

Is he referring to the rumors that he's a closet queen? The accusations of secret racism? Or just the common perception that he's mad, bad, and dangerous to know? All of these things or none of them? The questions are left deliberately, powerfully, provocatively—and characteristically—unanswered.

Hanging.

As the song reaches its dramatic, chest-heaving climax over drums that now sound more like a final, capital drumroll, it begins to dawn on us that Morrissey has placed himself on the scaffold the press has constructed for him, that the courageous resignation of *Vauxhall* is the courage of a condemned man, and these sardonically, sighingly sung last lines are his "last words," addressed to his audience, to his lover, to his dead God, but mostly to himself.

And the final, harsh snared drumbeat is really the sound of a trapdoor opening and a neck snapping.

VAUXHALL, PROBABLY DELIBERATELY, was an impossible album to follow. But of course, Morrissey did. Retirement, even after such a public and professional self-suspension, was not an option, however attractive it might seem. Even some of Morrissey's fans, though, might have wished that these really had been his last words. By the time the cacophonous-portentous Southpaw Grammar—an album that begins with a one-and-a-half-minute string-backed drumroll—was released the following year, in 1995, Morrissey appeared to have lost both his ruffian and his relative peace of mind. And also his muse.

There is no mention of Jake on the sleeve, but one of the better tracks is an up-tempo, hilarious, bitingly sarcastic song called "Best Friend on the Payroll," which is about that point in a relationship when someone realizes he's made a terrible mistake, not just about the other party but also perhaps about the very nature of love (that it's not about you, it's about him). A couple is having breakfast in bed and one of them is thinking: "No, no, no, it's not going to work out." Morrissey is still not the marrying kind.

> *When were you in love for the last time?*
> It's quite recent, but it's not a very realistic story, rather a sort of dream. Someone concrete, real, but an impossible romance.
> —*LES INROCKUPTIBLES,* 1995

This friendship, however short-lived it may have been, does appear to have achieved something that no one else and nothing else had ever done before—it changed him. Or at least it broadened his hopeless horizons ever so slightly. It no longer appeared to be just outsiders, lost boys, and rebels without a cause who captured Morrissey's imagination. In *Southpaw,* he allows himself to show open envy for the ease in the world of ordinary, working-class boys happily going nowhere (rather than mocking them as he did in *Viva Hate).* In the affectionate, endearingly daft if monotonous "Dagenham Dave" (also the title of a Stranglers track), Morrissey abandons his ambivalence, asks Sandie Shaw's roofer nephew out on a date, and declares himself a hopeless admirer of the apparent lack of self-consciousness of the "ordinary boys."

Dagenham Dave is a lad with his "head in a blouse" and "a mouthful of pie," everyone loves him, "and I see why." Dagenham Dave is happy going nowhere, rattling around in his car: "*'I love Karen, I love Sharon' on the window screen / With never the need to fight or question a single thing.*"

It's pure nostalgia, really, and there's very little truth in it. I'm well aware of that. I know that it's all pure fantasy, really, and 50 percent drivel. Everybody has their problems and there is no way of being that is absolutely free and fun-loving and without horrific responsibilities. It just isn't true. . . . I don't think I'm missing anything because I'm not a roofer from Ilford.

—*THE OBSERVER,* 1995

The fantasized bliss of normalcy—possibly of idiocy—is conveyed by the constant repetition of the name "Dagenham Dave," which so irritated many reviewers and fans, for whom it meant nothing except perhaps a rather embarrassing, artless crush on the part of the performer. But to Morrissey, the words *Dagenham Dave* are a magical mantra, literally music to his ears, conjuring up, as those two avowedly ordinary words do, all the things that he still doesn't have and knows he'll never have: happiness, contentedness, and peace of mind. And whose absence he feels even more after having experienced some kind of connection, however flawed and fleeting, with anOther. It may seem like a very small thing, but Morrissey's ability to "come out" as an admirer of such "normalcy," albeit of a highly retro and fetishized variety, was for him something of a breakthrough.

Happily, though, he can't behold such contented, healthy masculine innocence, even to idolize it, without corrupting it a shade or two: apparently, Dave *"would love to touch,"* but the problem is *"he's afraid he might self-combust / I could say more, but you get the general idea"*—the last line, of course, also being Morrissey's comment on most of his back catalog. (Deliberately contrasting with Dave's all-conquering likability, the B side to the single release of this track is the sinister "Nobody Loves Us," another paean to disgruntled outsiders . . . like Morrissey.)

Even the album's title hints at "self-combustion": "Southpaw" is boxing slang for "left-hander." Hence, *Southpaw Grammar* could mean simply "the school of hard knocks." But "left-hander" is also synonymous with *deviance*. *Southpaw Grammar* is, in other words, also the syntax of deviance, rather like Morrissey's Palare.

As ever, though, Morrissey can't quite make up his mind. In "The Boy Racer," a driving, literally driven song (this singer has a thing about being "driven" and taking the passenger seat: e.g., "This Charming Man," "You've Got Everything Now," "There Is a Light That Never Goes Out," "Break Up the Family," "Ammunition"—not to mention the fact that Jake was his driver), Morrissey complains that the animal beauty and contentedness of such carefree creatures that speed through life without *"ever getting pulled over"* is really too much to bear. As in "Dagenham Dave," the two words of the title are repeated over and over again, though this time in an increasingly frustrated, ultimately murderous fashion. The resentment is much more openly expressed here than in "Dagenham Dave." However, Morrissey doesn't rationalize his resentment. Instead, he frankly states his jealousy. It's entirely understandable, really: the lad at the urinal *"thinks he's got the whole world in his hands."* Morrissey obviously agrees. When he promises, over and over again, "We're gonna kill this pretty thing," it hardly seems so shocking. Even the use of the word *thing* seems unremarkable—creatures such as these are not fully human or even "animal" in the vegetarian scheme of things since *they don't suffer.* (*Southpaw* also contains the track "The Teachers Are Afraid of the Pupils," an interesting reversal of the message of "The Headmaster Ritual" from *Meat Is Murder,* an acknowledgment of changing times and, perhaps, advancing years.)

BY THE TIME *Southpaw* was released in the mid-nineties, three years after *Your Arsenal,* envy of the working-class lad's imagined lack of self-consciousness, his sexy physicality and ease in the world, his unshakable sense of who and what he was, and, above all, his authenticity, had become the dominant cultural trend in Britain.

The ruffian was no longer on the stair, but in the front room. Britain was entertaining Mr. Sloane in all mediums: music, fashion, television, and cinema. "New Lad," as this tendency was dubbed, was ostensibly a reaction to the nappy-changing sensitive "New Man" of the eighties and the emasculating effects of feminism. As its later uptake among women indicated ("New Ladettes"), however, it was as much a reaction to the inauthenticity and self-reflexiveness of modern life, where identity was increasingly uncertain and subject to massive change. Laddishness was in vogue and everyone had fallen for Dagenham Dave because, it seemed, "lads" knew who they were, what they wanted, and how to have a good time when more and more people were less and less sure of these things.

The bitter irony of the nineties was that now that the working-class had ceased to exist as a political force, as a class of itself and for itself, everyone was for it. Now that everyone aspired to be middle class home-owners, everyone wanted to be "working class" or, rather, wear working class–ness (no one wanted to be *really* working class—least of all the working class). Everyone wanted to like football, or at least be seen to be liking it. Everyone wanted to buy the football-terrace anthems of Oasis, the "singing plumbers" (as they were dubbed by Brett Anderson) from Manchester, who cannily upped their cultural capital by pretending they were car thieves when teenagers. Everyone, not just posh indie boy-band *Parklife* tourists Blur, wanted a "sexy," downwardly mobile "mocknee" accent. Everyone had an unhealthy fascination with lowlife and gangsters, and everyone—not just the rich art students of Pulp lyrics—wanted to sleep with common people. It even seemed as if everyone wanted a skinhead or suedehead haircut (especially those who worked in the City). And everyone, from Britpopsters to the Labour Party, wrapped himself in the Union Jack.

But no one wanted Morrissey. *Southpaw* (an admittedly "difficult" album, to the point of distraction) disappeared almost without a trace.

Ironically, many of the journalists who spearheaded this mainstream exploitation of rough English lads, writing excitedly in the new booming business of politically incorrect glossy men's magazines full of ads for men's vanity products about English football hooligans, gangsters, boxers, barroom brawls, and "yobbish" behavior in general, were journalists from the very music paper that had lambasted Morrissey for his unhealthy and uncouth interest in "scum" a few years earlier. (The first and most famous of these "lad" titles was produced by the publisher of the *NME* and was edited and staffed by *NME* journalists.)

Morrissey's unhealthy personal obsessions turned out to have anticipated the "hot" cultural trend of the nineties—just as he had done in the early eighties, when, with his narcissistic naked-male Smiths cover sleeves, feminist-inspired politics, and sexually ambiguous lyrics, he anticipated, fathered even, the so-called New Man. And that's hardly surprising, since, contrary to the propaganda, New Lad was an organic development of New Man—both were, after all, marketing strategies, both were wannabe products of glossy men's magazines (though New Lad turned out to be much more successful at selling men glossy, girlie things), and both were forms of masculine aestheticism. Of which Morrissey was the supreme, dandyish connoisseur.

The ruffian's greatest and most thoughtful admirer, however, could not be allowed to benefit from the ruffian's newfound fashionability. Partly because that's how commercial exploitation of art works, but mostly because Morrissey was the living, self-conscious, embarrassing proof of the connection and continuity between eighties and nineties masculinity—and the (homo)eroticism and aestheticism at its heart.

The literally hysterical disavowal and denigration of male-male erotics—while at the same time exploiting them to the elbow: e.g., the pretty-boys-together gangster films of Guy Ritchie—was an essential requirement of New Lad in its drive to reach a mass market. But this disavowal was symptomatic of an even guiltier secret, in which just the name "Morrissey" threatened to blow the gaff on: the closeted, self-conscious, and nerdy spectatorship of New Lad. In order for it to be salable to millions, it had to be advertised as something "natural" and "unaffected"; a cure for the symptoms rather than just more . . . symptoms. Worst of all, Morrissey wasn't terribly interested in the commodification of working classness for the middle classes to wear.

"Reader Meet Author" on *Southpaw* is a scathing attack on the middle-class tourism of working-class life. Morrissey gets straight to the heart of the strange, somewhat queer attraction, but also of the disingenuous appropriation of Otherness. Moz, of course, isn't blind to the irony of his own position as a sensitive mummy's boy who hid in his room for most of his adolescence and then became a somewhat pampered pop star, exploring his idealization of the boys who used to chase him down the street on his way back from the library (but then, he does appear to have occasionally actually lain side by side with one or two of them).

In live performances, he has been known to amend the lines in "Reader Meet Author" that refer to the prospect of real violence erupting, from: *"You'd be the first away, because you're that type"* to *"I'd be the first away because I'm that type."* As if by way of explanatory equivocation, he has also changed a later line in the song from: *"Have you ever escaped from a shipwrecked life?"* to *"Have you ever escaped from a Manchester life?"*

Is "low life" the right term for what you write about?
No, it's my life actually. It's not affected in the least.
Working class culture isn't particularly going anywhere. On
"Reader Meet Author," I sing, "The year 2000 won't
change anyone here," and that's true. It won't change their
lives. They won't be catapulted into space age culture and
mobile fax machines. The poor remain poor. Someone has
to work in Woolworths.
And it could have been you.
No. I haven't got the legs.
        —Q, 1995

For the final verdict, however, as to whether Morrissey is
really a ruffian or just another "tourist," perhaps we should look
to a higher authority, a professional expert on such wayward
boys, someone skilled in passing judgment on bad lads. Someone
like Judge Weeks, a High Court beak.

As Morrissey himself had predicted several times, his pop
career did indeed bring the judiciary cracking down on his
unruly head, but perhaps not in the precise manner he might
have imagined. In 1996, he found himself in court with Johnny
Marr contesting ex-Smiths drummer Mike Joyce's claim to
25 percent of the Smiths' performance royalties against the 10
percent he and Rourke had been allocated by Morrissey and
Marr, the founders, creative talent, and de facto administrators
and managers of the band (working-class lads together or no,
Morrissey was certainly not going to pretend that everyone in
the Smiths was equal).

In court, Morrissey showed that, matured or not, when
confronted with magisterial, paternal—and class—authority, he
still couldn't and wouldn't be a "good son." His rebellious streak
shone through and he displayed, perhaps for the first time in his
life, a lack of reverence for men who dress in wigs and stockings,

which the court inevitably interpreted as insolence. Morrissey was used to being cross-examined by middle-class men with degrees in pedantry, even if they were usually equipped with tape recorders instead of legal briefs, so for him, it was just more of the same. The difference was, however, that on this occasion, there was no jury—or readership—to play to.

QC: *Could I please finish my question?*
It's much too time consuming.
QC: *It's more time consuming if you don't allow me to finish the question.*
I don't agree.

> — MORRISSEY IN THE HIGH COURT BEING CROSS-
> EXAMINED BY JOYCE'S QC (QUEEN'S COUNSEL), 1996

Arguably, this Wildean loftiness was to cost him and Marr a cool one and a half million pounds, as Judge Weeks appeared to decide not so much for a polite Joyce (who was praised for his "straightforward and honest" testimony) as against the unbowed Morrissey. In a phrase that was immediately turned into crowing banner headlines by a deliriously grateful British press, which naturally saw this case as nothing less than a criminal trial with Morrissey's personality in the dock, the very grand Mr. Weeks (so grand, in fact, that he reportedly had to have *Top of the Pops* explained to him) pronounced the evidence of this Northern working-class Anglo-Irish radical who bears more grudges than High Court judges as being "devious, truculent, and unreliable when his own interests were at stake."

Of course, the first four words were the ones generally reported and were presented as a judgment on Morrissey's entire life.

It is open to debate what a High Court judge, or for that matter any member of the legal profession, might mean by "devious" and "unreliable." However, the use of the word *truculent* is more telling. According to the *Concise Oxford English Dictionary*, *truculent* means: "fierce . . . ; aggressive, savage; pugnacious."

An' they catch 'im an' they say 'e's mental.

SO MUCH FOR the verdict. Who actually finally won this confrontation, this showdown between Morrissey and the English Legal Establishment, is another matter, however. Seven years and several appeals on, Morrissey was still defiant while Joyce was still waiting.

He may have to suffer and cry slightly longer.

I was working class and I was made to feel like a peasant.
    —MORRISSEY ON JUDGE WEEKS, *THE IRISH TIMES,* 1999

TAKE HIM BACK TO DEAR OLD BLIGHTY

Only England could have produced him, and he always said that the country was going to the dogs. His principles were out of date, but there was a good deal to be said for his prejudices.

—OSCAR WILDE

I don't really think black people and white people will ever really get on or like each other. I don't think they ever will. The French will never like the English. That tunnel will collapse.

—MORRISSEY

11.

f the past is another country, then Morrissey, for whom England is the past he never had, has always been a stranger in his own land, an exile in the present. Long before he moved to L.A., in the nineties, Morrissey was propped up at the bar of the Olde English pub in Santa Monica, drunk on nostalgia for a Mother Country that had never really accepted him, that he had never really liked, and that had probably never really existed.

Despite the fact that Morrissey has come to be seen as "quintessentially English," his personal history runs counter to received "Englishness": Anglo-Irish, working class, provincial, Northern, *literate*. Even within the Northern, Irish-descendant working-class subgrouping of Englishness, his literacy marginalized him as a mummy's boy and bookworm; philistinism and uncouthness is prized in England by all classes, North and South.

In retaliation, Morrissey broke off diplomatic relations with the actual existing England, blockading himself in his bedroom for most of his adolescence, starring in his own remake of *Passport to Pimlico,* holding a torch for a preposterously idealized and romanticized Albion. He watched, observed, noted, analyzed, and desired ravenously from afar, trying vainly to consume, to possess her through old films, books, and records. England would be his; it would owe him a living.

In other words, Morrissey was a wannabe. Just like his literary role model, that other Anglo-Irish wannabe Wilde, he was determined to become more English than the English—partly because he ached to belong, to be loved, to be accepted by England, to wrap himself up in her green hills and satanic mills, and partly because he ached to destroy her. As the lover-destroyer of nineteenth-century polite society put it himself: Each man kills the thing he loves, the brave man with a sword, the smart man with a pop single.

> I am only attracted to the things I can never become or get. My pop career would be finished if I found total harmony.
> —*DAGENS NYHETER,* 1997

Morrissey's relationship to Englishness is, next to his relationship to fame itself, perhaps the most contradictory of all his contradictory relationships. How can such a radical be such a patriot? How can such an anarchist be such a nationalist? How can someone who wanted to drop his trousers to the Queen, who went one step further than the Sex Pistols and named an album *The Queen Is Dead,* who sang "Margaret on the Guillotine," and who openly regretted that the IRA bomb that exploded at the 1984 Tory conference in Brighton failed to assassinate the British prime minister be so fiercely loyal to the country of his birth, which has tormented him so? How, in other words, can such a cynic be such an idealist?

> I could never live anywhere else—I absolutely adore England, I really do. Not many people see what I see—so many romantic elements of English life buried beneath the corrosion. I'm the only person I know who can take a day-trip to Carlisle and get emotional about what he sees.
> —*MELODY MAKER,* 1987

Just as behind every cynic there is a disappointed idealist, the rebel, however much of a bastard, literal and metaphorical, he might be, can't help but love his mother country, which is why he finds it intolerable. The rebel patriot, like the expat, is in love with an idea, which is always the most passionate, most danger-ous, most *artistic* kind of love (D. H. Lawrence, another home-grown product of mother love, also loved to loathe England). Splendidly complicating matters, the rebel is often adamantly attached to the very things that oppressed and suffocated him and turned him into a dissident and sent him into internal exile: Manchester; flat, gray days; pitiless rain; numbing boredom; nar-row minds; petty jealousies; warm beer; dole queues; every day being like Sunday; class despair; pub fights. England was the Other for Morrissey, which he needed to tell him who he wasn't and thus who he wanted to be.

> I'm really chained to those iron bridges. I'm really chained
> to the pier. I'm persistently on some disused clearing in
> Wigan. I shall be buried there, I'm sure, and I shall be glad
> to go at that point.
> —MORRISSEY, 1984

Morrissey's patriotism, like his attitude to life, was a form of sulking—but then, so was the patriotism of many other fellow islanders. After the realization began to sink in, post-Suez, that the U.K. had lost both the Second World War and the Empire to the United States, Englishness had itself begun to deteriorate into a form of sulkiness, a kind of petulant pouting, exemplified by the endless but sometimes rather diverting industrial tantrums of the sixties and seventies. And most famously, most gloriously, with punk and its affected sneer to all things English, which, like Johnny Rotten himself, was fiercely in love with England and her blowsy beer gardens, her litter-strewn car parks, her hopeless housing estates, her ridiculously cluttered and overbearing history, and, probably, yes, her ugly, kitsch, ludicrous monarchy, even as it gobbed in her face.

With perfect supernatural timing, Morrissey arrived on the postpunk early-eighties scene with his own fully formed, poetic, sulky, sullen, I-want-it-back-I-don't-want-it Englishness when British sovereignty was being surrendered to Europe; the British establishment and the monarchy were on their last gouty legs, undermined by their own Tory Party (which was now treasonously in love with market forces); British society was beginning a process of crash, crass, and compulsory Americanization that seemed designed to produce a nation of crap Americans (by the next decade, it had succeeded spectacularly); and "Britishness" itself was beginning to unravel under devolutionary demands. (Significantly, presciently, Morrissey generally preferred to speak of "Englishness" rather than "Britishness").

> *Where do you go for your holidays?*
> I don't go on holiday. Not since they shut down Butlins at
> Bognor. No, I just hang around the East End in a long
> black cape.
> —Q, 1995

There was only one other figure in the eighties whose relationship to Englishness was as complex, powerful, and important as Morrissey's, and that was his hated Margaret Thatcher. Maggie was his dodgy doppelgänger, sharing not only his fondness for hairspray and old-fashioned blouses with frilly collars, but his animus. She was an outsider and a wannabe. She was utterly self-possessed. She didn't suffer fools gladly. She was Northern (from Grantham, the first truly Northern town as you motor up the A1). She spoke her mind in a profession in which insincerity was the lingua franca. She was a Little Englander. She possessed a gender that was all her own. She was the product of an especially intense and never properly resolved family romance (daddy's girl instead of mummy's boy).

And she was lower middle class, which, to the Tory Party in those days, before she refashioned it in her own petit bourgeois image, was literally as low as you could go. Maggie was in some senses the Northern Woman of Morrissey's dreams (and nightmares)—common, comic, glamorous, forceful, unstoppable, grotesque, driven, and quite, quite mad. No wonder he was obsessed with her.

In fact, if the Iron Lady had embarked on a recording career instead of a political one, and had somehow acquired the two attributes of the Northern Woman she lacked—a heart and a sense of humor—Morrissey might have written her fan mail instead of hate lyrics.

Like Morrissey, Maggie was a rebel-patriot with chips on both shoulders whose resentment against the British-English establishment was as strong, if not stronger, than her love for England. Gleefully she set about destroying the institutions that made England . . . Britain. The BBC, the universities, the corporate state, the monarchy were all put to the torch of the marketplace, though some of these edifices turned out to be slow burning and were not entirely consumed until long after her departure from the political scene. She was Janus-faced, idolizing the past in the shape of the nineteenth century rather than Morrissey's sixties, which she despised, seeing the decade, quite rightly, as cutting England off from *her own* past, but she changed the island more than Cromwell (his revolution, unlike hers, failed to endure).

Posing as Britannia wearing Boadicea's face paint, she oversaw Britain's last imperial adventure, the Falklands War ("the wishes of the islanders must be paramount"), and loudly broadcast her steely Europhobia while quietly taking Britain further into Europe, pushing Scotland into the arms of the secessionists and opening her legs to America, her real love. She may have destroyed the British working class, but she also ultimately destroyed the British institution that was its historic enemy and that had brought her fame and success, and that she had taken to the absolute limits of its endurance—the Tory Party.

> I don't like anything new—I'm really not modern to any
> degree at all. Take houses—I like old, dark properties,
> Victorian or Georgian preferably, with very old furniture. I
> can't stand maisonettes. It's really nothing to do with
> coming from the North—Southerners always regard
> having lived in the north as a strange medical phenomenon
> or the reason for having an unusual diet or peculiar haircut.
> —*MELODY MAKER,* 1987

Likewise, Morrissey also effectively destroyed or exhausted the British institution that had brought him fame and success and that he had taken to its absolute limit—pop music. He was also a Janus-faced figure in the world of pop in the eighties, countenancing both an exaggerated respect for British pop and the final destruction of it (as well as a secret Yankophilia). After Morrissey, there could be no more pop stars, which was actually how he wanted it. Like the Iron Lady, he was an impossible act to follow. And also like her, the much-reverenced bygone era was merely a plinth on which to mount his statue, where it would cast a long shadow over the future. His oft-repeated predictions about the imminent demise of pop music were accurate enough but were also plain wish-fulfillment born out of an intensely ambivalent, nay *apocalyptic,* love for pop. Like him, it was too good for the world.

Popular music is slowly being laid to rest in every conceivable way....The ashes are already about us if we could but notice them.

—*THE SOUTH BANK SHOW,* 1986

Morrissey was the ultimate, preposterous incarnation of English pop. He was the moaning messiah that it had prophesied for so long. Fathered by the unholy spirit of English pop culture, his was a virgin birth, and this was born testament by his life: Pop music took the place of human contact. He was both the final evolution of English pop and the fatal mutation spelling its doom; its apotheosis and its nemesis, its final justification and its final solution.

Not only was there no competition, there could be no descendants. His unrivaled knowledge of the pop canon, his unequalled imagination of what it might mean to be a pop star, his loopy ambition to turn pop into great art, and his total, single-minded, *desperate* investment in pursuing these things could only exhaust the form forever. Moreover, Morrissey's mastery of English and Englishness was so self-conscious, so ironic, so intense, so devout, so creepy, and finally so played out that English pop and even Englishness itself could never hope to recover from it. The unnatural, analyzing, stripping heat of Morrissey's love of Englishness, the knowingly iconic Smiths sleeves, the arch lyrical references, the longing nostalgia, the pronounced eccentricity, the humdrum towns, the frustration, the fucking iron bridges ended up separating Englishness itself from anything solid, anything lived—anything corrupting—turning it into a free-floating signifier.

When the Smiths expired in 1987 following guitarist and collaborator Johnny Marr's exit from the group, Morrissey may well have risen again on the third day (at Wolverhampton) and pursued a successful solo career, but it's now possible to see that English pop remained in the tomb, hopelessly extinct, wrapped in back issues of the *NME*. A large rock blocked the entrance, rolled there by Morrissey himself.

THE SO-CALLED BRITPOP phenomenon of the nineties that so excited some newspapers and a couple of hairdressers for a while may have had one or two interesting moments, but it certainly did not represent a resurrection of English pop, merely a galvanic motion induced by the application of large amounts of lucre (and cocaine). Britpop was little more than a commercial footnote to the Smiths, a belated and massively overhyped attempt by the record industry to cash in on the legacy of the original indie four-boys-and-guitars band whose commercial potential was never fully realized in its lifetime. It may be difficult for a generation raised on a diet of media hype to comprehend, but the Smiths, the band that is now almost universally hailed as the greatest group of the eighties, *were never played on daytime radio*. Their record company, because it really was indie and not some niche label for a record giant, spent less on publicity than most Britpop publicists (the real stars of the show) spent on cocaine. As a consequence, with the exception of "Sheila Take a Bow," which scraped in by the skin of its buck teeth in 1987, at the height of the group's "popularity," their singles always stalled before reaching the top ten (and often didn't even make it into the top twenty—in fact, the highest chart position of any Smiths single was the re-release of "This Charming Man" in 1992, five years after the group's demise; it reached the giddy heights of No. 8, which was an improvement at least on its original high watermark, in 1984, of No. 25). They certainly never made it into the popular press, except to be denounced, while the "serious" nationals merely ignored them. And to cap it all, they *refused to make music videos*.

By today's slaggy standards, then, they were a bunch of complete losers.

Yet they had a large, fanatical following across all classes, the like of which will never be seen again, and are now hailed as that decade's greatest band and, in fact, the most influential band ever. The media-PR-record-biz-fashion conglomerate known as Britpop, by contrast, had all of these things handed to it on a BPI-monogrammed velvet cushion with a complimentary line of charlie. While it may have been more "popular"—*indie,* after all, by now meant "mainstream"—Britpop failed to inspire even a single Kleenex worth of the devotion and passion the Smiths did when they were hidden under a bushel. Under the arc lamps they kissed, and although they ended up with sore lips, it just wasn't like the old days anymore.

Throughout the nineties, the blood pressure of English pop, measured in overall record sales, especially of singles, continued to plummet. The Britpop bands themselves seemed strangely deathly, much more slavishly, icily retro than the Smiths—who were denounced at the time for their nostalgia—had ever been. Blur was the Kinks for students and confused teenage girls from Epson who mistook Damon Albarn for someone sexy. Suede, who arguably began it all and who did, to be sure, show some early promise, was fronted by a man who seemed to think he was Ziggy Stardust exhumed from his shallow grave in the dressing room of the Hammersmith Odeon (and reanimated with countless *NME* front pages). Oasis, by far the most successful Britpop outfit and, in fact, its standard-bearers, was a Beatles tribute band for New Lads and New Labour MPs and who, by only their third album, *Be Here Now,* managed the extraordinary and admittedly rather impressive achievement of becoming their own tribute band.

These working-class Manchester boys with Irish antecedents were seen as the Smiths minus the troublesome, effeminate evil genius—which is to say Marr without Morrissey (a point of view supported by the doggerel lyrics of Oasis songs). And indeed,

Marr, the scally Beatles fan fond of partying, might perhaps have possibly trodden the same football-crowd-pleasing path if he hadn't had the Sandie Shaw–worshipping, Oscar Wilde–quoting, abstemious introvert from Stretford to nag and pervert him in a more difficult direction. Legend has it that Oasis's songwriter and guitarist Noel Gallagher decided to become a pop artist after seeing Johnny Marr perform with the Smiths on *Top of the Pops*. (Typically, Blur's Damon Albarn decided to form a band after watching Morrissey on *The South Bank Show*.) Marr bestowed his avuncular blessing on Oasis and became very friendly with Noel and his brother Liam; it was even rumored that Marr loaned Noel the sacred guitar with which he had recorded *The Queen Is Dead*. It was promptly, so the story goes, smashed onstage.

> If I were knocked down tomorrow by a passing train, I would be considered the most important artist ever in the history of English pop music, which today I am not considered to be. That's just a rough guess.
> —*MUSICIAN*, 1991

In a sense, the whole point of Britpop was to airbrush Morrissey out of the picture. Morrissey had to become an "unperson" so that the nineties and its centrally planned and coordinated pop economy could happen. (That, of course, was exactly what occurred after the Madstock gig in Finsbury Park in 1992, the year before Britpop took off.)

> If there's one thing I've grown to NOT expect it's good reviews. The ONLY thing from me that the British press will review positively is my death.
> —*ROLLING STONE*, 1999

With the possible and very brief exceptions of fabulously skinny Northerner Jarvis Cocker, who threw it all away with that embarrassing tantrum in front of Michael Jackson at the Brits (Jackson was being very annoying, but did the world really deserve to see Jarvis's bottom? Besides, doesn't turning up at such a record-industry pig-trough event somewhat compromise your self-righteousness?), and Taff band Manic Street Preachers' even skinnier Richey Manic, who sensibly disappeared before the Manics became famous, fat, and fatuous (*This Is My Truth, Tell Me Yours*). Britpop failed to produce a single star worthy of the name.

> Stand me next to Primal Scream and I'll eat the lot of them alive—and I know you worship the very hair that they stand on—but next to someone like that, there is no competition. Intellectually there is no competition at all in pop music any longer! Everybody is so boring! Relentlessly boring! Even those who are considered not to be, bore me stiff. And I can forgive people of anything except dullness.
> —*Q*, 1994

But then, it wasn't meant to. Pop stars in the nineties had devolved into mere celebrities, nothing but painted wooden horses for the media merry-go-round. Noel Gallagher's then wife sensibly formalized this arrangement by hiring out her celeb friends for openings and launch parties. The Gallagher brothers themselves, though undoubtedly talented, behaved like lottery winners with guitars, white trash with stacks of cash who spent it recklessly on the front pages of the tabloids. To be sure, the monotonous monobrows represented a kind of working-class revenge, mostly in the form of drunken looting and snorting among the ruins of English pop.

The bragging materialistic self-importance of all this was

somewhat punctured, however, by the fact that by the late nineties, the Spice Girls, the manufactured "girl power" band whose professed inspiration was Margaret Thatcher and who seemed to be a feisty, bollocked version of the eunuch boy band Take That (who in turn seemed to be modeled on the Village People), outsold the main boy bands Oasis, Blur, and Suede put together. Teen girls, not teen boys and thirtysomething New Lads, were the industry's paymistresses. Geri Halliwell, sweating bovinely in a stretchy Union Jack dress—the pop version of those tourist shops on London's Oxford Street, full of Union Jack mugs and Houses of Parliament ashtrays—was the real face of English pop in the nineties.

> How come, regardless of what happens, I'm "alternative"? And when alternative starts happening I'm still "alternative"?
> —MORRISSEY ONSTAGE, BOSTON, 2000

What would turn out to be the official wake for English pop was kindly laid on by the Oasis fan and ropy Margaret Thatcher impersonator Anthony Blair, the New Labour leader elected by a chart-busting landslide in May 1997, ending nearly twenty years of unbroken Tory rule (though many would later dispute that Tory rule had actually ended). Having decided to "rebrand" Britain as "Cool Britannia," "Tone," enjoying pop-star levels of approval, invited the usual suspects of Britpop round to Number 10 for a drink and some mutual publicity. After all, since everyone else was gnawing at the corpse of pop, why shouldn't politics? So the new executives of the English political establishment and English pop finally met in a morbid celebrity embrace for the cameras, and it was much more difficult to tell them apart than it should have been.

It was left to Elton John, that old seventies pop rocker

turned panto dame, to sing the music at the actual funeral of pop later that year in Westminster Abbey, in the form of the best-selling single-to-end-all-singles, the Diana dirge "Good-bye England's Rose." To the hundreds of thousands lining the streets of London on a warm September day and the hundreds of millions watching live around the world what was effectively the last ever *Top of the Pops,* Diana was the nearest thing to an English pop star in the nineties. Which was, of course, the greatest indictment of that decade.

Morrissey was probably thousands of miles away in Los Angeles (or perhaps hiding at his mum's in Cheshire). Nonetheless, his scornful, spiteful laughter still echoed through Westminster Abbey that day, unnoticed by the assembled feudal dignitaries and their heirs and successors, the celebs, but mightily frightening the pigeons nesting in the gargoyles and Dame Elton's wig.

BRITPOP WOULD HAVE been forgiven everything if it hadn't failed in the only thing that would have justified it and for which it was trumpeted as having already achieved: halting the advance of "dance music," or even just treading on its toes a little. In fact, since the late eighties, dance and its attendant drug culture had continued its speedy assimilation of England's youth without pausing to check its pupils in the gents' mirror. The programmed bass lines and drum sequences laid down a murderous barrage not only on pop music, but on Englishness itself. After all, Englishness relied on repression—class repression, sexual repression, emotional repression, any bloody repression you can mention. Repression made the English all that they were and, even more important, all that they could not be (and was the most "naturally" English aspect of Morrissey's character). Dance music, however, pushed the ear of English youth up against a ten-foot speaker, told them to "loosen up," to "groove with the beat," to have a "good time," to lose themselves in sensuality—or in the words of a nineties TV ad for a Swedish furniture store: to "stop being so *English.*"

> To me, acid house was never about music but a doorway for the drug culture. . . . People realized that they could take enormous amounts of drugs. Which the English never used to. And suddenly, on one or another, it was part of everybody's lives. It was, if you ask me, the only thing acid house achieved. The music was rubbish, just as the people who made it.
>
> —*THE HUMAN DAFFODIL,* 1998

Of course, dance music couldn't achieve this historic victory over the English all by itself; chemical warfare had to be deployed. To loosen their dependency on the magnificently ersatz drug of pop music, the English had to be persuaded to take drearily real drugs. English youth would be weaned off beer, pub fights, sharp dressing, and pop singles and on to designer drugs, chill-out room neck massages, and baggy clothes. Ecstasy—even the word was fiendishly un-English: until circa 1989, its use was only permitted by football commentators describing England winning the World Cup five-nil on the Queen's birthday—was secretly added to lager supplies by fifth columnists parachuted in from Ibiza. Ecstasy was nothing less than a nerve agent that destroyed the English sensibility. Unlike the love affair with aggro-inducing amphetamines in the mod sixties and punk seventies, this was really poisonous stuff that made your teeth fall out. By loosening inhibitions, releasing endorphins, provoking a sense of well-being and warmth toward others, and giving straight white boys the notion that they actually had a sense of rhythm, it promised to destroy English culture and its edge forever.

England may be a very small country. But why is it so important for pop musicians all over the world to be famous in England of all countries? Why? I tell you why, because the English have always been born with a sense for good taste. And in this particular case, we've had a lot to offer. Probably more than anyone else.

—*BLITZ, 1992*

E was ingested religiously by millions of young people every weekend. It broke down class barriers, racial barriers, gender barriers, and taste barriers. English lads and lasses were turned into vacant, sunny-natured Californians: "'Avin' a good night, mate?" became the Anglo version of "Have a nice day." Billions of conversations full of embarrassing, redundant intimacy were conducted with complete strangers, some of them foreign. Most horrifying of all, Ecstasy made the English finally feel worthy of love, at least for a night or two or three (if you had some really good shit). In an England of all-weekend raves, every day was no longer like Sunday. Even Sunday wasn't Sunday any more, it was just the second half of Saturday. And there were no more stifled Friday nights.

I know people for whom drugs make them very happy. And I personally know of many relationships that are built simply upon Ecstasy. On the surface it may seem like a good thing but one day it may all wear off. And physically, a lot of people will be in terrible, terrible trouble. The way I see it is people just breaking out and saying. "No more depression, no more repression. I'm not going to stay on the dole queue. I'm going to go out and dance and meet people."

—*THE FACE, 1990*

IT WAS NO coincidence that the invasion of England by dance music and its massive uptake by her youth began in

Morrissey's gloomy home town, the Rainy City. Funnily enough, most Mancunians were not cut out for a life of maudlin introspection amid the mossy postindustrial landscape and redundant wreckage of a once-proud working-class culture. Given the choice, they would opt for partying or Ibiza every time. Even Morrissey, for all his protestations of eternal fidelity to those iron bridges, chose escape: He left the North, traveled South, and knew he could never go back home again. Everyone wants to leave home, especially those who protest they never will. And drugs are the cheapest and perhaps the safest way to leave home.

The career of New Order, possibly Manchester's *second* most influential band and one that also promised faithfully never to leave its hometown (living in Manchester, like Englishness during the blitz, is or was a form of "don't worry, we're all in this together"), symbolizes just how much Manchester has to answer for. The group began as the gloomiest and most—gloriously— pretentious of gloomy pretentious Manc bands, called, perversely enough, Joy Division (actually, this was a double perversity, as the name was originally assigned to those forced to work as prostitutes in concentration camps). After its angst-ridden lead singer proved his sincerity/took it all too seriously and hanged himself in 1980, the band understandably changed its name and direction and began getting more interested in electronic music and hanging around in gay discos swallowing Ecstasy.

The New Order that bassist-songwriter Peter Hook and his initially charmingly, mumblingly reluctant and uncertain new lead singer Bernard Sumner would usher in was to turn out to be rather more interested in levity (though, thankfully, the band would never quite manage to completely lose its mournful, almost tragic quality: Sumner's vocals still sound like a lonely boy crying next door with his window open). Hence, the transitional 1983 megahit "Blue Monday"—a dance record whose greatness, like the band itself's, owes as much to the way it fights against its inner disco-dolliness as to its innovative bass line. Throughout the eighties, however this resistance was to decline, as the Dionysian gained over the Apollonian (i.e., the band appealed less and less to the head and more and more to the "handbag"), finally producing the MDMA-soaked end-of-the-eighties Ibiza album, *Technique,* and the literally crowd-pleasing "World in Motion" 1990 England World Cup team anthem—originally called "E Is for England." (Admittedly, even their Ibiza record, bless 'em, never really got away from that happy-sad-drunk-on-a-wet-Tuesday-afternoon-in-Whalley-range feeling.)

It was highly symbolic both in terms of the Manchester scene and the English pop scheme of things that after leaving the Smiths in 1987, reportedly after a long bout of depression, Marr joined up with New Order's Sumner to form the dancey-prancey-portentous Electronic; Morrissey was infamous for his implacable opposition to electronic music and dance. Their first collaboration was with the Pet Shop Boys' Nil Talent, who, predictably, triumphantly seized the opportunity of this association with Marr to realize the ambition with which he had started his pop career: Penning the limp lyrics for the debut single "Getting Away with It," he regaled the world with his bad Morrissey drag—"It was me doing Morrissey," he has since confessed eagerly, if somewhat self-deludingly, to anyone who would listen.

However, pop's flirtation with dance, which, granted, had a certain charm (though perhaps the best thing about it was that you couldn't really dance to it), didn't so much provoke a reinvigoration of English pop as a merciless, final gang-bang of it. A whirlwind of hard drugs and a stampede of unadulterated dance was to effectively undo New Order and their legendary label, Tony Wilson's Factory Records, the batty Svengali force behind much of Manchester's phenomenally creative pop scene since the seventies. Fittingly, it was the famous Manchester dance club the Hacienda, central to disseminating the new dance culture and its drugs, built and run by Factory with New Order profits, that proved, like Happy Mondays (New Order's label mates and antithesis), a swaying Frankenstein monster of Dionysian chaos—the "big wheel generator," where boys didn't get so much stabbed as peppered with semiautomatic fire—which eventually consumed the Apollonian Factory records, and with it much of Manchester's pop scene, as well as most of New Order's earnings. (It's difficult, though, not to admire the enthusiasm and consistency with which Mr. Wilson fed, trained, and encouraged his own baggy gravediggers.) New Order was then forced into the terrible, unimaginable humiliation of breaking its promise and leaving Manchester, moving to despised London and, worse, signing to a label called . . . *London Records.*

Little wonder, then, that by the early nineties, Manchester's youths had lost themselves in bass-heavy gay disco rhythms from Detroit—another decaying postindustrial northern town—and were taking masses of mind-altering drugs (instead of merely listening to music made by people on drugs, the more usual British division of musical labor). The rave scene ruled and DJs, the spawn of Jimmy Saville but with less style sense, were the new pop stars. Once again, Manchester and the North proved themselves the heart of the nation's youth, as pretty soon the whole country began really, like, feeling the music inside them. And forgetting they were ever, y'know, English. Man.

What do you think of the Criminal Justice Bill [an attempt to outlaw raves]? Do you think people in leggings have a right to live wherever they choose?
I don't think people in leggings have a right to live. I don't think people should hold raves because I don't like rave

music. I suggested the Criminal Justice Bill, so I'm glad that
it's been taken up.

—*Q,* 1995

Admittedly, E culture was as much a curative as it was a
calamity. The drugs that dance prescribed and the incessant fidg-
ety movement, sweatiness, and garrulousness that it provoked
represented a therapy for English melancholia—a jubilant, warm
dampness in place of a unhappy, cold, drizzly one; a sense of
belonging and contact instead of awkward isolation. After all,
Ecstasy had originally been developed to treat depression. *E is for
England.* But as is often the case with lifelong and congenital ill-
nesses, if you remove all the symptoms, how much of the patient
is left?

All the same, Morrissey understood that, like the pop music
they were replacing, dissolving, drugs could be a route out of suffocation. In the 1989 ballad single "Interesting Drug" (the B side featured a track called "Such a Little Thing Makes a Big Difference"),
he calls for some plain speaking amid the moral panic that was
endemic at the time: *"Interesting drug / The one that you took / TELL
THE TRUTH—IT REALLY HELPED YOU."*

Unlike almost any of the other pop songs about drugs that
emerged in the late eighties and early nineties, it doesn't beat
around the bush, and actually uses the word *drug* instead of
resorting to sniggering nudge-nudge, wink-wink "Ebeneezer
Goode"–type references (sub-Palare). Moreover, it puts the use
of drugs into a political, class context of late-eighties postboom-
heading-for-bust Thatcherism: *"There are some bad people on the
rise . . . ruining people's lives."* And in a reference to a government
"job creation" program, it echoes what is possibly his best-
known lyric (*"I was looking for a job and then I found a job / And
heaven knows I'm miserable now"*). The backing for "Interesting
Drug," provided by Kirsty MacColl, has an angelic-sounding

Village of the Damned childishness to it, familiar from "Panic" (the video is set in a school, and writing on blackboard spells out the lyric *"There are some bad people on the rise"* as "There are some bad people on the *right"*).

Morrissey doesn't appear to have a moral problem with drugs themselves—they make perfect sense to him—it's their disastrous effect on English culture that he cannot abide. Attached as he is to the very things that oppressed him and made him what he is and what he isn't and that forced him to invest so much in pop music, a substitute for drugs, sex, love, and life that, at its best, far surpassed what it stood in for, he couldn't help but lament their dissolution. The drugs were fine, but by removing the very critical faculties that imprisoned the English in their own self-consciousness, they made for banal music, which was, as we know, a hanging offense in Morrissey's book.

> England is not England in any real sense of the word; it has
> been internationalized and that's screechingly evident
> wherever you look around the country. The English people
> are not strong enough to defend their sense of history.
> Patriotism doesn't really matter anymore. So I think
> England has died.
> —*SPIN*, 1991

Morrissey's dogged defense of English self-consciousness can take some oddly provocative forms, however. *Viva Hate*'s "Bengali in Platforms" (1988), complete with an arrangement by Stephen Street that sounds as if it includes a sitar, could possibly be interpreted as mocking immigrant attempts to *assimilate:* "*He only wants to embrace your culture / And be your friend forever."* It hardly needs pointing out that Morrissey, the unrivaled pop sovereign of England and Englishness, is himself a product of immigration and assimilation.

"Bengali in Platforms" is a rather more ambiguous song than "The National Front Disco," though, oddly, it's generally not cited so often by the Morrissey-is-an-evil-racist-don't-play-his-records-or-you'll-burst-into-flames brigade. From a certain perspective, the song seems to question the Bengali's right to be "here" at all. From another, it is merely a mischievous examination of alienation. Unless you really *want* to believe that Morrissey is actually advocating the forcible repatriation of Bengalis in platforms, however, the most likely and most obvious interpretation, the one that is carried by the wistful tone of the music, is that Morrissey, the self-confessed grotesque, the homeless Anglo-Irish bedroom hermit who prizes his Englishness but also claims he doesn't belong anywhere and who is both a triumph of assimilation and a tragic failure, is unable to resist poking heavyhearted fun at someone else's social/cultural/sartorial displacement and uncertain attempts to fit in.

When you realize the song is, like Morrissey's disastrous childhood and his fragmented head, clearly set in the context of the seventies (platform shoes were a staple of glam rock), then it becomes even more apparent that he is singing, once again, more about his own awkward subjectivity than about anything else. The ambiguity of the song is at "worst" a symptom of Morrissey's artistic self-indulgence or at "best" another example of his reckless refusal to write about a subject in the officially approved fashion.

> There are many people who are so obsessed with racism that one can't mention the word *Bengali;* it instantly becomes a racist song, even if you're saying, "Bengali, marry me." But I still can't see any silent racism there.
> *Not even with the line "Life is hard enough when you belong here"?*
> Well, it is, isn't it?

*True, but that implies that Bengalis don't belong here, which isn't
a very global view of the world.*
In a sense it's true. And I think that's almost true for
anybody. If you went to Yugoslavia tomorrow, you'd
probably feel that you didn't belong there.
        —*SOUNDS*, 1988

It was rap that provoked the most bitter assault from
Morrissey, going much further than any of his denunciations of
dance. Perhaps this was because for him rap represented an accel-
eration of the Americanization of England, by far the most powerful foe of Englishness. And perhaps this was also because rap,
unlike dance music, appears to use words seriously. After all, like
Morrissey, it uses rather a lot of them; likewise, it also refuses
moon-in-June sentimentality and demands that you listen to the
lyrics, in this instance by actually refusing to sing them.

The increasing popularity of rap in the early nineties in the
U.K. and its attendant culture of "rap-ismo" could be interpreted—by an old-fashioned pop star—as an assault on the lyrical heritage of English pop (replacing it with a regime that had
no use for Morrissey). The disastrous aesthetic impact of rap also
has to be taken into account. By the early nineties, every white
male in Britain under twenty-five was required by local authority bylaws to wear basketball shoes and a baseball cap the wrong
way around and constantly talk about "bitches," "hos," and
"motherfuckas," especially if he attended public school. (If
Britpop can be credited with anything at all, it did at least succeed in making baseball caps unfashionable—though apparently
no one thought to mention this to William Hague, the balding
"young" leader of the Conservative Party in the late nineties.)

Perhaps jealousy also played a part—after all, Morrissey's
highly successful, acclaimed lyrical fascination with hoods and
hard men was being replaced and supplanted by a music form

that presented itself as actually being made by hoods and hard men. The propaganda of rap held that there was no need for the artist middleman anymore. Rap was coming direct from "da streets" (in the case of much of punk, which made the same claim, and certainly of Morrissey, it was more a case of coming from a box bedroom overlooking da streets).

> Rap is the degree zero of music. I know that what I'm saying sounds really corny, but I'm struck by the fact that it's enough for a rap group to break itself laboriously on a song with the thinnest of melodies to make people call it a work of genius and hail the song to the pantheon of classics. I know as well that the same speech has been held about punk. Except that punk didn't last. It had the virtue to bring us the Ramones and, above all, to revitalize rock and shake the system. On the contrary, rap never fails to repeat itself. It must be assumed that its only use is to sort out the swingers from the fuddy-duddies. Blokes who suffer while listening to rap just because they're scared to death not to be hip—I see some everyday! Sorry, but I'd rather be corny.
> —*ROCK SOUNDS,* 1993

Morrissey's criticism of rap music is nothing if not forth-right. It may be a tad overstated, it may be a little out of touch, but it is not entirely groundless. More to the point, almost no one else (white) dared to say it. Inevitably, Morrissey's honest critique of rap was used as more kindling by those who wanted to burn him at the stake: Rap was "black culture," therefore, white Morrissey was being racist in daring to criticize it. Of course, this argument is itself segregationist racism of the most patronizing kind.

Early rap in the form of groups like Public Enemy and

N.W.A was vital, creative, revolutionary even—artistically and politically. But rap quickly institutionalized itself, going through the rebellious motions, assembling the stale iconography of outsiderdom, and, with gangsta rap, finally becoming a form of "carni" bling-bling-bragging showbiz. Even though it managed to produce the occasional dead (black) body, rap had largely become a smoothly oiled mechanism for making record companies very rich and conservative white suburban boys who wanted to piss off their Midwestern mothers very happy.

Perhaps this is why at the end of the nineties, hip-hop finally produced a white rapper from Detroit called Marshall Mathers, a.k.a. Eminem, a.k.a. Slim Shady, whose songs and ranting interviews and, in fact, whole motherfucking point, or so he would have you believe, was all about pissing off his mom and revenging his allegedly "fucked-up" childhood. With Dr. Dre (formerly of N.W.A) standing behind him, gifted hands on the mixing deck, Em's neurotic, twisted, and highly sexually confused investment in words, delivered over a fat, funky, and very nonneurotic bass line, seemed to have produced a new music form, a genuinely pop hip-hop.

The troubled-troubling smash-hit single "Stan," from *The Marshall Mathers LP* (2001), told a tragic, twisted, and hilarious Gothic love story about a male fan who becomes obsessed with the rapper and ends up killing himself and his pregnant girlfriend in a fit of pique, driving off a bridge, because Slim didn't write back. His young male and female fans cut and died their hair like his bleached-blond crop, becoming queer-looking clones of this bastard star, who was disowned at an early age by his father, then reconstructed and reproduced himself through the perverted alchemy of pop/hip-hop. Controversy followed him everywhere and he was denounced (by Lynne Cheney, the Gay and Lesbian Alliance Against Defamation, the National Organization of Women, and his mother) for his violent and hate-filled lyrics. Not surprisingly, comparisons with Morrissey began to be made.

However, aside from the observations that Morrissey's lyrical chain saw was rather sharper and funnier and that he wouldn't be seen dead in dungarees, the crucial difference was that the British music press did not campaign to silence this "alarming" man, Slim Shady.

Eminem is the new Morrissey. Discuss.
Pigfarmer's Weekly is the new *City Life*. Discuss.
　　　—*CITY LIFE*, 2003

On the contrary, American-born big mouth Slim Shady was awarded gongs by the *NME* and accorded the honor of being defended by British broadsheet journalists (anxious to show how hip-hop-happening they were) as a "great artist," "humorist," "genius lyricist," "free speecher," and "truth teller" who was anatomizing the way things are rather than the way they should be—despite the fact that he sang gleefully and unambiguously about beating and murdering women (including his own wife) and the joys of raping lesbians and stabbing gays in the head, and was even arrested for threatening someone with a gun and pistol-whipping him (smartly, blacks were not targeted by Em, who was not exactly an "equal-ops" misanthrope).

By contrast, when homegrown big mouth Morrissey had been accused of the r-word after being found in possession of a Union Jack and some vaguely ambiguous lyrics, there was no general stampede to his defense.

I didn't invent the Union Jack, you do realize that, don't you? I didn't knock it up on a spinning wheel in the front room. I can't account for people's reactions. Some people adore it; others are embarrassed by it. I don't get it. I don't

understand the Fascist implications of it. I think it happened because it was time to get old Mozzer. Nothing more sophisticated than that.
—Q, 1995

Despite being an artist of much greater achievement and nuance—or perhaps, because of this—Morrissey the Mancunian misanthrope was not afforded a smidgen of the creative freedom later awarded the Michigan maniac, who, it would turn out, after countless actressy acceptance speeches at record-industry awards ceremonies and some dubious duets with Dame Elton, was anyway rather less interested in artistic integrity and truth-telling than suckcess.

> *If you were forced to leave England at the point of a gun, where would you go?*
> Jersey, Guernsey, anywhere with a decent postal service.
> *Not Los Angeles?*
> No. I need grit and struggle and Los Angeles is terribly nice, but people, once they get there, cease to be real. Constant and repetitive fulfillment is not good for the human spirit. We all need rain and good old depression. Life can't be all beer and skittles.
> —Q, 1995

During the early nineties, Morrissey had begun looking to Los Angeles, if not for the language he used then certainly for his audience, record sales, and record label. As his popularity began to plummet in the U.K., as he denounced the Americanization of Britain most loudly, his popularity in the U.S. reached unheard-of proportions; he sold out the Hollywood Bowl in just ten minutes and the Los Angeles Forum in fourteen. In the States, he was hailed as a living sign and invited on prime-time TV chat shows;

in England, he was branded irrelevant at best and a clapped-out embarrassment.

As the nineties progressed, his stock in the U.S. continued to wax as much as it waned in the U.K. Inevitably, he found himself spending more and more time in the U.S., especially in L.A. In 1996, he bought a house in Hollywood designed by Clark Gable for Carole Lombard, with cult actor Johnny Depp for a neighbor. Morrissey, the archpatriot, found himself in the very situation he would have lambasted ten years previously: an English pop star selling out to America, betraying his roots and perhaps—most unforgivable of all—finding some kind of approximation of contentment.

> Initially, I had a naive view of America. I hated the fact that it seemed to have so much while I had nothing. I feel differently now. Guess why?
> —*THE BIG ISSUE*, 1997

But, of course, it wasn't a betrayal, or it was at least no more a betrayal of England than his whole pop career had been. The anti-Americanism of his past, like his anti-Southernism before he left Manchester for London, was the simultaneous product of envy and a refusal to admit his aspirations even to himself. In an important if offbeat sense, Morrissey was always American—and not just because he was a James Dean devotee. His ambition was much too big to be contained in the Old Country, with its petty resentments, class envy, and twitching net curtains (even if he was responsible for much of the twitching). He was always heading for that West Coast penal colony for uppity working-class English types.

Above all, Morrissey's *loneliness* is quintessentially American: All Americans are strangers in their own land. The Native Americans were wiped out or forced onto unfamiliar reservations not just to steal their land but to make them as rootless as the white man—to make them "American." The "United States" is a big, drafty, empty place without enough history or public houses or fish-and-chips shops to go around, and so Americans wrap themselves in the flag, hug the cross, huddle on the sports field, or religiously attend the movies. From time to time, they even invade foreign countries, hoping to make friends with the newly conquered/liberated people. Most famously, they invented popular culture and consumerism to keep them company and have very generously exported this form of canned loneliness around the world.

For his part, Lancashire's patron saint of solitude, perhaps the strangest but also perhaps the aptest product of pop culture, its ultimate victim and ultimate master, probably admires American affability, friendliness, and *neediness* as much as he finds it ludicrous and frightening. Besides, he often performs Englishness just as self-consciously, just as desperately—and endearingly—as Americans perform Americanness (though, since England is on the verge of extinction while America engulfs the globe in its smotheringly friendly bear hug, his performance is perhaps somewhat more arch).

> Everything that happens in America is constantly reported
> on the English news while, in America, England is never
> referred to and British politics are completely meaningless.
> I mean, the country could completely explode and
> disappear into outer space and America would not mention
> that on the daily news.
> —*ALTERNATIVE PRESS,* 1993

Morrissey's Englishness was virtual—an idealized Englishness that could actually be much better sustained in the U.S., away from the increasingly compromised contemporary reality, in a California town where "England" only exists as an underused set on the back lot of Universal Studios. With the perversity for which he is famous, by settling in "Loose Angela" as much as anyone can settle in such an insubstantial place, Morrissey was being true to his vision of Englishness, which increasingly had even less to do with the actual existing England than it ever did.

> Please don't imagine I came to Los Angeles to surf or work out. I know it's happening here somewhere, but I could never do any of that.
> —*WORD*, 2003

Morrissey in L.A. is a joke, of course, but a predictable one, not just because L.A. is the natural home of narcissistic, dysfunctional, agoraphobic types with great profiles everywhere, but because, in a globalized postmodern world where, so it seems, all meanings become "free-floating," all meanings and those interested in producing them gravitate to the city of signs. Arguably, Morrissey himself, through the success of his art, finally separated England from Englishness forever, watched it drift across the Atlantic like an untethered fairground balloon caught in a prevailing wind, and then upped and followed it.

Besides, America offered this Anglo asylum seeker uncritical, all-embracing, all-conquering love. And to someone from England's resentful shores, America in love is an awe-inspiring, intoxicating, life-transforming revelation; one far more potent and therapeutic than even Ecstasy.

Everyone leaves home in the end, especially those who say they never will.

> I'd like all the vilification to end now and just the love to come through and feel, for 24 hours a day, unbridled support from all quarters.
> —*Q*, 1994

Of course, Morrissey's pessimism, misanthropy, and "miserabilism" are technically capital offenses in the U.S., but he is from the Old World, which everyone knows is a terrible cross to bear, and so allowances are made on compassionate grounds. By the same token, if America was in love with the future and Morrissey was in love with the past, then that was okay, since the past that Morrissey was in love with was an English one and Americans consider the Old Country washed up anyway.

> Everybody is beautiful all the time and that heat, every
> single day . . . I understand that some people find it
> unbearable. It really is the Mamas and the Papas all the
> time. It really is.
> —*POP,* 1998

To young, perhaps slightly unpopular Americans, Morrissey represents not so much "Englishness" (which, quite rightly, most know little about) as a country, or a world, in his own right—Morrisseyworld is a place where they can wander through his vast back catalog, lose themselves in his mysterious references, ride his ready wit, and tour his gothic neuroses and childhood hang-ups. With his impressive oeuvre, now spanning more than two decades, Morrissey has created an unrivaled richness, depth, and, yes, peculiar kind of love from his own imagination. Morrisseyworld is a place to meet other outsiders, a community of loners and losers; alienation and shyness is nice, but it's better to have someone to share it with. Hence, Manchester's prodigal son has spawned myriad fanzines in the U.S. and a host of websites where lonely young people typing in their bedrooms can connect with other lonely young people typing in their bedrooms and talk about the lonely records they like to listen to . . . alone.

I like the light. It's astonishing to wake up in the morning
and see that light and say, yes, you can do things today. That
really doesn't happen in Manchester.
　　—*THE BIG ISSUE*, 1999

To a certain American audience, Morrissey is familiar but
exotic, American but un-American, alternative but timeless. He
is the pop-cultural soul in a world made soulless by pop culture;
a distinctively Catholic voice in a distinctly Protestant country.
A man who lives between borders, an insider-outsider. And that,
along with his refusal of rap music, his tendency to wear his
heart on his sleeve, his fascination with, exploration of—and
penetration of—machismo, his dramatic defiance, and, of course,
his highly cultivated sideburns, is probably a factor in his famous
appeal to many young Mexican-Americans—effectively California's hidden, and "homeless," working class. Or perhaps it is
merely due to Mexican-American evident good taste.

　　Oddly, the people sweating, without health insurance and
frequently for less than the minimum wage, to sustain California's luxurious lifestyle (including, of course, the one that
Morrissey enjoys), to maintain those immaculately clean homes,
those neatly tended gardens, those shiny cars, those sparkling
swimming pools, that staggering abundance of food and eateries,
tend toward a doomed and romantic view of the world, one at
odds with that of cosseted, entitled, "realistic," mainstream, prosaic middle-class Californians for whom these things appear
almost by magic, or entitlement: *"When you're rich and white you'll
be all right"* ("Mexico").

I spend hours just driving around the small, rundown
Mexican areas of Los Angeles—that is, the areas where the
small, rundown Mexicans live. And have become quite
fascinated by that. And so, yes, you could say I've come

from Salford to Lincoln Heights. It's a short walk, really, and there are very familiar types in each place.
—*THE TIMES MAGAZINE,* 1999

Morrisseyworld is also a place where malcontent, adolescent Americans of all descriptions can go and drop out, going against the jock-prom-queen-college-fund values of the suburbs and the piped, choreographed snarly "rebellion" of MTV. Morrissey is, after all, much cheaper than Paris, and slightly less hassle than a high-school massacre. On the American scene, Moz remains a resolutely almost-mainstream cult performer, triangulated somewhere between Kurt Cobain, Lou Reed, and Benny Hill.

THEN AGAIN, MAYBE this is patronizing old-world horseshit. Maybe American fans, like Morrissey fans anywhere else in the world, simply recognize him as an authentic individualist—and in a country ostensibly built on individualism but frequently more slavishly conformist than Switzerland, this means a lot. In particular, this is seen in the fatal integrity that shines through his work and his career choices like a beacon (luring the innocent onto the rocks). His refusal to compromise, to chase the money, to give the audience what they want, to listen to the record-company men with their focus-group findings who tell him how much there is to be made if he cashes in his chips and goes chasing the Serious Moonlight, is an especially extraordinary thing to achieve in a land—a world—where the customer is always right, the artist is always wrong, and money does all the talking.

I've lived for the best part of the last two years in Los Angeles, where I remain, and which I even quite like. All the awful clichés about Los Angeles are, of course, true. But

I feel less affected by them than most, because I happen to think that ALL PEOPLE EVERYWHERE are mad.
 —*ROLLING STONE,* 1999

With the exception perhaps of Oscar Wilde and that other failed Morrissey prototype, Quentin Crisp, who were fortunate at least not to have to deal with record companies, most other English pop stars who have found success in the U.S. have promptly lost themselves. Since the Beatles, the "British invasion" of America has been a constant motif of British pop music, if not the whole point of it. Making America notice us, or at least hearing their daughters screaming at us, seems the greatest form of success we can conceive of. After all, "success" is an American idea and, hence, it isn't quite the genuine article until it is something that Americans recognize, too.

But we're terribly conflicted. We condemn our bands for "selling out" to America, but ridicule them for not selling *in* America. We in England like to imagine that we can reverse the result of the War of Independence with a fancy hairstyle and a few catchy tunes, that we can stake our claim in the American sun without having to sacrifice our charming English pallor or penniless integrity, only to rudely discover that America always, always wins. It is too big, too coarse, and the climate altogether too intemperate for the overdressed–underdressed urban dandies, professional eccentrics, and out–and–out psychotics who periodically launch themselves from these shores in an attempt to stamp their image on the place.

It's also far too grown-up. The naive British cult-artists say coquettishly to the almighty dollar, "Let's Dance," but the American record company just bends them over their three-album deal, reams them out, and pins their broken hymen to the Washington Monument. Like Antaeus, the undefeated wrestler of Greek myth, or, for that matter, David Jones, the Kabuki mime artist from Bromley, English pop stars find their power ebbing away when their feet are no longer touching their mother soil.

Does this include Morrissey, the most "English" of English pop stars? Probably. Possibly. After all, since he moved there in 1996, he has not exactly been what you would call *prolific*. But not inevitably. While L.A. may represent the nearest thing to retirement for Morrissey and possibly a kind of mummification (it is, after all, Hollywood, that crumbling, cryptlike part of L.A. guarded by the ghosts of Bette Davis and Marilyn Monroe, in which he has immured himself), he may yet turn out to be the most durable Limey pop star in the New World precisely because he has always been homesick; he's always been an Englishman abroad. Like an Anglo Count Dracula, he carries his Mother Country around with him; the soil in the bottom of his coffin is his books, records, films—and his own back catalog.

> It's very important that you heat the pot before you put the water in—if you use a pot, I know most people just throw a teabag into a cup. But in England, of course, you have to make a pot of tea. And you have to heat the pot first with hot water, and then put the teabags in. I can't believe I'm saying this. And then put the hot water in and then just throw it all over yourself. Rush to outpatients' and write a really good song.
> — MORRISSEY EXPLAINING TO AMERICANS HOW TO MAKE TEA, KROQ, 1997

AND THEN, JUST when you had got used to, resigned to, relaxed to the notion of Morrissey buried in L.A. forever, he turns up with a flourish of his cape in . . . Whitby. Well, the Royal Albert Hall, to be more exact.

The year 2002, the same year in which he was acknowledged as the "most influential artist ever" by a recanting *NME,* saw a triumphant, albeit brief, return to the U.K. for the Prince of Gloominess to play two sold-out nights at the Royal Albert cake tin. Onstage, Morrissey, looking leaner than he has in years, performed songs mostly from his early solo period—and also some new material. This included the almost spoken-word passionate defiance of "Irish Blood English Heart," part musical gauntlet, part antiestablishment auto-martyrdom: a speech from the scaffold; the exquisite "The First of the Gang to Die," a Los Angeleno update of his lifelong ruffian romance, with an intro of buzzing guitars and mandolins sounding for all the world like Moz's heart swooning, which, with its very first line—*"You have never been in love / Until you've seen the stars / Reflect in the reservoirs"*—announces the return of an incomparable, irresistible talent; and the celeb-bashing "The World Is Full of Crashing Bores" (*"so scared to show intelligence / It might smear their lovely career"*), an acute critique of the illness of modern fame, full of the pathos and comedy of his unique brand of self-dramatizing scorn and self-pity. His voice, stronger and more seductive than ever, easily overcame the prim resistance of the Victorian building's notorious acoustics, not to mention its sense of morality, filling the packed, oddly-shaped building with his strange, oddly-shaped music-hall love.

He began by setting about the audience with an enervatingly boisterous, shockingly youthful, note-perfect performance of the Smiths song "I Want the One I Can't Have," the song that is literally the song of his life, but that night, the last night of the Poms, it seemed addressed to the whole of England.

England responded by shouting out she was his for the taking. For the first time since the early nineties, Morrissey was greeted with adulatory notices in the press; even his old tabloid enemy *The Sun* sniffed which way the wind was blowing and saw fit to rave about his show and assure us that "Morrissey is on his way back."

Rehabilitation was definitely under way for one of England's most famous exiles. After all the years of vilification, the prophet without portfolio was finally being honored in his own land.

Why?

Perhaps because the nineties were finally over. Perhaps because Britpop and in fact English pop music itself was dead and buried, just as Morrissey had predicted, supplanted by TV talent contests, tacky showbiz values, and makeover programs. Perhaps because no one could be bothered to pretend to believe Morrissey was Manchester's answer to Adolf Eichmann anymore or could even remember the reasons they had to in the first place. Perhaps because it had been some time since he'd released an album and reminded them of how difficult and contrary to fashion his work could be. And perhaps because it was hoped that Morrissey, now forty-three, had lost most of his teeth and could be indulged as the Grand Old Gummy Man of Pop (if so, they were in for a sharp surprise).

Or maybe, just maybe, it was because everyone had forgotten what a true star, as opposed to a celebrity, looked like and what he was capable of until Morrissey showed up again with a quip and a flash of his disdainful talent.

And perhaps it was also because the media, and the world in general, now had within its upper echelons quite a few aging Smiths and Morrissey fans: Beautiful Bastards grown older but not necessarily up—just hideously compromised. Probably these clever swine were engaging (rather like this author) in a little personal thirtysomething nostalgia for a poorer, less sophisticated time when they were just better, more likable people, dreaming big dreams and planning big plans before the big ship sailed on the alley-alley-o. A time when they still had tremendous, tremulous, foolish faith in the power of pop music and words and their lying promises. A time when that charming-alarming man, the unchallenged and wicked master of both, accosted them and stole all their hearts away in a swooning, crooning manner that no other performer or, for that matter, any "real" "live" person, whatever that may be, ever came close to matching.

You see, of all the disappointments the pop Cassandra sat and prophesied about, none proved truer than his claim that there would be no one like him again. Ever.

> *Does it scare you that you still inspire such devotion in people?*
> No, but it might scare them.
> —*CITY LIFE,* 2003

By the following year, Morrissey began to be sighted more frequently in the U.K., particularly in secondhand cardigan shops near his mother's home in Cheshire. Unusually, he granted interviews to magazines other than his archfavorite, the homeless weekly *The Big Issue,* threatening to become, well, almost *ubiquitous.* He also popped up in Manchester's *City Life,* which had just voted him "Manchester's Greatest Ever Frontman," beating Liam Gallagher, Ian Curtis, Shaun Ryder, Ian Brown, Richard Ashcroft, Mark E. Smith, and the blessed Tim Burgess—and promised to play in Manchester soon, ending the (real or imagined) feud with his hometown that had lasted more than a decade: The last time he played Manchester was in 1992.

> *How does it feel to be voted Manchester's greatest ever frontman?*
> I'm absolutely exhausted from sending all those votes.
> —*CITY LIFE,* 2003

He was even seen on the box in his first major U.K. TV appearance since 1987: an hour-long Channel 4 documentary about him made during the previous year was aired in May to a frisson of media excitement. Most of the talking was done by various famous fans, including J. K. Rowling, Bono, Kathy Burke, Noel Gallagher, and Alan Bennett, expressing their admiration for this prickly star; Morrissey, for his part, gave very little away and pulled off the remarkable feat of appearing a reluctant guest on his own doc. Perhaps the most significant moment was when he was filmed outside his eccentric Hollywood home, which looks like a gingerbread windmill, squinting against the Southern Californian sunshine and promising us that he hadn't "adapted" to Los Angeles.

In the same week, after six long years without a record contract, it was announced that he had signed to a British record company Sanctuary Music Group, home to Black Sabbath, the Libertines, and the Strokes and also, following a takeover in the early nineties, the Smiths' old record label, Rough Trade. Morrissey threatened to begin work immediately on a new album, reportedly called *Irish Blood English Heart,* also the title of one of the new songs he had performed at the Royal Albert Hall the previous year, a song that bragged, all too credibly, *"There is no one on this earth I'm afraid of,"* and went on to look forward to a time when to be English is to not feel *"shameful / racist or racial."* The LP was eventually released in 2004 as *You Are the Quarry,* the title no doubt a comment on the British media's treatment of him as a national blood sport for much of the previous decade—and, given the press's largely adulatory response to the album, another delicious Morriseyan irony).

Morrissey, it seemed, really had come home.

Why did it take so long to re-sign? You can't have been short of offers. . . .
I honestly didn't have any decent offers. For example, three major U.S. labels said, "We want you, but we don't want your band," so I turned them down. Another label said, "We want to sign you, but we'd first like you to make an album with the musicians from Radiohead," and another label said, "We'll sign you if you agree to make an album with Tracey Thorn." Absolutely bewildering. People don't know what I've been through.
    —*CITY LIFE,* 2003

In a classic, deeply Morrisseyan twist (of the stiletto), it emerged that he had so impressed Sanctuary's chief executive with his connoisseurship of its Trojan catalog that the CEO had readily agreed to Morissey's request to resurrect for his use the old Attack label, which in the seventies brought the world the Pioneers, Gregory Isaacs, and the Upsetters, giving him the license to its back catalog and the power to sign any new talent that caught his eye.

In other words, that alarming man who had once famously outraged the *NME* by daring to criticize music that happened to be black in origin, who was nearly destroyed by his criminal refusal to feel ashamed of Englishness, and who would not save his skin by genuflecting to political correctness by talking loudly about the black music he did happen to like (which, of course, was the favorite music of real skinheads, as opposed to Nazis with no hair), was a decade later back in town, back in business, and in charge of a reggae label called Attack. Irony is probably the only sensual pleasure that rude boy Morrissey enjoys more than pouring scorn.

If all identity is based to some extent on contradiction, Morrissey's is *all* contradiction.

> I once said, "Reggae is vile," did I? Well, several tongue-in-cheek things were said in those days, which, when placed in cold print, lost their humorous quality. "Swan Lake," by the Cats, along with "Double Barrel" and "Young, Gifted, and Black," were staple teenage necessities to me. Anyway, annoying the *NME* always has value.
> —MORRISSEY EXPLAINING THE INCLUSION OF A
> SKA TRACK ON HIS COMPILATION ALBUM
> *UNDER THE INFLUENCE, WORD,* 2003

TOO BUSY THINKING ABOUT MYSELF

I have often wished I had time to cultivate modesty. . . . But I am too busy thinking about myself.

　　—DAME EDITH SITWELL

Sisyphus, proletarian of the gods, powerless and rebellious, knows the whole extent of his wretched condition; it is what he thinks of during his wretched descent. The lucidity that was to constitute his torture at the same time crowns his victory. There is no fate that cannot be surmounted by scorn.

　　—ALBERT CAMUS

If George Michael had to live my life for five minutes, he'd strangle himself with the nearest piece of cord.

　　—MORRISSEY

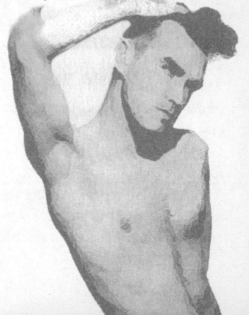

12.

veryone knows that Morrissey is mad.

It's an official fact of which every household is informed by a government leaflet pushed through their letter boxes every year, usually around Whitsuntide.

The stories proving his madness are legion: the canceled concerts; the canceled tours; the refusal to be interviewed; the refusal, when he actually agrees to be interviewed, to be nice to interviewers; the imperiousness; the spontaneous disappearances; the unanswered telephone; the unanswered telegrams; the unanswered doorbell; the summary excommunications (sometimes by postcard—legend has it that one hapless former confidant, after some perceived betrayal, received three postcards through his letter box, one after the other, with a single word allocated to each: *LOSE, MY, NUMBER*); the ditched record companies; the sacked managers; the refusal to get married in *Hello!* magazine. Above all, the refusal to be a proper pop star and do all those proper pop-star things that pop stars are supposed to do, which anyone in his right mind would be happy to do and which are, in fact, the only reasons that most people become pop stars in the first place.

A churlish refusal, in other words, to suck Satan's cock.

Morrissey's "madness" is actually a passionate, not to say rabidly jealous, self-possessiveness rare enough in ordinary punters but almost unknown in the tarty world of pop. Morrissey's "looniness" is an extreme form of self-preservation, self-regard, and self-love that compels him to say the one thing people don't want to ever hear from a pop star: "No."

Over and over again.

No to the loss of himself. No to the ravenous, slavering demands of everyone who wants a piece of him: fans, the music industry, associates, biographers, even and especially friends. Albert Camus once asked, "What is a rebel?" and came up with the answer: "A man who says 'no.'" Obviously he meant to say: "Morrissey."

The resentment felt by Joe Public at Morrissey's refusal to paint a vulgar picture is understandable. After all, they're used to the idea that a pop star belongs to them, that he or she is their creature, entirely and always available for their pleasure and, most particularly, their displeasure. It's not a groundless expectation. Most people who become famous do so by inviting the public to buy shares in them. They float themselves on the stock exchange of public opinion, surrendering their destiny and personality to interested parties and spending the rest of their pop careers trying to manage, play off, and reconcile the various interest groups that own them. Morrissey, on the other hand, a self-capitalized and very private company, will not let his fame and his success be about anything other than *him*. He wants recognition, he wants adoration, but not at the cost of his self-love. Morrissey's madness is really just a simple form of stinginess: He refuses to pay anyone else a dividend in his own fame, a percentage of his own personality.

So he rejects the deal that almost every other star strikes with the world—a world that says, "We will make you a legend across the globe, a giant among men, an immortal of the early-evening news and a regular on *The National Lottery*, on one tiny, teensy-weensy condition: That it is not actually you who we make famous. Yes, we will put your name in lights, but it will not be your name anymore. Your face will rotate around the clock on MTV, but it will not be your face. You may cash the lottery-size check we send you, but it is not really your money. You will sing to millions, but you will not sing your life. You will be loved but not for who you are, rather for who we decide the audience wants you to be. And in the meantime, don't you EVER unplug your telephone again or leave town without checking with us first, okay?

> *Which words or phrases do you most overuse?*
> "No, I won't," "Why should I?" "What's the point?" and
> "I'd like to terminate our agreement."
> —*KILL UNCLE* TOUR BOOK, 1991

To describe this deal as Faustian is to do a disservice to Dr. Faustus's business sense. In his deal with Old Nick, he at least gained a lifetime of doing exactly what he pleased before the Sulphurous One came for him. Most pop stars happily sign away not just their immortal souls (which, frankly, no one is terribly interested in) but their *mortal* lives as well. They live in gilded cages paraded around town by their record or film company, which hands out tridents to the public with which to prod the star for its amusement. Why do celebs agree? Why do they sign such a patently bad deal with their own blood? Because their ambition is just so desperately mundane. Most pop stars are, by definition, secondhanders. They don't want the world, just acceptance. They don't want to be great, just popular. They don't want to be feared, just rich. They don't want to destroy, just to belong. They sign away their lives because they want the sweet, fluffy, sticky celeb trappings of fame, not its bitter, lonely essence. And the essence of real fame is . . . revenge. While the essence of revenge is . . . Morrissey.

Do you regard success as a form of revenge?
Oh absolutely and entirely a form of revenge, yes, I do.
And is it sweet?
Remarkably sweet. I like the taste, yes. More, please!
But revenge for what?
Well, for everything, on everybody. . . . So now I can just sit
back every night—when *Minder* is finished—and just
chuckle, deafeningly.
  —*THE HIT,* OCTOBER 5, 1985

Just what does a strong-willed but oversensitive boy sitting
out his adolescence in his bedroom do after he has memorized
The Picture of Dorian Gray and masturbated three times that afternoon already? Why, he plans his *vengeance!* Every day he rehearses
his boundless vindictiveness against a world that tramples him
underfoot with its indifference.

Over time, his anger cools, but it solidifies it into something
tangible, something familiar, something that he could love as the
most valuable and virtuous part of himself. Hence, Morrissey's
hunger for fame was not a cure for his misanthropy, a walking
into the light and the laughter, as it so often is—or is hoped to
be—with lesser talents, but a bubble for it that would sustain and
channel his enmity beyond his excruciatingly disappointing adolescence. Fame was the route by which Morrissey could leave his
fetid bedroom but continue to breathe the same air, a way of
entering the world without ever having to change, without having to compromise, without having to relinquish his familiar passions. Without ever having to grow up: *"I'd like to drop my trousers
to the world."*

How do you want to be remembered?
As Manchester's answer to the H-bomb.
  —*KILL UNCLE* TOUR BOOK, 1991

Inevitably, this victory over the world was a Pyrrhic one. In a sense, he never *did* leave his bedroom. In the eighties, the success of the Smiths allowed him to leave Manchester for the arms of national fame—which inevitably meant London. But by the nineties, he found that London had become Manchester (and so he left Britain for the arms of America). Moz was still the strange boy on his own whom everyone around these parts laughed at; the "nutter," the "basket case." His bedroom may have been more spacious, better decorated, and now came with room service, and he may have had rather more pen pals, but he was still living in a mental bedsit. As in those gray, resentful Manchester days, people suspected that this secluded, introverted creature thought himself that most unforgivable of things—particularly in a star—"special." And they were right.

> I'm not a phone person. I can't quite get used to the telephone.
> *Why? Lack of intimacy?*
> Lack of interest. There's usually a person on the other end.
> —*MODERN ROCK LIVE,* 1997

This isn't to say that Morrissey wasn't sorely tempted by the promise of global fame. The desire for recognition and acceptance always sits alongside the desire for retribution and destruction (though it is always a mistake to see the former as merely being masked by the latter, as in: "Oh, he's a nice person really—he's just a bit bitter, that's all"). In the days of the Smiths, he frequently boasted about their/his worldwide ambitions, and songs such as "Frankly Mr. Shankly" and "You Just Haven't Earned It Yet Baby" appeared to pour scorn on the "righteous" and "holy" scruples, or simple incompetence, of those such as his hippie Rough Trade boss Geoff Travis, whom Morrissey deemed to be standing between him and the vast unlimited fame he felt should be his by rights.

I'm ready to be accepted by everybody. I want to be heard
and I want to be seen by as many people as possible.
—*MELODY MAKER, 1983*

But his own actions spoke differently, betraying an uncon-
scious refusal to grant the necessary concessions, to make the necessary dilutions of himself to achieve the level of fame he craved.
Morrissey's ambition was bigger than that of the rest of the Smiths
put together, but he was the one persuading them, often against
their better judgment, to renounce Satan and all his works and
live on a diet of fame gruel and celeb abstinence. He wanted the
Smiths to be as big and as modest as the Beatles but with the
(early) cred of the Rolling Stones—the Beatles, in other words,
without Brian Epstein. Later, it became clear that he wanted to be
Elvis without Colonel Tom Parker. Of course, this was just more
evidence of his "madness." Without Colonel Parker, Elvis was just
a hillbilly truck driver no one had ever heard of. Everyone
knows—even Jesus H. Christ, who would have been just another
bastard carpenter who thought he could walk on water without
his go-getting Jewish manager, Saint Paul—that what is Caesar's
must be rendered unto Caesar, because Caesar is the master of this
world and all who would succeed in it. But no one had told
Morrissey.

Sometimes I do have a great physical need to be reasonably
blunt, which most people find quite taxing. That's the side
of me which is unmarketable, totally unpromotable. . . . But
the songs, and the album title, and the sleeve, and whatever
else you might wish to investigate, are simply . . . me.
—*MUSICIAN, 1991*

So, with the brief and reportedly reluctant exception of the
venerable Joe Moss, who managed the Smiths on an ad hoc basis

until the first album, he refused to deal with managers. He signed to an independent record label without the resources to market his records. He wouldn't make music videos (which meant, among other things, that they didn't get played on MTV, and so big, sleepy America didn't wake up to the Smiths until they were the Stiffs). And he canceled major international tours, literally at the airport gate. Given that Morrissey's fear of flying seems metaphorical as well as literal, Marr's departure from the Smiths at the very moment when they were threatening to go global makes one wonder whether he jumped or was unconsciously, half intentionally pushed, however bereft Morrissey was at the break. (Self-sabotage is a proud Mancunian habit: e.g., Oasis's antics in the U.S., and, most impressively, Ian Curtis, the lead singer of Joy Division, who hung himself on the eve of his first American tour.)

> Can you imagine anything so boring as world domination.
> I mean, what would you do in your spare time?
> —Q, 1995

The bizarre story of "Hand in Glove" illustrates Morrissey's total disrespect for the way of the world, the workings of the pop business in particular, and his refusal to give the public what it thinks it wants instead of what he knows it needs. When it was originally released in 1983, "Hand in Glove" disappeared almost without trace, barely charting at No. 124. Morrissey, however, was not satisfied with this unambiguous public verdict on his debut and, instead of drawing a veil over his stillborn firstborn, began an unprecedented campaign of browbeating. He proceeded to bang on and on and on about the song in every interview, insisted it appear on *The Smiths, Hatful of Hollow,* and the U.S. compilation *Louder than Bombs*—even including the taunting lines "Hand in glove . . . / The sun shines out of our behinds" at the end of *The Smiths* track "Pretty Girls Make Graves." He finally beat the British public into abject submission, which made it a top-ten hit after he persuaded Sandie Shaw to cover it in 1984 (only a year after the original).

> *What brings you here today?*
> The 138 to Streatham Hill.
> —MORRISSEY TO AN MTV REPORTER AFTER HIS
> ACCEPTANCE OF AN IVOR NOVELLO LIFETIME
> ACHIEVEMENT AWARD, 1998

In his solo career, Morrissey may have relented and given Caesar/the record industry some burnt offerings of music videos, but only because now, with most of his audience in the United States, he would simply fade away without them (mind you, MTV exhibits an extreme aversion to actually showing them). However, this appears to have been his only concession. Far from becoming more pragmatic, more pliable with age, this stubbornly, devoutly self-obsessed character shows no signs of relinquishing his "control freakery."

> As soon as people get to work with a group they have the impression they have full powers. Guided by money and covetousness, they start doing anything. It's one of my biggest regrets in life: I've never found any person clever enough to represent me. This person doesn't exist.
> —*LES INROCKUPTIBLES,* 1995

By dint of a sustained and superhuman effort of skill and cunning, Morrissey managed throughout the nineties to snatch defeat from the jaws of victory and prevent his career from going supernova in the U.S., somehow keeping it forever bubbling under, just short of major, full-fledged, all-formats, all-media, general-release, vulgar fame. (By 1998, he had managed to bring about a state of affairs in which he was such a "special" pop star that he was actually without a record deal of any kind, and was to remain that way into the early noughties.)

> I know I'm making your stomach churn as I say those
> words, but I do feel like a one-off. You can hate the sight of
> me, or you can cherish every word I've uttered. But I do
> feel reasonably unique, I do. It's a terrible, terrible curse. I
> wish I could just blend in.
> —*MUSICIAN*, 1991

Despite his tendency to blame record companies/the press/ the Marylebone Cricket Club for these things and the fact that he stubbornly remains "merely" the most famous cult performer in the world, one whom everyone has heard of even if most don't actually own any of his records, he knows he has no one to thank but himself. His solo career has turned out to be a perfect rendition of that truth. His solitary image on the album covers, his lonely monomoniker (without even a first name to keep it company) hovering above like a halo, like a crown of thorns, like a bloody albatross; the way, post-Marr, his voice occasionally seems to be trying to impose a melody where there isn't one by sheer willpower; and above all, his strangely moving stage per-formance, where he seems a thousand miles away from his band, from his "profession," and, in fact, from any kind of human soci-ety at all—except the adoration of his fans—is a distillation of the essential drama of Morrissey's life: one man and his "mad-ness" against the world.

> *What does it feel like to see your proliferated image about, on*
> *hoardings, in magazines, to hear your voice on the radio?*
> It's very odd. I was in a shop once, buying scented candles,

and on the radio came Steve Wright with a collage of Smiths songs, and I got a distinct chill, almost as if the hand of Death was tapping me on the shoulder, saying, "Put yer candles down, it's time to go!"
—*MELODY MAKER,* 1988

Whatever it might do for your mental health, not to mention your bank balance and marriage prospects, this is a great strategy for holding on to one's artistic edge. Nosing into middle age, surrounded by the evidence of his past successes and acclaim and, of course, the continuing love from his fans, Morrissey is still a voice sobbing in the wilderness, still complaining bitterly of the things he complained about to himself as a child: that he is unloved, underrated, overlooked, neglected. His love, in other words, is still as sharp as a needle in our eye.

Dirk Bogarde sent me a card the other day, and I almost cried with joy when it arrived. I thought, Put it this way, Mozzer, you have a card from Dirk Bogarde here [and he slapped the settee]. You have Alan Bennett sitting in your kitchen having tea. You have David Bowie having sung one of your songs quite beautifully. What else are you looking for? What right do I have to be sour-faced and complaining, queuing up at Waitrose in Holloway being annoyed because somebody in front of me has got a leg of lamb? What more could there be?
—*SELECT,* 1994

Anyone needing to be convinced that he has held on to his edge—and exclusion—with white knuckles needs only to listen to his eve-of-middle-age 1997 album (his eleventh), which was not called *Help Me Put My Kids Through College* but *Maladjusted.* Although much of the music ranks several celestial circles beneath the sustained brilliance of *Vauxhall and I* or *Your Arsenal* and was not received well by the critics or the fans, it has moments, such as the shudderingly powerful "Trouble Loves Me," that more than equal anything from his back catalog and have a directness and an unaffected, uncloying poignancy and pathos that, say, Radiohead or their many (very) well-brought-up imitators, such as Coldplay, will never achieve, no matter how much angst they sprinkle on their Coco Pops in the morning. Moreover, as a document of an artist's willful failure to "settle down," *Maladjusted* is incontrovertibly, startlingly genuine.

Remaining true to the thirteen-year-old promise of "Suffer Little Children" to make society pay for causing such suffering (by, paradoxically if perhaps inevitably, reversing its subjectivity) is a track called "Ambitious Outsiders," a mournful string arrangement with threatening kettledrum accompaniment over which Morrissey croaks eerily, poking fun at the imagined security of domestic bliss, apparently speaking on behalf of faceless, threatening figures committed to spoiling other people's happiness: *"Top of the list / Is your smiling kids . . . DON'T UNDERESTIMATE US."*

While this may be the universal ransom note of all pop music at its best, this really isn't the sort of thing a wealthy, famous, globally acclaimed thirty-eight-year-old should be singing. It's an irresponsible statement of a continuing artistic identification with those on the fringes who avenge themselves on society; a statement that performers half his age and with rather more piercings wouldn't dare to make. Nevertheless, pop's most unapologetic and most pernicious pied piper is perfectly well aware that he's also his own worst enemy, especially when he's blaming someone else. The piano-led "Trouble Loves Me," reminiscent of "I Know It's Over" from *The Queen Is Dead,* builds and falls like the self-intoxicating moods of, well . . . a manic-depressive—a heartrending mixture of confession and accusation. Musically, it's the tortured anthem that Queen was forever trying to write but just didn't have the neuroses for. With a hymnlike piano-chord intro (Morrissey is our Ancient and Modern), he croons at the high end of his range in a voice on the verge of cracking.

Quavering and wobbling in that characteristically engaging-annoying way, he confides the drama and pathos of his scorn. And, indeed, the more he considers his condition, the more he reflects on his treatment, then the more agitated he becomes and the worse he makes things for himself. The accompaniment escalates from warm piano to searing electric guitar as he begins to flagellate himself with gusto, decrying his foolish "ready wit" and deluded desires, which keep him "running 'round."

As he implies, his famous ready wit is both the function and the cause of his disenchantment. He won't allow himself the peace he says he craves, even after all these years. He's still chasing his demons, stopping to catch his breath, and then turning around and inviting them to chase him again. He is discontented, malcontented with everyone and everything, most especially himself and his achievements. He wants not to want. Almost.

Contrary as ever, he's proudly resigned to his condition, his art, and its consequences. Often, Morrissey's songs seem to take the form of an imagined conversation with an imagined lover (which is literally true in a sense: He's addressing his fans almost as much as he's talking to himself). "Trouble Loves Me" is a classic example of this. The opening lines suggest that the lament is directed to, in typically accusatory, ironic fashion, an "ex" (certainly "Trouble" could be the name of any or all of the ruffians he admires). By the end of this turbulent song, fraught with emotional drama, defiance, and weary resignation, he finally confesses that, at midnight, *I can't get you out of my head."*

The frustration and anger in the dark, midnight thoughts

still running 'round his head are emphasized by the unusual, almost clumsy length of the line: "I-can't-get-you-out-of-my-head," which Morrissey shakes out with musically balled fists. It is a syllable longer than the next-longest line, which occurs in an earlier, more tranquil part of the song: a caressing, sibilant phrase of which the longer line with the shorter, harder words has deprived him.

But is it Morrissey himself or his "ex" who he can't get out of his head and who leaves him with a disenchanted taste? Is it an unhappy experience of love, or is it the uneasy residue of his life that leaves him sleepless and anxious at night? As ever, and as in most people's experience, it isn't clear. The lines *"Go to Soho, oh / Go to waste in / The wrong arms"* could be a dismissive rebuke delivered to a former, unfaithful, perhaps male lover (Soho is famous today not only as London's gay district but also as a "party" district, especially for media types; in Morrissey's much-loved fifties and sixties, though, it was the center of bohemia and criminality).

Or it could merely be Morrissey offering himself some more sarcastic advice: It is better to acquiesce, to be the person society wants you to be, and to embrace the predictable and the inauthentic. Settling for the attainable—which is to say what you don't want—and going to waste in the wrong arms is at least a safe option and certainly less trouble than pursuing the unattainable. At your age.

Whatever his enemies might attack him for, whatever the crimes they might accuse him of, Morrissey always beats them to the punch. No one is harder on him than himself; no one would want to be Morrissey.

There's nothing difficult about going to a psychoanalyst. Especially not for me, who is by nature rather keen on confession. I've given a great number of interviews in my

life, which has probably constituted an excellent warm-up.
... I'll certainly need centuries to settle everything.
—*LES INROCKUPTIBLES,* 1995

The title track, "Maladjusted," is perhaps the most powerful
and mordant statement of Morrissey's awareness of his position
in the world—and the seriousness of his condition. It opens with
some distorted feedback followed by a sample from the classic
stiff-upper-lip British war movie *Cockleshell Heroes* (1955), an
account of the heroic if slightly silly attempt by ten Royal
Marines in canoes to take on the might of the Nazi navy (almost
all were killed). Before the mission, the lads get into a punch-up
with a pub full of sailors. Black-and-blue and back in the bar-
racks but in high spirits, Anthony Newley, having grown up from
his Artful Dodger role and playing a cheeky-chappie bootneck
from the ranks, announces mock-formally, *"On this glorious h'occasion of the splendid defeat"*—which can only be Morrissey's own
wry appraisal of his own career and life. (*Maladjusted* was released
in the year following his drubbing by Mike Joyce and "m'learned"
friends in High Court.)

Sounding like a voice from beyond the grave and before the
womb, Morrissey moans, *"I wanna start from before the beginning"*
(a twisted echo perhaps of "Do-Re-Mi" from *The Sound of
Music,* which opens: *"Let's start at the very beginning / A very fine
place to start"*). Morrissey almost speaks the lyrics over the doom-
laden drums and guitars; it seems like he's making a statement to
the police, or his Maker. Then, suddenly changing his mind, he
grabs his car keys and trilby and takes us on a night out, during
which we loot some wine, avoid some "Stevenage overspill"
(Stevenage is a deathly dull dormitory town a half hour north of
London, as well as a pun on his disowned "dull" first name), and,
as usual, toss a half brick at normality without bothering to hide
our resentment.

The lights of the Fulham Road (a lively, well-to-do part of London, full of bars, restaurants, and animal life) are inviting but, somehow, their promise is not delivered, at least not to us. Life fails us again and instead we end up back where we started, with Morrissey complaining and boasting of his masochistic relationship with the machinery of fame and the pimping record industry (and the lawyers that infest it).

But his loathing isn't all outer-directed. Self-loathing, after all, is always the B side to self-loving. Morrissey here expresses a distaste for his own words.

It's an astonishingly brave, not to mention despondent, confession for an artist of Morrissey's stature to be making; the idea that he might entertain such profound doubts about the merit of his work, that he might even have taken that remark of the Lily Law Lord to heart, when his genius is founded precisely on his singularity, his willfulness, his arrogance, his self-conceit, his scorn, is perturbing. Then you remember that, of course, without the self-doubt, without the merciless, neurotic questioning of everything, the disrespect for all assumptions, even about his own achievements, there could be no genius. Self-indulgence might not be altogether uncommon in Morrissey's life, but self-deceit, a necessity for most people in order to survive life, is to him a luxury he rarely affords himself.

This, after all, is the terrible personal cost of Morrissey's greatness—but it is a price, you sense, that Morrissey, for all his brilliant whining, is ultimately willing to pay. "Maladjusted" ends with the ethereal repeated falsetto, as he tells himself, over and over again, that he isn't mad, ironically recalling the echoing, falsetto line *"I need advice, I need advice"* at the end of *The Smiths'* "Miserable Lie." Although here, thirteen years on, the irony works in the opposite direction—actually, he really does need advice (not that he's going to take it, mind).

Yes, the refrain could be interpreted as yet another rebuff to

his critics, the press, the courts, the music business, the family—
all the institutions that have effectively sectioned him and packed
him off to the funny farm—but it is just as likely that Morrissey
is actually mocking those around him, including himself, who
like to tell him that it's not him but the world that's a wrong 'un.

Taking the self-analysis and humility of "Maladjusted" one
stage further is "Ammunition," a bizarre, splutter-inducing track
that, by Morrissey's standards, is almost Buddhist: He claims that
he *"doesn't need more ammunition"* and that instead he's pleased
"with the things I've found."

For a moment, it seems as if poor old Mozzer has finally
accepted that bitterness doesn't become someone of his years
and jawline, that he ought to try on a more dignified sensibility.
That he ought to become a distinguished old man of pop, resting
on his comfy and extensive laurels, take up painting, and perhaps
launch an Internet service provider. Gratifyingly, "Ammunition,"
which otherwise would seem to mark the end of Morrissey's
serious musical career, is violently contradicted by the spleneti-
cally and unremittingly hateful (not to mention tuneless)
"Sorrow Will Come to You in the End," a song whose concept
of bad karma is just a little bit too proactive (perhaps for this reason it was dropped from the U.K. release of the album).
Addressed to *"Lawyer . . . liar!"* it advises him not to close his eyes
because *"a man who slits throats / Has time on his hands."*

*Hey! Um, yeah, Morrissey, your new song "Ammunition," you
talk . . . you say that you have no place or time in your life for
revenge. I was wondering, is that true and did something happen
that triggered that?*
It's not true, I'm afraid. It's not true. It's a nice idea, but not
true. I've got lots of space for revenge and, uh, long may it live.
—MORRISSEY ON MODERN ROCK LIVE RADIO
PHONE-IN (U.S.), 1997

It is left to the mellifluous (if perhaps somewhat pale descendant of "Everyday Is Like Sunday") "Alma Matters" to explain what really keeps him going. He admits the strangeness of choices he's made, and then asserts, in the words of that willful 1960s Northern girl Jo, the pop-star manque, the role model who has brought him to this pretty pass, *"It's my life to wreck my own way."*

"Alma" is probably a reference to Alma Cogan, the "girl with a giggle in her voice" who was the fifties prototype of the sixties girl singers Morrissey still worships and who died in 1966, underrated and largely forgotten. But the word has many resonances. Alma was also the name of Mike Baldwin's wife in *Coronation Street* from the eighties through the nineties. Baldwin was the show's live-in "love-rat," while Alma was a classic example of the tough-but-vulnerable Northern Woman who suffers valiantly the slings and arrows of outrageous fortune, especially in matters of the heart, and with whom Morrissey still identifies. In fact, as the pun on *alma mater* (old school or college) implies, this autodidact early-school-leaver was tutored in during his Manchester childhood. In a further Morrisseyan twist, *alma mater* is also the name given to a university or college song. The line *"It's my life / To wreck my own way"* is from his favorite hymn sheet, Shelagh Delaney's *A Taste of Honey,* which is Morrissey's college song.

Just as his connection with such misfit, touchingly freakish, gender-ambiguous characters sustained him when he was young, the connection his fans have with him today, when he is not so young but not very much older either, sustains *them* in their misfit, freakish, confused years, however long they might last. And the knowledge of that sustains him now. Quite possibly, it maintains him in his perpetual adolescent agony.

It is this peculiar, decidedly unhealthy relationship with his fans that explains the oddly intense nature of Morrissey's cult fame, which more than makes up for in devotion what it lacks in numbers. The unique and unrivaled fervor with which his fans love him is a function of their certainty that their relationship is something special, that it isn't like any other love, that this one is different because it's just *us*. They know that their love affair with him is as pure and unadulterated and direct as it gets in pop music. There is no percentage proof higher, no stronger distillation available, even under the pop-music counter for ready money, than the Morrissey brand. They know that he has always been true to them in his own strange, sick way. *Because he's remained true to himself.* The very things that have cost him his happiness—his bitter integrity, his scorn—are the things they love him for.

> *Do you receive a lot of fan mail?*
> Yes, a great lot. Mostly complaints, actually. . . . It's often
> parents of fans who write and ask me to stop existing.
> Someone wrote that she couldn't manage to walk past her
> daughter's room because she constantly played records by a
> man having his legs sawn off.
> —*BLITZ,* 1992

Through his work, he gives them the only love he knows—himself. Never what he thinks they might like to hear (although his music is full of jokes at his expense, shared with his audience, such as, for example, the end of "Disappointed"— *"This is the last song I will ever sing* [audience cheers] / *No: I've changed my mind again* [audience boos]"—and perhaps the whole of *Kill Uncle*). It is all, apart from the occasional half-decent tune, that most Morrissey fans want. Even the canceled concerts, which some point to as evidence of a fickle or callous attitude toward his fans, are, in a sense, merely part of the package, a reminder that Morrissey is not and never has been an *entertainer;* that, in the end, though he may depend on his relationship with his fans rather more than most performers (partly because it stands in for real flesh and blood ones) and take strength from the knowledge that his love is arming them in their own struggles with the world (or withdrawal from it), it's definitely, decidedly about him and not about them.

> *What is the source of this extraordinary love your fans display?*
> Trust. I think admiring me, shall we say, is quite a task.
> Because if you say you like Morrissey, then you have to explain why.
> —*DETAILS,* 1992

When the fans rush the stage, flattening hefty security guards, and succeed in wrapping themselves around the indulgent singer—head on his shoulder or pressed against his neck, or somewhere in his bosom, beaming preposterously rapturously, like an adopted child reunited with his (un)natural mother—they're proving their love, forgiveness, and acceptance of him and all his glorious shortcomings in an outpouring of demonstrative affection that no other contemporary performer comes close to provoking.

They are also, of course, hugging themselves, trying to claim his willful loneliness and the tremendous, foolish strength it betokens as their own—without, hopefully, actually having to suffer the full consequences of it in their own lives. They are consoling themselves with the entirely fanciful notion that the world can reward integrity, when, as they know very well, no matter how much they try to change the fact of it with their adoration of him, Morrissey is the exception that proves the rule of mediocrity. The Way of the World is the Way of the World for a very good reason. Only a blessed man, a man of saintly and perhaps slightly unhinged virtue, can resist it. Such a man is admirable, but definitely not enviable.

I think that there is a great sense that I have been always
overlooked. I think that the audience is perfectly aware of
this and they feel that I have been enormously short-
changed . . . by the entire music industry and all of their
relatives! I've been dumped into the "out" tray.
    —*SPIN*, 1992

Truth is, Morrissey is far too preoccupied with posterity to
achieve full-blooded, real, here-and-now *News of the World* fame.
The hereafter is what he has his eye on. It is fatal fame he really
wants; every song must be sung as if it were his last.

Hence, the obsession with suicide—death as a performance
that the suicide hopes will be extensively reviewed. After all, taking one's life can, like fame, also be a form of revenge. The wrists
slashed, the neck snapped, the brains spattered, are symbolically
someone else's ("*Now* they'll be sorry . . ."). The suicide's body is
a metaphor—the most violent and powerful of all, perhaps
because unlike most metaphors, it can only be used once. In the
self-mutilating, self-perpetuating words of Richey Manic, it's
"4 REAL."

So how much revenge there is to be had in a famous
suicide! The famous suicide is an artist-zealot who dies in the
service of an idea, which is the sign of true dedication and fanaticism. Jesus Christ was, of course, the most famous artist-zealot.
His death, an elaborate form of suicide, was literally the linchpin
of his fame, turning him into an idea—transcendence—as well as
a timeless logo (one that a famous vamp[iress] named after his
mother would find, a couple of thousand years later, rather
kinky). Even ordinary, common-or-garden suicide can be a stab
at immortality, or at least notoriety. Not so much the ultimate
victory over Death as the ultimate revenge on . . . Life. (The
Universal Church, of course, decreed that Christians who were
unable to persuade someone else to martyr them and who

decided instead to cut out the middleman and organize their own martyrdom were guilty of an irredeemable sin, otherwise known as cheating, and would be buried in unconsecrated graves.)

> I look upon suicide as this incredibly brave thing, having maximum control over one's body, yet, ludicrously, suicide has been looked upon as some severe disorder of somebody who doesn't know what she or he's doing. I always saw it as the height of self-awareness and control over one's destiny. . . . The desire to live for as long as possible is really quite cowardly. I find these issues quite easy to confront in the comfort of one's living room, but perhaps in a high speed jet, I'd rather talk about something else.
> —*SQUARE PEG*, 1984

Suicide, in other words, is the most spectacular form of sulking and also, perhaps, the ultimate form of self-possession, a refusal to become what the world wants you to become: pragmatic, reasonable, sensible, corrupt, *older*. Saint Augustine saw it as nothing less than a defiance of God, perhaps not just because it was the "easy" way out of this veil of tears but also because, in the right hands, it could be a blasphemous attempt at godhead. Rock and roll recognizes this very well and has always been an extremely "morbid" art form (though not quite as morbid as Christianity), preoccupied with the idea of an authentic life, which, of course, means a life that can't be lived: "Death is the only thing left to respect," as Jimmy Dean, that strange boy who crucified himself on the steering wheel of his Porsche and will now never grow old, put it.

Even when the death of an idol is not officially suicide, we like to imagine that it amounted to as much—Marc Bolan's crash, Janis Joplin's/Jimi Hendrix's/Johnny Thunders's overdoses, James

Dean's smash, Buddy Holly's disappearance, Elvis's heart attack. Of course, it was a "terrible tragedy" on the one hand. But on the other . . . well, they were *asking for it,* weren't they? We like to conceive of them if not actually, literally taking their own lives, then at least loitering with intent in the Garden of Gethsemane. Kurt Cobain's shotgun fellatio in 1994 was not, in rock-and-roll terms, a "mad" or "sad" act, but a perfectly logical development, a sign of his dedication to his art. Suicide was, as it was for Ian Curtis before him, his greatest hit.

> *What did you think of Kurt Cobain's suicide?*
> I respect his decision.
> —MORRISSEY

Some thought Morrissey might be miffed that Cobain had beaten him to it. After all, the theme of suicide, premature death, and being remembered is a constant in his work, and it had been long before Kurt's brand of grungy sulking arrived on the scene. In fact, the suicide note as a musical form is Morrissey's speciality, as in "Shakespeare's Sister" (*"Throw your white body down!"*); "There Is a Light That Never Goes Out" (*"And if a double-decker bus / Crashes into us"*); "Well I Wonder" (*"Gasping—dying—but somehow still alive / This is the final stand of all I am"*); "Death at One's Elbow" (*"You'll slip on the / Trail of my bespattered remains"*); "Asleep" (*"Don't try to wake me in the morning, for I will be gone"*); "I Know It's Over" (*"Oh, Mother, I can feel the soil falling over my head"*). To name just a few.

And, of course, the suicide note to end all suicide notes, the spectacularly, *heroically* passive-aggressive "Speedway" from *Vauxhall and I,* a song so blasphemous in its disdain, so astounding in its self-pity, so moving in its self-dramatization that it seems, like the Galilean Fisher of Men, to offer the world the ultimate yes, when it is, in fact, the ultimate no, one so perfectly beautiful that it almost renders suicide unnecessary or, at most, a bureaucratic formality hardly worth bothering with. Morrissey enacts his own death every time he performs it, usually as a last number, in a single spotlight surrounded by darkness, nimbly stepping out of the circle of light as the final trapdoor drumbeat falls and the spot extinguishes, and then gliding away quickly into the backstage gloom.

Of course, this means that unlike most suicides, Morrissey can read the notices the next day.

Arguably, if childishly, the only authentic and genuinely free response to being given a life you didn't ask for, the only way to own it, is to give it up—which is perhaps why we talk about "taking one's own life" (in both hands).

But Morrissey, as his fans know very well, is not very likely to take this option—the gesture wouldn't be nearly as dramatic as continuing to live in spite of everything and, most important, everybody. To live on . . . *in spite*. As he sings in "He Cried" on *Maladjusted: "He was stoned to death but he's still living."*

For all the dark hints of Dean-inspired auto-thanasia in his work, Morrissey is not likely to exercise his final artistic option and bring down the curtain at the moment of his choosing by veering cliffward or into the path of an oncoming double-decker bus. Partly, this is because he doesn't need to. He has achieved in life the transcendence that other performers have only achieved in death (or real, clinical, certifiable madness). This is the twisted miracle of Morrissey's life that his fans, his congregation of Beautiful Bastards, bears witness to. Morrissey is the only "saint" to be canonized before his death, and the only one to intercede on behalf of his supplicants not from heaven but from his bedroom.

As "Speedway" chucklingly implies beneath its morbid but undeniably witty death wish, the old moaner is not likely to be found swinging by his neck from his antique Victorian chandelier. The cord that binds him to this world, keeping him dangling here, choking and gasping but somehow still alive, is not simply his defiance or even his sense of drama, but more important, his very twisted sense of humor. Staying alive and staying Morrissey is just too big a joke to play on the world to pass up.

> *Do you find that there are certain subject matters where you might belittle it by putting it in a three-minute lyric?*
> No.
> —MORRISSEY ON GREATER LONDON RADIO, 1999

Humor, albeit of the funereal black variety, permeates almost all of Morrissey's work, making him easily the funniest and most self-mocking lyricist around. Yet Morrissey's black-creped comic talent is resolutely overlooked by all his detractors, who, inevitably, accuse him of being humorless. Perhaps this is partly because his humor is quintessentially Northern, both in its darkness and its self-deprecation: *"As the flames rose to her Roman nose / And her hearing aid started to melt."* Perhaps it's also because there is something to his gallows humor that is frighteningly Other and yet familiar at the same time, as old as the hills yet original, impossibly wicked but also somehow too good for this world.

But mostly it's because, for such people, recognizing or even acknowledging Morrissey's sense of humor would compromise their useful defense mechanism that Morrissey is mad and/or sad in some simple, hygienic fashion that doesn't implicate *them*. It would no longer simply be Morrissey's problem. After all, to laugh at Morrissey's jokes is to let him inside your head, something that, understandably, terrifies most normal people.

> I have always had to laugh at myself. If I hadn't found my social position when I was a teenager so amusing, I would have strangled myself.
> —*BLITZ*, 1998

Nonetheless, it is precisely Morrissey's "darkness" that is so liberating. Just as a joke makes us laugh because it shakingly releases an idea or a feeling we hadn't dared or thought to express ourselves, Morrissey's "miserable" songs have saved many fans from suicide—when someone on this "unhappy planet" has gone to the trouble of expressing your own dark thoughts so charmingly and so wittily and in a fashion that makes it clear he's lived with them for a thousand years, before you were even born, it would be the height of bad manners to leave it prematurely. And anyway, Morrissey has blocked all the exits with his talent; he's met us at the cemetery gates on a dreaded sunny day with some muscle in the form of Mr. Wilde at his side: He's felt it, thought it, looked at it, sung it, quipped it, and laughed his head off at it infinitely better—and much more exquisitely—than you or I could ever manage. So why the hell should we even *bother?* We'd only make a bloody mess of it.

Another reason why Morrissey isn't about to make a quick getaway is the small question of where he would actually *go.* A question addressed in the teasing, ticklish but "tragic" final track on *Maladjusted,* "Satan Rejected My Soul." A breezily bleak parting shot, "Satan" suggests that Morrissey was so desperate to find some kind of peace, some kind of home, that he tried to cut a deal with Old Nick but found himself rejected even there: *"He won't be dragged down / He's seen my face around."*

It's a joke, of course, but one that relies on us to know that Morrissey's entire career, avowedly depraved as it is, has been a struggle to renounce Satan's works in the form of the Way of the World—or corruption. He is much too originally wicked for old Beelzebub, and his soul much too heavy for hell, or, for that matter, the balance of a Manichaean universe. Morrissey is forever trapped somewhere between heaven and hell, life and art, good and evil, lying in his bed thinking about life or thinking about death, and neither one particularly appealing to him. Even purgatory would be a relief; like Gatwick Airport, there may be a long wait, the food may be execrable and the décor distasteful, but at least the lost souls there, unlike Morrissey, know they're eventually going *somewhere,* they're just not sure whether they'll have a sea view.

> Artists are not really people, are they? Not really. Because eventually you end up having had a lifestyle or an experience which most other people have never had. Because before you had the fame or success you were working towards it. And your mind was very locked into that. And then when it happens to you, it takes you further away from the human race. But it is a great journey.
> —*MELODY MAKER,* 1997

Understandably, Morrissey, the poor dear, becomes desperate and begs for Satan to take it off his hands—even when actually trying to make a deal with the Devil, Morrissey can't bring himself to put a price on his immemorial soul. He goes on, trying to reassure Satan that it won't bring him down as well.

Wicked and vain as Morrissey might be in his heart and in his art, his lived life has been anything but sinful or venal, if it has been anything at all. Morally speaking, he is *The Picture of Dorian Gray* in reverse: All the sin and corruption and genius has gone into his ravishing art, which walks the world while he remains locked up, hanging in his attic. Hence, Lucifer won't be persuaded, not even by Morrissey's cooing "oo-ooh, oo-ooh" noises over the last few bars of the song. Contrary to the timeworn phrase, you can't go to hell in your own way, and Morrissey can't even give his soul away. He's stuck with it, poor lad.

And so are we.

Morrissey may not be happy in his own special purgatory, but at least it is unquestionably his own. This is the real Faustian pact that the boy from the mean Stretford streets who refused to forgive or forget the trick that life, love, and lust played on him has made, not with the Devil or with a record company or even with his hairdresser but with himself.

His art, and what passes for his life, bear testament to his greatest virtue and his greatest vice: He would always rather be unique than happy.

But then, isn't that the nature of True Love? The kind of love that pop music is always whispering in our ear about if we would only hear it, encouraging us to feel so singular in our sadness, so achingly good about feeling bad—to hug ourselves and to never ever let go?

The kind of love that isn't like any other love, the kind that if you go about it the right-wrong way, shines out of your behind.

"I'VE ALWAYS BEEN TRUE TO YOU IN MY OWN SICK WAY I'LL ALWAYS STAY TRUE TO YOU."

ACKNOWLEDGMENTS

'd like to thank Mum and Dad, Mark LeFanu and the Society of Authors, the late Shulman Livesey, Alan Jackson, Meirion Todd, Suzi Feay, Paul Simpson, Jake Arnott, Mary Lawton, Lorraine Gannon, Simon Blow, Brian Pera, Dave Clemens, David Baker, Simon Casson, the Readers Wifes, David Tseng of Morrissey-solo.com, David Toube, Tim Lusher, Daniela Bernardelle, Gareth Davies, Mr. Hughes, Mr. Lowe, Mr. Bulcock, Mr. Mitchell, and very particularly Mr. Zeeland.

INDEX

ABOUT THE AUTHOR

MARK SIMPSON is the author of several books—*The Queen Is Dead, Sex Terror, Anti-Gay, It's a Queer World,* and *Male Impersonators*—as well as a regular writer for Salon.com and *The Independent on Sunday,* among other publications. Infamous as the man who, according to *The New York Times,* fathered the "metrosexual" buzz-word, he lives in London.